When Ladislav Holy precipitately left Czechoslovakia for the UK in 1968, he was already one of the leading anthropologists in Central Europe. In the following decades he carried out important field studies in Africa. Since 1986 he has been engaged in research in the Czech Republic, and he brings to this timely study of national identity the skills of a seasoned researcher, a cosmopolitan perspective, and the insights of an insider. Drawing on historical and literary sources as well as ethnography, he analyses the particular Czech discourses on national identity and the changing but always problematic relations between nation and state in a period of revolutionary transformation. He argues that there were specifically 'Czech' aspects to the communist regime and to the 'velvet revolution', and paying particular attention to symbolic representations of what it means to be Czech, he explores how notions of Czech identity were involved in the debates surrounding the fall of communism, and the emergence of a new social system.

D0939959

Cambridge Studies in Social and Cultural Anthropology

103

THE LITTLE CZECH AND THE GREAT CZECH NATION

Cambridge Studies in Social and Cultural Anthropology

The monograph series Cambridge Studies in Social and Cultural Anthropology publishes analytical ethnographies, comparative works, and contributions to theory. All combine an expert and critical command of ethnography and a sophisticated engagement with current theoretical debates.

A list of books in the series will be found at the end of the volume.

THE LITTLE CZECH AND THE GREAT CZECH NATION

National identity and the post-communist transformation of society

LADISLAV HOLY
University of St Andrews

CAMBRIDGE
UNIVERSITY PRESS

Published by the Press Syndicate of the University of Cambridge
The Pitt Building, Trumpington Street, Cambridge CB2 1RP
40 West 20th Street, New York, NY 10011–4211, USA
10 Stamford Road, Oakleigh, Melbourne 3166, Australia

First published 1996

A catalogue record for this book is available from the British Library

Library of Congress cataloguing in publication data

Holy, Ladislav.
    The little Czech and the great Czech nation : national
identity and the post-communist transformation of society / Ladislav
Holy.
      p.   cm.
    Includes bibliographical references.
    ISBN 0 521 55469 1 (hc.) – ISBN 0 521 55584 1 (pbk.)
    1. Czech Republic – Politics and government.   2. National
characteristics, Czech.   3. Social change – Czech Republic.
    I. Title.
    DB2238.7.H65   1996
943.7105–dc20   95-48157 CIP

ISBN 0 521 554691 hardback
ISBN 0 521 555841 paperback

Transferred to digital printing 1999

For Kate

Contents

Acknowledgements		*page* x
	Introduction	1
1	Nation against state	16
2	Freedom, nation, and personhood	55
3	Self-stereotypes and national traditions	72
4	National traditions and the imagining of the nation	114
5	National traditions and the political process	138
6	Nation and state in the context of Czech culture	168
	Notes	205
	References	213
	Index	220

Acknowledgements

Most of the material for this book was collected during my research in the Czech Republic from July 1992 to January 1993. My trip was sponsored by the Nuffield Foundation and I am very grateful for their generosity. In the Czech Republic my work would have been impossible without the continual help I was given. Jindřich and Soňa Švecovi, Josef and Olga Kandertovi, Milouš and Hana Stárkovi, Karel and Míla Dolečkovi, and Eliška Fučíková provided a much appreciated hospitality. Josef Kandert, secretary of the Czechoslovak Ethnographic Society, put the society's facilities at my disposal and helped with bibliographic searches. Soňa Švecová, Miriam Moravcová, Václav Hubinger, and Zdeněk Uherek gave constructive criticism of my various interpretations. Furthermore, I wish to acknowledge the help provided by my two research assistants, Radim Tobolka and Štěpán Žežula. My thinking and writing has been profoundly influenced by invaluable comments on the earlier draft of the manuscript made by Nigel Rapport and Roy Dilley. Special thanks are due to Barbara Metzger for having edited the final draft for style, Jiří Všetečka for allowing me to use his photograph for the cover illustration, and Jessica Kuper for her editorial help.

Some of the material in chapter 5 was first published in *Contesting markets*, ed. R. Dilley (1992) and *Socialism: ideals, ideologies, and local practice*, ed. C. M. Hann (1993); and part of chapter 6 was first published in *Man* (N.S.) 29 (1994). I gratefully acknowledge the permission of the Edinburgh University Press, the Association of Social Anthropologists of the Commonwealth, and the Royal Anthropological Institute, respectively, to use this material in this book.

Introduction

Most of the sociological and political-scientific writing on Central and Eastern Europe is still grounded in a sociological universalism (Kapferer 1988: 3) which treats this region as a politically, economically, and, to some extent, even culturally undifferentiated whole. Various Central and Eastern European countries up to 1989 had essentially the same political and economic system and at present are undergoing what is again seen as essentially the same kind of transformation from a totalitarian political system to democratic pluralism and from a centrally planned to a market economy. Although various countries of the former Eastern bloc displayed many common features which made it possible to perceive the socialist system as radically different from the capitalist and liberal-democratic systems of the free world, there were also considerable differences among them. In so far as Western observers and commentators paid attention to these differences, they explained them by reference to pre-socialist history and political culture (Brown and Gray 1979; Rothschild 1989).

Social equality was an important aspect of the ideology of all former socialist countries, but in Czechoslovakia it was realised in practice to a far more significant degree than anywhere else in Eastern Europe. Czechoslovakia eliminated the private sector to a much greater extent and had a more egalitarian income policy than the other states of the socialist bloc. The political system in Czechoslovakia also had its specific features even under communist rule, particularly in retaining the office of president of the republic (Taborsky 1961: 167–72, 182–95).

The 'velvet revolution' of November 1989 which abruptly ended communist rule in Czechoslovakia differed significantly from the way in which the communist system was overthrown in other Eastern European countries. The political change in Czechoslovakia, in contrast with, for example, the Soviet Union or Bulgaria, was not instigated by the ruling elites and largely accepted below, but brought about by the open revolt of the population. Perhaps the most significant feature of the 'velvet revolution' was that it was initiated by students, actors, and other intellectuals, whose publicly expressed opposition to the communist regime was swiftly followed by the masses. Although the creation of a post-socialist social order in Czechoslovakia and in what became the independent Czech Republic in 1993 has many similarities with the process which is now under way particularly in Poland and Hungary, it too has its unique features.

The differences in the form of the socialist system, in the way in which it ended and in the process of political and economic transformation which is now taking place in the countries of Central and Eastern Europe, are the result of the different historical development of these countries and of the different cultures which are the product of this development. The aim of this book is to investigate the specific ways in which Czech cultural meanings and in particular the notion of Czech identity and the accompanying nationalist sentiments have affected life under communism, its overthrow, and the political and economic transformation of post-communist society.

Culture and politics; discourse and text

In discussing the role of cultural meanings in the post-communist transformation of Czech society, I make a distinction between culture and discourse. Following the line of thought developed, among others, by Geertz (1973), Schneider (1976, 1980), and Spiro (1982), I understand culture as a system of collectively held notions, beliefs, premises, ideas, dispositions, and understandings. This system is not something that is locked in people's heads but is embodied in shared symbols which are the main vehicles through which people communicate their worldview, value orientations, and ethos to one another.

Politics has for the most part not been the subject of study as a cultural system. It is still often conceptualised as governed by strictly rational considerations of a purely utilitarian kind, of which considerations of costs and benefits are a classical model. Numerous books by historians and political scientists on the political history of the Czechoslovak state are informed by this conceptualisation of the political, and many anthropological studies of politics have also been grounded in it. Anthropologists have examined politics as a give-and-take in which people follow their material interests as consumers in the market of benefits, rights, duties, and privileges. For many, politics is about interest groups, economic forces, and power relations.

I do not conceptualise politics simply as the pursuit of group and sectional interests independent of any particular culture. My assumption is that politics is an aspect of the overall cultural system and every political action is embedded in a wider cultural context. Thus cultural presuppositions and values which in themselves would not be seen as political (in the strict sense of the term) inevitably influence political action (in the narrow sense of the term). In referring to specific political events I pay less attention to particular policies than to the various symbols through which people make sense of the political process.

A similar conceptualisation of the political has been suggested by those anthropologists who see political action as first of all symbolic. In their view, symbolic action is the main form of interaction of political elites with the public and with each other when they are in public view; it is used to assert the legitimacy of power and to bolster the rulers' authority. Symbols are widely used to arouse emotions and enthusiasm for politics. They are used to express identification with particular policies or political forces and are the main means by which people make sense of the political process, which presents itself to them primarily in symbolic form. All in all, attitudes are shaped more by symbolic forms than by utilitarian calculations (Kertzer 1988). The potency of symbols in political processes derives from the fact that they are vehicles for conception, as Geertz expressed it (1966: 5). In my discussion of specific political events in recent Czechoslovak history, I concentrate on the myths, symbols, and traditions which make possible the identification of people as members of the Czech nation and create Czech national consciousness.

The shared cultural notions underlying and giving meaning to events are invoked not only in symbolic form but also in specific discourses as either implicit or explicit assumptions which underlie their logic or are their explicit subject. The term 'discourse' derives from many different sources and scholarly traditions and in social scientific practice carries different meanings which are often purposely vague (Scherzer 1987: 296). For many writers it is employed in reference to a particular view, model, definition, argument, or even relation. In a more rigorous usage the term has two different senses. Whereas linguists tend to see discourse as units of language that exceed the limits of a single sentence and are produced in everyday communication (see, e.g., Halliday 1978: 109; Halliday and Hasan 1976: 10), anthropologists and some discourse analysts, following the usage shaped largely by Foucault (1972, 1979), tend to see it as a corpus of 'texts' taking spoken, written, iconic, kinesic, musical, and other forms (Seidel 1989: 222) and produced in a variety of contexts (see, e.g.,

Fairclough 1989: 24; Fairclough 1992; Seidel 1989; Milton 1993). Adopting the latter view, I take discourse to be socially constituted communication which leads to the production of a set of 'texts'. These need not be written or oral but may be constituted through other modes of expression, for example, through the representational or performative arts. Even in their written or spoken form they need not be restricted to a single genre. 'Culture' I take to be a system of notions, ideas, and premises which is not exclusive to any particular discourse but underlies a multiplicity of them.

My discussion concentrates on discourses which gained prominence in Czech society after the fall of the communist regime, and either could not have emerged under communism or had been driven underground and restricted to a narrow circle of dissidents: discourses on the market economy, various forms of ownership, democratic pluralism, civil society, the environment, gender relations, individualism and nationalism, modern Czech history, and Czechoslovak and Czech statehood, among others. These are all public discourses concerned with issues which the fall of communism and the post-communist transformation of society brought into prominence. In limiting myself to the consideration of this type of discourse I do not imply that they are the only ones which currently exist in Czech society.

Linguistic anthropologists have examined the ways in which grammatical categories are used in poetic, magical, and political discourse and reflect culturally specific ways of expressing meaning and the unconscious patterning of thought (Scherzer 1987). Their insight that to 'study culture we must study the actual forms of discourse produced and performed by societies and individuals' (Scherzer 1987: 306) has, however, been hampered by the fact that they have concentrated mainly on 'the formal patterning principles that organize forms of oral discourse' (Bauman 1986: ix). In focusing on structure they have largely overlooked the fact that discourse also always says something about something (J. B. Thompson 1984: 8, 100; J. B. Thompson 1990: 287ff.). In my analysis of Czech discourses I concentrate not on their structure but on their content. All of them creatively seize on and make explicit what can be seen as basic premises of Czech culture. This is not, however, the only reason I consider discourse an important entry into Czech cultural meanings.

The concept of culture as an ideational system has often led anthropologists to consider culture as a product or object, 'a unitary code of meaning that passes down over time without fundamental alteration and that operates apart from individual or collective action' (Fox 1985: 154).

More often than not, this conceptualisation of culture has limited our insight into the dynamics of cultural processes, particularly the simultaneous processes of continuity of tradition and constant cultural change. An adequate conception of culture must account for the mechanisms which produce both continuity and change. As many discourse analysts have pointed out, discourse is the locus of such mechanisms (Halliday 1978: 124–5; Scherzer 1987: 296, 306; G. Urban 1991: 17). In discussing contemporary Czech discourses I pay particular attention to the way in which what Czechs consider their time-honoured traditions and deep-rooted cultural notions are reproduced and thus perpetually re-created in the present. These discourses are the locus of '"a management of meaning" by which culture is generated and maintained, transmitted and received, applied, exhibited, remembered, scrutinised, and experimented with' (Hannerz 1987: 550). As Czech culture, like any other, is continuously re-created in contemporary discourses, it is 'always in the making' (Fox 1985: 137, 199) and always a 'work in progress' (Hannerz 1987: 550). Czechs themselves are able to see it as an enduring and unchanging tradition because any particular discourse is always constructed in opposition to some other (Thomas 1992). The post-communist transformation of society is a situation of dramatic social change. The discourses which have emerged in this situation either have explicitly invoked discourses current in pre-socialist Czech society or have been constructed in conscious opposition to the official discourses current during the socialist period. In either case, by referring to previous historically situated discourses, they keep alive and, in a new historical situation, make relevant the notions expressed in them and thus create the impression of an unchanging cultural tradition. At the same time, because the current discourses are always conceived of as in contradistinction to past ones, they also foster the impression of change. These two seemingly contradictory impressions form the background for my discussion of the notion of Czech identity.

Czechs and Slovaks

National identity, like all other identities, is always constructed in opposition to those perceived as the Other (Cohen 1974; Grillo 1980; Heiberg 1980; Schlesinger 1987). During their nineteenth-century 'national revival', Czechs constructed their identity in conscious opposition to the Germans with whom they shared geographical, political, and economic space within the Austro-Hungarian Empire. Their pursuit of national sovereignty culminated in 1918 with the creation of the Czechoslovak Republic as one of the successors of the defeated empire. Although established on the principle of every nation's right to self-determination, Czechoslovakia was in fact a multinational state. Most importantly, it had a sizeable German minority. The Czechs did not feel numerically strong enough to assert themselves against the German element, and therefore the new state was conceived as that of the Czechs, until then part of Austria, and the Slovaks, until then an ethnic minority in Hungary. The inclusion of Czechs and Slovaks in a common state was to the advantage of both. For Czechs it meant the achievement, together with the Slovaks, of an indisputable majority in a multiethnic state. For Slovaks it meant the preservation of their national identity, which had been under constant and ever-increasing threat.

Although Czechoslovakia was a multiethnic state, the Czechs identified fully with it, considering it the restoration of their statehood after three hundred years of Habsburg rule. A growing number of Slovaks were, however, dissatisfied with the dominant role of the Czechs and began to perceive the new republic as replacing their former subordination to Budapest with subordination to Prague. Uneasy Czech–Slovak relations eventually led to the declaration of an independent Slovak state under Nazi tutelage in 1939, the constitution of the Czechoslovak Socialist Republic as a federal state in 1968, the confirmation of the federal structure after the demise of communism in 1989, and the eventual separation of Czechoslovakia into independent Czech and Slovak states in 1993.

There were only three federated states among the former socialist countries whose political systems were divided along national lines: the Soviet Union, Yugoslavia, and Czechoslovakia. All three disintegrated in the aftermath of the fall of the communist system amidst increasing national tensions. The upsurge of nationalist sentiment in Czechoslovakia did not take the violent form that it did in Yugoslavia and parts of the former Soviet Union but manifested itself in prolonged constitutional crisis and political paralysis. The prevailing feeling in the Czech lands – Bohemia and Moravia – is that the disintegration of Czechoslovakia in 1993 was the result of Slovak nationalism, anti-Czech sentiment, and Slovak separatism.

This book is not a study of Czech–Slovak relations but a study of Czech national identity. In it I try to formulate what it means to be a Czech to those who describe themselves as such. The reason I pay some attention to Czech–Slovak relations is that since the expulsion of the German population from Czechoslovakia in 1945, Czechs have been constructing their national identity mainly in opposition to Slovaks, perceived as their most significant Other. In discussing Czech–Slovak relations, I describe them solely from the Czech point of view. As I lived and worked only among Czechs, I can talk only about how Czechs see the Slovaks but not about how Slovaks see the Czechs. I suggest, among other things, that against Slovak nationalism stands what may be called Czech nationalism: awareness of a separate Czech identity, the deep-rooted conviction of the existence of a Czech nation, and an explicit or tacit identification with it. This Czech nationalism tends to be overshadowed by the manifest Slovak nationalism even for many Czechs, who, paradoxically, manifest it through its vehement denial. This is because it is the nationalism of a dominant nation which, unlike the Slovak nation, had in its own view already achieved sovereignty in the Czechoslovak Republic.

Czech national identity

The disintegration of Czechoslovakia is generally seen as one instance of a general process of transformation taking place in the former communist countries whereby the ideology of communism is replaced by that of nationalism. The disintegration of the Soviet Union and Yugoslavia, accompanied by the rise of an often violent nationalism, as well as the peaceful disintegration of Czechoslovakia along national lines, reinforces the image of nationalism as 'the last word of communism' (Alan 1992: 8). According to this image, the disintegration of the 'communist empire' is accompanied by the proliferation of nation-states.

However, the image of the rise of nationalism as an ideology which has filled up the ideological vacuum created by the demise of communism is to a great extent an illusion. Verdery (1993) has argued that the roots of ethno-national conflict in the former socialist societies are not to be sought primarily in 'age-old enmities' and that it would be a mistake to imagine that ethnic and national conflicts had been simply suspended and held in 'cold storage' under socialism. On the contrary, national ideology and thinking in national terms were fostered by the political economy of socialism itself, particularly by its 'economy of shortage'. Although this particular explanation does not fit the Czechoslovak case, Verdery is right to point to the presence of nationalist sentiment under socialism, in spite of the suppression of its political expression. As far as socialist Czechoslovakia is concerned, hand in hand with the officially proclaimed ideology of 'proletarian internationalism' went the recognition of the national principle in the organisation of communist society and the communist state. In fact, the importance of this principle pre-dates the communist state. A constitutional decree of August 1945 deprived of Czechoslovak citizenship all Germans except those who had officially adopted Czech or Slovak nationality before the war. Until then, Germans and Hungarians living on Czechoslovak territory had formally been Czechoslovak citizens, although, except for active anti-fascists, they had been considered 'unreliable' ones. The decree automatically confiscating their property took into consideration only their nationality. Consciousness of national identity and membership of a nation have in many other ways been strengthened by official policy. Post-war Czechoslovakia declared itself the common state of Czechs and Slovaks officially conceptualised as two equal nations. The federation of 1968 was a federation of two republics created on a national principle. The parliament – the Federal Assembly – included both the Chamber of the People and the Chamber of Nations, the deputies of which were representatives not of the citizens but of their respective nations. People were made aware of their nationality and reminded that it mattered in the occasional population censuses and in the inclusion of nationality on their identity cards.

The national principle in politics and the division of the political scene along national lines remained in place after the revolution of 1989 in spite of the new political rhetoric emphasising the ideals and values of civil society. The constitutional law of 1991 stipulated once again that the Czech and Slovak Federal Republic was a voluntary union of the two equal republics of the Czech and Slovak nations based on the right of self-determination of each. The post-communist state retained the pre-war system of separate Czech and Slovak political groupings. The most important political organisation to emerge from the 'velvet revolution' was the Civic Forum, operating in the Czech lands; its Slovak counterpart was the Public Against Violence. All but one of the newly established political parties were either Czech or Slovak. The single exception was the Civic Democratic Party, a Czech party that in the 1992 elections campaigned and fielded its own candidates in Slovakia as well. However, the feeling of Czech political commentators was that the party began presenting itself as truly 'federal' too late in the campaign, and because of this failed to gain the 5 per cent of the popular vote in Slovakia necessary for representation in the Slovak National Council (the Slovak parliament).

Verdery (1992) points to various other causes of the rise of nationalist sentiment and xenophobia which are now observable in all former socialist countries of Eastern Europe. Among other things, she mentions that nationalism provides a convenient answer to the question of who is to blame for the economic and political backwardness of the former socialist countries in comparison with their Western counterparts. The idiom of national difference has become a convenient means of assigning blame to others. In post-1989 Czechoslovakia, Slovaks habitually blamed the Czechs and Czechs blamed the Slovaks for all the ills of their common socialist past. According to opinion polls conducted in 1991, most Czechs and most Slovaks felt that they were financially subsidising the other nation (*Respekt*, 1991, no. 16: 1).

Because Czech nationalism since the creation of the republic in 1918 has been for the most part the nationalism of a dominant nation, Czechness has not needed to be openly asserted. This has led to the view, expressed some fifteen years ago in the discussion in Czech émigré circles about the meaning of Czechness, that the Czech nation no longer existed – that all that was left was a Czech-speaking population. Awareness of being Czech is tacit (Macura 1993: 11). It is grounded in an implicit awareness of the common historical fate of the collectivity spoken of as 'we', but is seldom the subject of an explicit discourse. It becomes such either in situations which are perceived as national crises or when what is tacitly taken as the Czech way of doing things is threatened by those perceived as the Other. In my exploration of Czech identity I concentrate on certain such recent situations which are of special methodological significance because they represent moments of explicit symbolic manipulation. Just as this manipulation makes assumptions about shared national identity transparent to its participants, it makes them transparent to the observing anthropologist. This is in no small measure due to the fact that in such situations symbols are often contested, verbally interpreted, and in numerous other ways explicitly linked to the values, notions, and ideas for which they stand. For these reasons, I use as my main ethnography a few selected events from recent political history, which I discuss more or less in the order in which they unfolded in historical time: the demonstrations in Prague in 1988 and 1989 which preceded the 'velvet revolution' of November 1989 (chapter 1), the events of November 1989 and the discussion surrounding the beginning of the transformation of Czechoslovak economy (chapter 5), and the political negotiations over the structure of the post-communist state and the discourse about the independent Czech state (chapter 6).

Examining the first public demonstrations against the communist regime in 1988 and 1989 and the overthrow of the communist system in 1989, I argue that the opposition to the communist system was carried out in the name of the nation and was construed as the nation's rising against what was generally perceived as foreign oppression. The rise of nationalist sentiment, far from being a result of the fall of communism, in fact preceded it and stemmed from the perception of socialism as an alien, Soviet imposition which had ruthlessly destroyed the traditions and values which people saw as 'theirs'. The opposition to this alien system was construed and understood as 'us' (the nation) standing against 'them' (the alien system embodied in the socialist state), and the overthrow of socialism took the form of a national liberation. Since then, national awareness has been nourished by the pro-European rhetoric of those advocating privatisation, a market economy, and democracy, which has a long history in Central Europe (on Hungary, see S. Gal 1991) and has been instrumental in constructing the dichotomy between culturally specific (i.e., national) and universal (i.e., European) values.

In all the recent political events and situations which constitute my main ethnography, frequent references were made to Czech history, and for the participants themselves what happened became meaningful because of their shared historical knowledge. To understand these events and situations in the same way as they were understood by their participants requires some degree of historical knowledge, and to provide it one could begin the discussion of Czech identity with a brief outline of Czech history. This history is not, however, a straightforward narrative of everything that happened in the past but a selection of certain past events which are ascribed specific meaning because they are understood as contributing in some significant way to the shaping of the present. Just as any other history is constructed from the point of view of the present-day understanding of its subject, Czech history is a narrative of past events constructed from the present-day understanding of what it means to be a Czech. In other words, what is understood as Czech history is a construction which makes possible the understanding that 'we are what we are today because this or that happened in our past'. It is a construction which is an integral part of the discourse which perpetually constructs and reconstructs Czech identity. If one began the discussion of Czech identity by offering any particular outline of Czech history, rather than analysing this discourse, one would be constructing it or participating in it. This is what Czech intellectuals are doing when they construct the narrative of the Czech past or 'at last tell the truth about our history'. And this is also what ordinary Czechs are doing when they either accept the intellectuals' constructions as valid, reject, reinterpret, or simplify them, or select from them what they see as significant for understanding who they are.

To be able to analyse rather than shape the discourse, I cannot therefore begin with an outline of Czech history. Instead, I start my exploration of the cultural construction of Czech identity by describing the sharp separation between the public and the private domains brought about by the almost total abolition of the private ownership of the means of production in socialist Czechoslovakia (chapter 1); I then move on to an analysis of the symbols invoked in the events which eventually culminated in the 'velvet revolution' of 1989 (chapters 2 and 3). Many of these symbols are meaningful only in terms of what is understood as having happened in the past and as having particular significance for the present. Like the symbols themselves, these past events are often contested and endowed with different meanings by various participants in the events, who nevertheless understand the events in which they are taking part as the result of a certain course of history. To be able to interpret what it means to be a Czech, I often refer to what this course of history is understood to be. Czechs, of course, argue among themselves over which understanding is right, truthful, or correct and which is false and incorrect. It cannot be the anthropologist's job to arbitrate the actors' dispute. What I see as my main task is to explain why different understandings of the past exist, what contemporary interests generate them, and how they shape the ongoing discourse about Czech identity (chapter 4).

Czech culture

Our understanding of culturally specific meanings is always the result of either explicit or implicit cross-cultural comparison (Holy 1987: 10–11). My understanding of the basic aspects of Czech identity is also the result of comparison. I was born in Prague and lived in Czechoslovakia for the first thirty-five years of my life. Having left Czechoslovakia in 1968, I revisited it for the first time in 1986, having by then lived fourteen years in the United Kingdom. My anthropological interest in Czech culture began in 1989, and I spent six months in Czechoslovakia from July 1992 to January 1993 collecting most of the data on which my account is based. Czech is my first language, and unless I was driving my British-registered car, people who did not know me did not suspect that I was not a Czechoslovak citizen until I told them. Most Czech customs and ways of doing things were familiar to me, but others struck me as distinctly odd as the result of my constant comparison of the situation in Czechoslovakia with that in Britain. My renewed exposure to Czech culture and the Czech way of life generated a peculiar sense of both familiarity and strangeness. I am sure that the problems on which I concentrate in my account are the result of my comparison of the two cultures – Czech and British – to which I have been intensively exposed during my life and that someone with different experience would probably identify quite different ones.

Given my middle-class background, it is not surprising that most of my 'informants' in Czechoslovakia were persons with whom I would normally associate if I lived there: middle-class, university-educated men and women, many of them my old friends, colleagues, and acquaintances. To eliminate the danger of presenting exclusively a view of the educated Czech middle class, I did some of my fieldwork among the workers in a locomotive depot in Prague and among farmers and workers in a small village in northern Bohemia. Although most of my fieldwork was conducted in particular communities, my account deliberately moves beyond the conventional framework of the community study. An anthropological focus on social and cultural processes operating beyond the local community has long been called for (Boissevain 1975; Crump 1975; Cole 1977; Grillo 1980; Wolf 1982), and my account is meant to be a contribution to such an endeavour. It aims at the description of Czech culture, by which I mean that complex of tacit knowledge, ideas, and notions expressed through the shared system of signs and symbols that enables Czechs to communicate meaningfully with each other.

Czech society is stratified in terms of economic and educational status, differentiated along the urban–rural divide, and increasingly embraces a wide variety of political orientations. The social, economic, and political differences are paralleled by cultural differences. The culture of a small farming village or a small market town is in many ways different from the culture of Prague, the political and cultural capital of the country, or that of other large towns. The culture of manual workers is considerably different from the culture of farmers, on the one hand, and the culture of university-educated elites, on the other. Nevertheless, in spite of this cultural diversity, Czechs recognise a common level of cultural identity and in numerous contexts talk about themselves as an undifferentiated community sharing a single culture. This feeling of cultural commonality is much stronger among Czechs than it is, for example, in Britain. The shared system of cultural notions which makes it possible for Czechs to make sense of each other's attitudes and actions is to a great extent the creation of the 'discursive practices of intellectuals' (Foster 1991: 235) and is effectively reproduced through the mass, public, compulsory, and standardised education system characteristic of modern industrial society (Gellner 1983). The school system disseminates not only knowledge and awareness of the national high culture in the sense of literature, drama, music, and art but also the shared cultural meanings which enable people to make sense of the world in which they live, of their interactions, and of the constantly changing events in which they are involved.

The book is aimed at analysing these shared cultural meanings. By situating my account on this level I certainly do not intend to imply that all

Czechs have appropriated Czech high culture to the same extent or that no differences in cultural awareness exist among them. Such differences, correlated with level of education and/or socio-economic status, manifest themselves in the degree of clarity, explicitness, or coherence with which particular individuals express shared cultural meanings. But a shared core of basic assumptions about the world underpins them and this book is concerned with elucidating these assumptions. Even so, however, my account is inevitably selective. The core of shared cultural assumptions and meanings is itself too vast to be comprehensively treated in a single book. I concentrate on those assumptions and meanings which were invoked in symbolic form during the political events which I describe or explicitly in the discourses which emerged in connection with the fall of the communist system and the post-communist transformation of Czech society. In particular, I concentrate on the relations between nation and state and between individualism and collectivism.

I also discuss Czech notions of egalitarianism and freedom and the images which Czechs have of themselves as individuals and as a nation. I tease these cultural conceptualisations out of the symbols invoked during the first public demonstrations against the communist regime which I describe in chapter 1; in chapters 2 and 3, I discuss them in detail. The images which Czechs hold of themselves as a nation are expressed in terms of what they see as their national traditions: the tradition of culture and good education, and the tradition of democracy. In chapter 4, I argue that it is the existence of these traditions that makes it possible to imagine the nation as a whole which transcends the individuals who constitute it, and that nationalism both makes history a necessity and generates thinking in historical terms. Nationalism is a discursive agreement that history matters without necessarily agreeing on what it is and what it means. In this chapter, I describe the two constructions of the national past which underlie the Czech historical discourse. In chapters 5 and 6, I concentrate on the role played by Czech national traditions and other premises of Czech culture in giving meaning to recent political events. In chapter 5, I describe how the images of the democratic and well-educated Czech nation became the effective rallying force for the political mobilisation of the masses during the 'velvet revolution' and in support of the radical economic reform on which the post-communist government embarked.

In the final chapter, I discuss the way in which Czech cultural notions underpinned the discourse about Czech statehood which preceded the peaceful disintegration of Czechoslovakia and the creation of an independent Czech state. The selection of the premises of Czech culture on which my discussion concentrates was determined by the nature of the symbolic manipulation or of the particular discourses which accompanied the events described. During these events, the Czechs invoked their shared cultural meanings from different perspectives, and I do likewise. Although my narrative follows the historical sequence of events from 1988 to 1993 in its broad outline, my discussion of the Czech cultural notions in chapters 2, 3, and 4 of necessity draws on events which I then describe in greater detail in chapters 5 and 6 as well as on events which pre-date the fall of communism in Czechoslovakia and the post-communist transformation of Czech society.

Because I was concerned with cultural meanings shared by different strata and sections of Czech society, only some of the data could be generated through participant-observation and discussions with particular individuals. Many of them come from the writings of various Czech intellectuals, who of course are themselves contemplating the problems to which I address myself, as well as from newspapers, magazines, television, and radio broadcasts. There is a reason for this mixture of data, unusual in anthropological monographs. Besides the school, television, the press, and other mass media are nowadays the main means of communication of shared cultural meanings. Those who produce television and radio programmes and write and publish newspaper articles are intellectuals, but their production is 'pitched to the cultural common denominator' (Herzfeld 1982: 647). Television and newspapers are of course not the only settings for the production of texts in which particular topics are discussed and which at once draw upon and reproduce the 'collectively held dispositions and understandings' (Foster 1991: 235) that constitute Czech culture. However, in aiming to reach the widest possible audience, they resort to the 'lowest common communication factors' (Parkin 1984: 353) and thus concisely reflect the twists and turns of orally produced discourses. For this reason, I draw on them quite extensively in my discussion.

This does not mean, however, that the views which I describe are exclusively the views of the politicians and intellectuals who make pronouncements on television and the radio and write articles for newspapers and magazines. The period following the fall of the communist system and preceding the dismantling of Czechoslovakia was politically highly charged, and virtually all Czechs participated in the various discourses it produced in one way or another. People talked about the ills of the communist past and the way communist rule ended, debated the process of privatisation, discussed the latest developments in the negotiations between Czech and Slovak politicians, commented on the latest political events and pronouncements, and expressed their views on the overall situation in the country at all possible times and in all possible settings: during their coffee breaks, at parties, in pubs and shops, at bus stops, on trains, or at family dinner tables. They read newspapers, watched television, and listened to the radio, and commented on what they saw, heard, and read.

The anthropologist who writes about the common culture of a society as large and diversified as the Czech one faces a problem not experienced by those who write about clearly bounded local communities or fairly homogeneous 'primitive' societies. I have often been forced into formulations which may seem unjustified generalisations, particularly when they describe attitudes of Czechs in general to issues on which there are obviously differences of opinion among the various sections of the population. All such generalisations are meant to point to significant trends emerging from conversations with a number of people in various fieldwork settings. Opinion surveys conducted by professional Czech and Slovak sociologists – for example, the Institute for Public Opinion Research, the Centre for Empirical Research, and the Agency for Independent Social Analysis – served for me as an indication of the extent to which the trends I detected among the people to whom I spoke and listened were in fact representative of the Czech population as a whole.

A national culture has not so far been the subject of much anthropological research. Perceived as a level of reality that is not susceptible to investigation by standard anthropological methods of participant-observation, it has become almost exclusively the preserve of historians or political scientists. It is, however, a level of reality that is becoming increasingly important in a world divided into nation-states which nowadays affect more aspects of their subjects' lives than ever before. In my view, it is an area of reality on which anthropologists should have something useful to say, and this book is a modest attempt at grasping this reality by specifically anthropological methods.

1

Nation against state

The recent demise of socialism in Eastern and Central Europe has produced an avalanche of writing on various aspects of the socialist system. Unlike economists, political scientists, and sociologists, who have analysed the socio-economic organisation and political systems of the former socialist countries, the anthropologists who have done fieldwork in the region have concentrated on the description of the life experiences of people living in these countries, the ways in which they have accommodated to the reality of the socialist system, and the effects of such accommodation on their interpersonal relations. They have paid particular attention to the fact that in most socialist countries, 'most of the time, most "ordinary people" simply took the system for granted, accommodated to it, and got on with their lives without joining either the Communist Party or a dissident group. In other words, they "muddled through", just as people do in other kinds of society' (Hann 1993: 11–12; see also Sampson 1984).

The anthropologists' effort to understand what it means to live in a socialist state has paralleled the interest of numerous Central European writers, playwrights, and other intellectuals, who have paid more attention to the effects of socialist reality on interpersonal relations than to the analysis of socialism as an economic and political system. Local intellectuals have viewed socialism first of all as a system which debased not only specifically Christian but also generally Western cultural values of moral rectitude by fostering 'living a lie', as the Czech playwright and now president of the Czech Republic Václav Havel expressed it (Havel et al. 1985). The Civic Forum's policy document, published on the eve of the general strike in November 1989 that eventually brought down the communist regime, spoke of the deep moral, spiritual, ecological, social, economic, and political crisis in which the country found itself. By mentioning the moral issue first, the document was emphasising a crisis which manifested itself in the generally felt destruction of the basic norms of honesty and politeness and the collapse of what the dissident intellectuals who produced the document often referred to as 'standards of civilised behaviour'.

The public and the private in socialist Czechoslovakia

Public opinion concurred with the Civic Forum's conclusions. According to a poll conducted in June 1993, over 80 per cent of Czechs considered the possibility of free travel, the freedom to engage in private entrepreneurial activity, and the increased supply of goods in the shops among the most important results of the socio-economic transformation on which the country had embarked after the fall of the communist system. Over 90 per cent mentioned as important problems poor interpersonal relations, the widespread fraud accompanying privatisation, and the general decline of morality (*Sociologické aktuality*, 1993, no. 6: 8–9). The survey suggests that Czechs see the destruction of basic moral principles not only as the major failing of the socialist system but as the legacy which will probably take longest to change. It is therefore appropriate to begin the discussion of the post-communist transformation by considering it. Another reason for taking this approach stems from the fact that there is a distinct irony in the Czech summary condemnation of socialism on moral grounds. In Czechoslovakia, socialism was not imposed by the bayonets of the Soviet army at the end of World War II, but grew out of the wishes of the majority of the population, to whom the justice and equality it promised seemed morally superior to the injustices and inequalities of capitalism.

The Czechoslovak government established in 1945 was composed of representatives of the four Czech and the four Slovak political parties, which together formed the National Front. Its composition was agreed upon toward the end of the war among the Czech and Slovak politicians in exile in London, the most prominent of them being the pre-war president of the Czechoslovak Republic, Edvard Beneš, and the politicians in exile in Moscow led by the chairman of the Czechoslovak Communist Party, Klement Gottwald. This 'Government of the National Front of the Czechs and Slovaks' was led by the left-wing Social Democrat Zdeněk Fierlinger, and it pursued a vigorous socialist programme, the main elements of which were land reform, taxation on wealth, and wide-ranging nationalisation of banks, large insurance companies, mines, and key industries.[1]

This programme, though it met with the opposition of the right-wing parties in the National Front and of many ordinary people, was backed by the majority of the population. In the first post-war elections in May 1946, in which all the parties of the National Front participated and which were the last free elections before the communist coup d'état of February 1948, the Communist Party polled 40.17 per cent and the Social Democratic Party 15.58 per cent of the popular vote in the Czech lands. The strongest party in Slovakia was the right-wing Democratic Party which polled 62 per cent of the vote; the Communist Party of Slovakia polled 30.37 per cent. The Czech and Slovak Communists won 114 seats in the 300-strong parliament (National Assembly), and together with the Social Democrats, who held 37 seats, and the Slovak Labour Party, which held 2 seats, they had an overall, if tiny, majority in it. The elections of 1946 changed the composition of local government councils. In the Czech lands, the Communist Party gained an overall majority in 37.5 per cent of local councils, and 128 of the 163 chairmen of district councils were Communists. Gottwald became prime minister.

The popular support the Communist Party enjoyed in the 1946 elections indicates that socialist principles were embraced by the majority of the population in the Czech lands if not in Slovakia. This stemmed from the general endorsement of the state's provision of basic social security to all citizens in the form of state pensions, free medical care, and free education and from the endorsement of the duty to work imposed in September 1945 on all men between the ages of sixteen and fifty-five and on all women between the ages of eighteen and forty-five.

Dunn has argued that as

a response to the morally and practically anarchic aspects of capitalist production, socialism is above all else an attempt to reimpose order upon modern social experience through the benign exercise of political authority: to replace the aesthetic, moral, and practical anarchy of capitalist production with a new, benign, and spiritually compelling order.   *(1984: 64)*

The popular support for socialist policies undoubtedly stemmed in no small measure from the endorsement of this 'restoration of a moral component to economic life, from which morality was effectively expunged following the rapid expansion of European industrial capitalism' (Hann 1993: 13).

Numerous studies of the collapse of the socialist system have emphasised its moral dimension (Runciman 1985; Hankiss 1990; Chirot 1991; Clark and Wildavsky 1991). Socialism proclaimed itself the first just social order in modern history, abolishing exploitation and making it possible for people to work according to their abilities and be rewarded solely according to their merits. This self-proclaimed moral superiority to the capitalist system, with all its inherent injustices, was achieved through the abolition of private ownership of the means of production. Although a number of economic activities in socialist Czechoslovakia took place outside the state sector (Wolchik 1991: 232–9), in contrast with the situation in Hungary and Poland there never developed what might properly be called a 'second economy' (Galasi and Sziraczki 1985) around which crystallised a 'second society' (Hankiss 1990; see also Skilling 1989). Many Czech dissidents themselves were of the opinion that one could at best speak only of the 'germ' of such a society in Czechoslovakia and only 'tendencies, or first manifestations of independence' (Skilling 1989: 223; on the debate over the 'second society' among Czech dissidents, see Skilling 1981: 75–7, 183–4). However, what the abolition of private ownership of the means of production led to was a separation of the public and private domains of life hitherto unprecedented in modern society. In this respect, throughout the socialist period – with the exception of the brief period of liberalisation in 1968 known as the Prague Spring – Czechoslovak society was more like the 'paralysed society' (Hankiss 1990: 11–45) of Hungary before 1965 than like post-1965 Hungary or post-1956 Poland. Ironically, it was precisely this sharp separation of the two domains and the resulting alienation from the public domain which led to what critics and opponents of socialism perceived as a deep moral crisis permeating virtually all aspects of socialist society.

Although many countries of the socialist bloc retained at least vestiges of a private sector (in services, retail outlets, and particularly agriculture), all private businesses in Czechoslovakia – including services, shops, and artisans' workshops – were fully liquidated and the collectivisation of land (the last of a series of measures undertaken to abolish private ownership of the means of production) was completed by 1960.[2] This systematic transformation was expressed in the new constitution of 1960, in which Czechoslovakia was declared a 'socialist state', second in history only to the USSR.

With the private ownership of virtually all means of production abolished, labour power was employed exclusively in the public sphere; irrespective of the type of work performed, people had to earn their living from employment in state or cooperative enterprises. As a result, the division of life into public and private spheres was inevitably sharpened. But the boundary between the public and the private in socialist Czechoslovakia permeated many more aspects of life than production and consumption: it affected morality, the value of time and property, modes of conduct, patterns of hospitality and socialising, etc., and it was maintained and made manifest by its own appropriate symbolic devices.

Mrs Thatcher's famous pronouncement that there is no society, only individuals and families, might have been bad sociology, but it was a good ideological slogan for encouraging private home ownership and small private business ventures in a situation of decreasing opportunities for wage employment. If a similar slogan had been coined for socialist Czechoslovakia it would have to have been the exact opposite: there are no individuals and families, only society. 'Society' (more than the alternatives 'people', 'citizens', or 'the toiling masses') was the term used to construct the collective identity which was the subject of the political and economic endeavour and in whose name and on whose behalf it was carried out. This term was employed by party and government spokesmen and their opponents and critics (who sometimes referred to the same collectivity as the 'nation'). For both these categories, society was the agent with goals, aspirations, and wishes, possessing its own will and morality. It was an entity which embraced or excluded particular individuals or from which particular individuals excluded themselves as a result of their actions, views, or opinions. It was society which achieved spectacular successes or, alternatively, failed to achieve them and which, in the process, transformed itself in the desired way or, again, failed to do so.

If society as a whole and not its constituent groups or individuals was to become an active subject of history and create a new social order superior to all previous ones, it had, of course, to be constantly guided in the right direction. Such guidance was provided by the idea of a 'new man' who considered work for society and its future of supreme value and whose actions were 'directed towards the good of the society rather than to his individual or group interests' (Paul 1979: 175). School curricula in both the humanities and the sciences were aimed at creating this 'new man' (see Krejci 1972: 50–1). The ideal inculcated through formal socialisation was reinforced by encouragement of forms of behaviour which conformed to it. To this effect, a great deal of effort was directed at strengthening collective forms of living.[3]

The appropriate relationship between the interests of the society and those of its individual members was bluntly specified in a lead article in the Communist Party newspaper *Rudé právo* (28 August 1979):

Only through the realisation of the interests of society can the interests of individuals also be fulfilled in the spirit of the socialist way of life. If the interests of individuals are different from the interests of society, they are not only contradictory but also in deep conflict with the efforts of socialist society and harmful to its interests.   *(quoted in Fidelius 1983: 142)*[4]

One expression of this desirable hierarchy of interests was the precedence of loyalty to society and its causes over loyalty to one's family and friends.[5] The ideal of unreserved devotion to the interests of society was constantly communicated through appropriate symbolic means, one of which was systematic omission of details of the private lives of party and government officials from their official biographies. In marked contrast to the situation in the West, where politicians' wives play important roles in their political campaigns, are objects of public interest, and often pursue their own particular political agendas, wives never accompanied party officials and government ministers at public functions. The absence of wives, assumed to be there but never mentioned and often seen for the first time at their husbands' funerals, potently symbolised the separation of politics and public life from private domestic life. This symbolism created the image of the politician as a man (rarely a woman) entirely dedicated to the public cause from which he was not distracted by his private familial ties and interests. One of the signs of the change which occurred in Czechoslovakia during the Prague Spring was that Dubček, unlike his predecessors and successors, made public the details of his private life. Similarly, Gorbachev's wife, Raisa, known by name and seen at his side during his public appearances, later became a powerful symbol of the change which he tried to bring about. More than any verbal proclamation, she demonstrated to the world that things in the USSR were different from what they had been in the past.

The banishment of politicians' wives from the public domain was only one manifestation of the sharp separation between public and private spheres. Another was the contrast between the neglect of public space and the cleanliness and tidiness of private flats commented upon in virtually every travel report from socialist Czechoslovakia. The Czech writer Bohumil Hrabal dwelt at length on this striking difference between public and the private spheres in an intermittent interview with the Hungarian publicist Szigeti in 1984–6, interpreting it as a kind of protest triggered by the fact that most people did not enjoy their jobs and wished for different ones, although it was mostly unclear to them what such jobs should or might be (Hrabal 1988: 59).

The boundary between public and private spheres was also marked by the clear distinction between the people with whom one interacted in each sphere. The co-actors in the public sphere were typically co-workers, officials, those who provided the necessary services, and the general public; in the private sphere they were relatives and friends. The overlap between these two categories of co-actors was minimal; according to a survey conducted in an electronics factory in the Czech town of Pardubice, 24.33 per cent of employees had their most frequent social contacts with relatives, 15.58 per cent with friends from outside the factory, and only 8.35 per cent with their co-workers (13.64 per cent of respondents had no regular social contacts with anyone) (Ulc 1974: 111). As a rule, friends were selected from among people of the same educational and cultural background who shared particular interests. Rather than from among co-workers, they were often chosen from among the members of various 'interest organisations'[6] ranging from associations catering for specialised interests such as philately, gardening, fishing, etc., through general and specialised sports clubs, to religious congregations and many others. A notable exception to the sharp separation between co-workers and friends occurred among academics, researchers, artists, writers, musicians, actors, and other members of the intelligentsia. Even under communism, their personal friends were typically other members of their professions and fellow employees of the same institute, theatre, or orchestra. This was because intellectuals were likely, to paraphrase Hrabal, to enjoy their jobs and not to wish for different ones, the congruence between job and interest resulting in a congruence between colleagues or fellow workers and friends.

In contrast to the considerable narrowing of other status differentials (income, education, and lifestyle), 'the structure of power positions was not redistributed towards greater equality, but on the contrary within a few years after 1948 acquired a distinct and steep differentiation with all the important decision making concentrated in a comparatively small body at the top' (Krejci 1972: 106). This concentration of power shifted the basic division within society from the structure of the ownership of the means of production to the structure of management of not only the means of production but also the means of education and what Ossowski calls the 'means of compulsion' (1969: 185–6) – in brief, to the management of the whole structure of social life.[7]

Conceptualising the main division of Czechoslovak society as that between managers and the managed tallies with the Czech folk model. Of the respondents in a 1967 sociological survey, only 11 per cent subscribed to the then-official view of Czechoslovak society as divided into three non-antagonistic social classes (workers, cooperative farmers, and intelligentsia); 20 per cent advocated a complex hierarchical model of society and 25 per cent a non-hierarchical one. The four other models elicited from 44 per cent of respondents were basically dichotomous: mass and elite (Machonin *et al.* 1969: 371). This type of folk model was alternatively expressed as the division of society into rulers and ruled (a favourite expression of dissidents and intellectuals) or into 'us' and 'them', with 'them' being variously called *papaláši*, *načálstvo* (from the Russian), or *velení* ('command', which is a pun on the official expression *vedení*, 'leadership').

The number of those who made active decisions in the public sphere remained too small to override the image of it as a sphere in which the individual was the object of manipulation, pressure, and coercion and of the private sphere as that in which the individual was a free agent restricted only by the conventions of custom, economic possibility, or morality. But even within these inevitable constraints, people's agency was felt to be greater in the private than in the public sphere, for through their own actions they themselves maintained and re-created the norms which restricted them. The prevailing feeling in the public sphere was helplessness.

Different kinds of morality prevailed in the public and in the private sphere. Šimečka points to one aspect of this difference:

The omnipresent lie of the state has a devastating effect on morality in general. It establishes the norm of a lie being rewarded rather than punished. The citizen accustomed to this point of view has a tolerant attitude to the lie in the non-private sphere. After all, he has been taught to lie at school, to hide his convictions; he has learnt to lie in his workplace, becoming convinced that it pays. In consequence, he lies when filling in forms, in his dealings with authorities, in the courtroom, to his superiors – in fact, he lies wherever he can. Morally, lying to the state does not worry him; it is a lie in self-defence, for he is aware that the state cheats him too. Generally, skilful swindlers and liars who succeed in tricking the state are more appreciated than honest people who grind away for the state which does not deserve it. I knew only one exemplary honest man among the workers. He would, for example, jump into a trench to save a tile or a brick for the state. The others would look at him and tap their foreheads . . . The citizen, like the state, considers lying a useful tactic especially in the political sphere, where it is precisely established what is to one's advantage. He lies in response to direct questions about his political profile according to what has been established as being to his advantage. He is fully committed to the socialist order and the Communist Party, he loves the Soviet Union, he has solved the problem of religion, he participates in meetings and demonstrations, he has no doubt of any kind. This type is exempt from moral evaluation. This same citizen at home views with horror and indescribable sadness his child's lying to him for the first time and turns away in disgust from a friend who has lied to him or concealed a secret from him. This is different. The lie outside the strictly delimited private domain is subject to different moral laws, and no one mixes the criteria of the outer and inner circles. Lies and pretence reign in the outer circle; inside the private sphere a man must be careful of his moral defence.   *(1984: 148–50)*

The different moral evaluations of lying in the public and the private sphere lent great intensity to friendship. Because in friendship 'each person discloses something about himself that would be embarrassing or damaging in a less restricted audience' and hence the 'logic of friendship is a simple transformation of the rules of public propriety into their opposite' (Suttles 1970: 116), lying and deceit were of course unimaginable among friends. Knowing the truth about each other's views, opinions, and life histories, friends were in collusion against the world in which deceit and lies were strategically exploited to one's advantage. Friendship was thus built on the utmost trust, for if this trust were betrayed the consequence might be job loss or even imprisonment. Friendship literally meant putting one's security or even one's freedom into another's hands.

Under communism, charity did not begin at home; it ended there. It was appropriate for parents to care about their children and for children to care about their ageing parents; it was appropriate to help others in the domestic group and to expect their help; it was appropriate to be courteous to one another in the private sphere; and it was particularly expected that the young would be courteous to the old and that the able-bodied would take care of the old, the ill, and the otherwise incapacitated. The norms of care and courtesy did not, however, apply in the public sphere, not even when care was the essence of the job. Courtesy was something regularly commented upon by Czech travellers to the West, and, correspondingly, the lack of care and courtesy in any kind of public interaction struck visitors to Czechoslovakia. Smiles were reserved for communication among friends; shop assistants, waiters, postal or bank clerks, petrol station attendants, and so on served customers with solemn faces. Verbal utterances were restricted to the barest minimum and replies to questions were brisk and snappy. How exceptional was the opposite is attested to by the fact that a reader felt compelled to write to *Rudé právo* (5 August 1989) about a 'fairy-tale' guard on a provincial train line who greeted passengers with a smile, and while collecting tickets wished them a pleasant journey, reminded them to collect their personal belongings before leaving the train, and on top of that even managed to announce the name of the next stop.

Different moral norms also applied to the theft of private and of public or 'socialist' (i.e., state or cooperative) property. Whereas according to the official judicial view the theft of socialist property was more serious than the theft of personal property because it reflected disrespect for the collective ethic which should guide the 'new man', the folk morality saw the latter crime as much more abhorrent. Widespread pilfering of socialist property was greatly encouraged by the prevailing economic situation. Given the chronic shortage of building materials, tools, and other goods, pilfering them from building sites and other places of work or buying them from those who had pilfered them was for many people the only solution. Czech public lavatories were notorious for their lack of towels, soap, and toilet paper, which as a rule disappeared as soon as they were put there. Pilfering of socialist property was also for many people a way of augmenting their incomes which most considered inadequate. (According to an opinion survey conducted in 1969, Kčs 3,153 was considered an adequate monthly income for a family with two school-age children; in 1966 only 2 per cent of the population had incomes as high as this (Ulc 1974: 57).) A widespread Czech saying clearly endorsed the morality of this course of action: 'Anyone who does not steal is robbing his family.'[8]

Because everyone worked in the public sphere for a living, the separation of the two spheres also affected time: on the one hand there was the time which one was required to spend in the public sphere, and on the other there was the time in which one lived fully in the private sphere. Private time had to be saved and used to the fullest – even if only for doing nothing. Public time was not a commodity with the same value. For many, time spent at work was seen as time lost for private life, and the amount of private time could be increased if a number of things of a private nature could be done in time officially allocated to work. Those whose work allowed them to do so did their shopping or attended to other private business during working hours.[9] This habit was also encouraged by the fact that the hours during which most shops were opened coincided with working hours, as well as by the fact that to be able to obtain goods one often had to be in the shop when they were delivered. Those who could not use working time for their private purposes (such as assembly-line workers) felt truly exploited. If they could not save time, they could at least save their energy for release in the private sphere. At one time, cards with a picture of the Good Soldier Schweik[10] and the slogan 'Take it easy' (*To chce klid*) could be seen in every workplace, from the garage to the ministry. The situation in which production became a matter of workers' goodwill was one of the aspects of the deteriorating economy which the reform of 1968 aimed to rectify. *Literární listy* commented critically in May 1968 that

to exert only as much energy and effort as have been accepted tacitly and with absolute solidarity in a given place of work [is] a kind of collective norm. As a rule, it is not the able and efficient who raise to their level the average and below-average workers, but vice versa: it is the mediocre who set the norm.   (*Ulc 1974: 54*)[11]

The chronic shortages of material goods and the unpredictability of supply made the theft of socialist property and the use of working time for private purposes almost inevitable. This inevitability was, however, conditioned by the priority assigned to the satisfaction of private over public needs – the rejection of the ideal of the 'new man' morally committed to the interests, goals, and aspirations of society. The misappropriation of socialist property and the misuse of working time may well have been economically motivated, but ultimately they were manifestations of alienation from socialist ideals and from the society which should ideally have been their embodiment. Czechs characterised this alienation as 'inner emigration' (Wheaton and Kavan 1992: 9), as the lack of 'self-realisation' in the public sphere and full 'self-realisation' in the private circle of the family and friends, or as an 'escape' or 'withdrawal' into the private sphere. The journal *Tribuna* (1970, no. 10: 5) criticised 'individuals who have achieved their "private communism". They have nice jobs, a house, country cottage, etc.; all they need is time enough to enjoy their possessions' (quoted in Ulc 1974: 171, n. 17). Although pensions were low, people looked forward to retirement, when they would be able to withdraw completely from the public sphere, and it was not unusual for them to retire at the earliest possible time even if not forced to do so.[12]

Prior to the process of 'normalisation' following the 'crisis period' of the 1960s, a great deal of the party's rhetoric was concerned with the moral crisis of society. Its root was seen to lie in the 'building of one's private imaginary world and flight into this substitute for true self-realisation', as the *Reportér* expressed it in April 1969 (Ulc 1974: 92). Party ideologists saw the causes of this attitude in the party's failure to eradicate the survival of 'bourgeois morality' because of the 'formalism' of its socialising efforts (see, e.g., Ulc 1974: 144). They perceived the moral crisis as the cause of the economic crisis and saw the remedy in increased attention to 'ideological work' and to educating the 'new socialist man'. The journal *Novinář* stated this policy clearly in 1972: 'This is once again the beginning of a process of moulding a socialist man, a conscientious builder of socialism, a man who is pure and firm' (quoted in Paul 1979: 36).

Paradoxically, during the late 1970s and 1980s, alienation and withdrawal into the private sphere were considered moral problems more by the dissidents than by the party and the government. The reason is that these trends were to a very great extent encouraged by official party policy adopted in the course of 'normalisation'. Political stability was achieved by giving in completely to the demands generated in the private sphere and abandoning any serious attempt at mobilising the working masses to increased effort in the building of socialism (Wheaton and Kavan 1992: 10, 23) which, paradoxically, was the essence of the Communist Party's action programme of 1968, supported by the overwhelming majority of Czechs. Economic priority was ascribed to the satisfaction of consumption needs, instead of to increasing the productivity of labour (the main economic aim of the 1968 reform), and to their stimulation by a limited import of Western consumer goods. In official rhetoric, the rising standard of living was construed as a sign of socialist achievement.

The situation in Czechoslovakia at the end of August 1988 was described by a Czech publicist who kept a diary throughout the year as follows:

Turning one's back on politics began to manifest itself from the beginning of normalisation. Because politics ceased to pretend that it was concerned with national interests and became only a well-paid job, because it transpired that lying paid and people without conscience prospered best, because it transpired that stupidity had better prospects of advancement than vision and education, most people left all public activity to those who had the stomach for it. An unwritten social contract thus emerged according to which the state and the party would do their thing and the people would do theirs. The functioning of this contract was of course conditional on the changed image of the regime. In its post-totalitarian[13] mutation, the regime no longer required that everyone be devoted to socialism, believe in the ideology, and be full of enthusiasm and ready to make sacrifices; it was enough for each individual simply to respect the rules, even if with obvious cynicism. Two worlds thus emerged: the artificial world of politics and the real world of little human histories bounded by the fence of one's own garden . . . An 'as if' state emerged from this contract. In this state, we 'as if' built communism, 'as if' scientifically guided society, 'as if' increased the standard of living, 'as if' elected state representatives with 99 per cent of the vote, and 'as if' did not see that everyone worked only for himself. Real life was dominated by practical interests: where to pluck this and where to gather that, where to cheat, how to grasp an opportunity, how to drag oneself up the social ladder, how to provide for the children, how to manage to travel abroad, and most of all how to have anything when something is always in short supply.   (*Šimečka 1990: 104–5*)

Opposition to the communist regime

A lifestyle oriented solely toward increasing material well-being and full self-realisation in the private sphere may appear to contradict the ideal of a 'change of people's consciousness [and] their identification with the aims of socialist society' (*Rudé právo*, 28 July 1978; quoted in Fidelius 1983: 128). It nevertheless served a positive political function in that withdrawal from the public sphere meant lack of support not only for the policy of the Communist Party but also for the political aims of its opponents and critics. In terms of pragmatic politics, the latter consequence was much more important than the former, and the normalisation policy of the Communist Party appears to have borne fruit. Twenty years after 1968 the economic and political transformation of the socialist system and the campaign for human rights were the concern of only a small group of intellectuals. Although the underground publications which expressed this group's political aims were more widely circulated than before and the foreign broadcasts which publicised them had a large audience, holiday cottages, cars, and family pets rather than efforts to change the structure of society remained the priority of the overwhelming majority of the population.

Attitudes expressed through the invocation of the material symbols of a fully meaningful human life were shared by those who shunned any active participation in public life and by the guardians of the existing social system. According to Šimečka, every police interrogation of a dissident ended with a rebuke:

Why do you do it, it is pointless, you only harm yourself and your family, you have a flat, a car, you are not hungry, what more do you want? We shall build socialism even without writers, journalists, and philosophers. Take care, like everybody else, that you have something and we shall leave you in peace.   *(1984: 106)*

Discouraging interest in any kind of political and economic alternative to the existing system by construing material well-being as a symbol of life fulfilment gave the communist system in Czechoslovakia remarkable stability. In the final analysis, this stability was achieved at the price of alienation from any broad public concern. Anthropologists who have done research in Central and Eastern Europe have argued about how much popular support the socialist regimes there enjoyed (Hann 1993: 11). Although the Communist Party in Czechoslovakia, as elsewhere in the socialist countries, had its leading role and hence its right to rule the country forever enshrined in the constitution, its legitimacy was a constant concern. The May Day parades and the results of regularly held elections[14] were presented by official propaganda as unmistakable signs of the people's support, but legitimacy required more than that. The obvious reluctance of the majority of the population to address any public issue contradicted what official propaganda construed as support for socialist principles and made it transparent that what the party proclaimed was indeed only propaganda. This meant that the ideal of the 'new man' committed to the goals of society rather than to individual or group interests could not be abandoned. The symbols of such commitment could, however, be manipulated, and through the use of appropriate symbols anything could be construed as support for the socialist order and for the Communist Party, its guardian and guarantee.

Such symbolic construction was part of the pragmatic policy which the party adopted from 1969 on. To achieve self-realisation in the accumulation of possessions, workers and employees of course had to earn money from work, and what they had to do in any case was construed as a symbol of their commitment to society. This symbol was no longer 'work enthusiasm' and 'work heroism' but everyday 'honest work'. In the late 1970s and the 1980s it was invoked in virtually every issue of *Rudé právo* and was probably most lucidly summed up in its lead article on 23 May 1978:

It is pleasing that the overwhelming majority of working people give the most persuasive proof of their political consciousness and their full confidence in the party and its policy through their everyday honest work and their concrete action for the socialist homeland.   *(quoted in Fidelius 1983: 154)*

A nice flat, a holiday cottage, a car, and a reasonable standard of living were concrete symbols of everything desirable in life in the final years of the communist regime in Czechoslovakia, and the pursuit of any other kind of achievement became meaningless. This realisation lay at the root of the dissidents' perpetual concern with the moral crisis of Czechoslovak society. The following quotation well summarises this concern:

A society which unashamedly proclaims the slogan 'Anyone who does not steal is robbing his family' is a sick one. The consumer mentality predominates – people are mostly interested only in 'living well' . . . higher goals, higher values are desperately missing. Only a minority has any religious beliefs; the idea that a man should do something for his nation has almost disappeared; people long for freedom and democracy, but hardly anyone is willing to sacrifice anything for these values; a number of people are interested in the arts and the sciences but those interested in science in particular are often bogged down in a narrow specialism which lacks wider perspectives.   *(Meznik 1989: 19)*

Withdrawal into the private sphere and the effective pursuit of private economic and social interests in the public one largely account for the lack of any mass opposition to the communist regime. Before November 1989 the opposition remained limited to a number of 'independent initiatives' of which the oldest and best-known was Charter 77. Others were the Committee for the Defence of the Unjustly Prosecuted (Výbor na ochranu nespravedlivě stíhaných, or VONS), the Independent Peace Association, Czech Children, the Movement for Civic Liberty, the Jazz Section, the Friends of the USA Club, the Ecological Committee, and a number of smaller groups (Skilling 1981; Kusin 1983). The Communist Party considered all of them illegal and hostile to socialism and state interests. Particularly during 1988 and 1989, various party documents and the official press paid increased attention to these groups in connection with what the party construed as their increased activity, their growing attempts to influence public opinion, and their gradual move from a campaign for the moral and democratic reform of socialism to open calls for its destruction and the re-creation of a bourgeois society. The party admitted the existence of some twenty such groups with 500 active members and 5,000 supporters and sympathisers (*Listy* 19 (1989), no. 2: 32). Although it is likely that even in its internal documents the party tried to play down the number of people actively involved in opposition to its policies, the fact remains that political opposition in Czechoslovakia was weak in comparison with Poland, Hungary, or East Germany. Although the number of 'independent initiatives' had steadily increased in the last few years before 1989, it remains doubtful whether this increase was matched by an increase in their active membership, which was characterised by considerable overlap. The public was informed about their activities mainly by foreign broadcasts, which after Czechoslovakia had signed the declaration on freedom of exchange of information were no longer jammed. Despite greater awareness of their activities in the late 1980s, the small circle of intellectuals involved in them lacked the support of the working class. As Václav Havel put it,

When friends from the Polish Solidarity whom we meet occasionally at the Czech–Polish border ask how many people Charter 77 has behind it, I feel like answering that while there are millions of people behind Solidarity, there are only millions of ears behind Charter 77.   *(The Times, 12 August 1988)*

Among the numerous reasons for the failure of most ordinary Czechs to identify with the dissidents' campaign, the construction of material well-being as a symbol of life fulfilment certainly played its role. In July and August 1989 *Rudé právo* published a series of letters in which readers denounced the authors and signatories of Charter 77's *Several Sentences*, a call for democracy, respect for human rights, and a dialogue with the government. Their typical targets were artists, whose behaviour was particularly puzzling because, being the best materially provided of all people in Czechoslovakia, they possessed all the recognised symbols of the good life. For example, railway station employees asked,

How can such people, whom our socialist society often provides with very good material security, stoop to such anti-socialist actions? How can cultural workers and even artists identify with such actions?   *(Rudé právo, 4 August 1989)*

Similarly, a house painter expressed his astonishment that most signatories were 'very well provided for materially by our society, and many of them have been highly honoured by orders and titles'. A worker told a reporter,

We have read in the newspapers what the Chartists want – in essence to abolish socialism. But what the famous actors who signed the pamphlet *Several Sentences* are up to I really do not know. Perhaps political power, when they already have everything.

The reaction of another worker was similar:

We do not live badly. But what have the authors of *Several Sentences* done for the republic during the past twenty years? What can they boast about? How have they contributed to the development of socialism? By those pamphlets and calls? Excuse me, but that won't fill my stomach.

The letters were selected by the editors of this Communist Party newspaper because they expressed ideologically desirable opinions, and one can reasonably assume that at least some of them were written to order. Nevertheless, even if most Czechs did not subscribe to the views expressed, the fact remains that as private individuals they had reached a more or less acceptable *modus vivendi* with the communist state. They cheated it and used it for their private benefit in numerous ingenious ways, and they devised effective strategies for eliminating its interference in their private lives. This accommodation of individuals' 'lifeworlds' to the socialist system was expressed in a joke which circulated widely in Czechoslovakia in the 1970s:

The first peculiarity of socialism: everybody is employed and nobody works. The second peculiarity: nobody works and the plan gets fulfilled one hundred per cent. The third peculiarity: the plan is fulfilled one hundred per cent and there is nothing to be had in the shops. The fourth peculiarity: there is nothing to be had in the shops and people have everything. The fifth peculiarity: people have everything and everybody grumbles about the regime from morning until night. The sixth peculiarity: everybody grumbles about the regime all the time and in the elections everybody votes for it.

Another reason for the lack of support for the active opposition to the communist regime was that many of the dissidents had at one time been communist intellectuals, active supporters of the creation of the 'new social order', and therefore their sincerity as dissidents was doubted. Their earlier writings, although officially banned and removed from libraries, were still remembered, and many people saw them simply as turncoats. Those who had never joined the Communist Party and did not actively support the communist system particularly disliked being lectured on its evils by those who had seen the light only too late. Many dissidents had been activists of the Prague Spring and suffered the reprisals that followed, and ordinary people tended to view them as politicians desperately trying to stage a comeback. That they were now campaigning under a different banner from that of 1968 was seen by many as a sign that being in the limelight was more important to them than the principles they espoused.

More important was probably the fact that most dissidents were intellectuals, some of them internationally renowned. This guaranteed them a certain degree of protection from persecution by the regime that ordinary dissidents would never enjoy. The frequent excuse 'We cannot all be dissidents' reflected recognition of this fact. The leading dissidents were themselves fully aware of their privileged position and tried to defuse it by every available means. The danger to the communist regime represented by the Committee for the Defence of the Unjustly Prosecuted stemmed precisely from the fact that it deliberately undermined the privileged position of well-known dissidents by publicising the persecution of unknown ones. For good reason, the actions of the secret police were targeted against the committee to a far greater extent than against Charter 77 (Možný 1991: 22–8).

Given the limited impact of the opposition groups, the scale of the popular demonstrations which broke out in Prague in 1988 and early 1989 took both the public and the government by surprise. It also surprised the dissidents themselves, who formed only a small minority among the demonstrators. In retrospect, it is difficult to specify who the demonstrators actually were. Prominent among them were young people, but a considerable number of very old people also took part. It is impossible to say that they were predominantly students, workers, or intellectuals; they seemed to represent a cross-section of the population as a whole. It is also difficult to determine the reasons for the spontaneous outbreak of the demonstrations. A strong motivating force was probably the belief that the Soviet Union under Gorbachev's leadership would not come to the defence of the Czechoslovak government as it had in 1968 under Brezhnev. The social-political development in Poland and Hungary certainly constituted an effective example – if only in that it indicated to the Czechs that change was possible. However, changes do not happen merely because they are possible. They have to be carried out by people who have an interest in instigating them. The mass exodus of East Germans to West Germany through Prague undoubtedly contributed to the open expression of dissatisfaction with the communist regime in Czechoslovakia. The ease with which East Germans left their Trabant cars behind in Prague was a clear indication that what most people had so far considered a highly desirable possession paled into insignificance against what they believed they could achieve through a radical change of political system.

Communist ideology had always proclaimed that the Communist Party was the vanguard of the working masses, whose interests it represented. The impact of public demonstrations on political development in Czechoslovakia was much more significant than the impact of the dissident movement because they showed that the masses refused to be led by the party. They were a public, unmistakable, and, most of all, mass rejection of the existing regime. In this respect, they were of course political acts and were clearly understood as such by the government and the Czechoslovak and international media. However, if they articulated any political demands, it was in a highly symbolic way. Political attitudes may be shaped more by symbolic forms than by utilitarian calculations, but there is more to the relation between the symbolic and the political than this. Symbolic action is used not only to assert the right to rule or to demonstrate political allegiance but also to bring about change in political and economic structures or to defend these structures against attempts to change them, to institute new policies, or to defend existing ones. Not only are political actions for the most part symbolic but symbolic actions become political ones. The political significance of symbolic actions seems to me to have been much greater in the totalitarian political systems of the socialist countries of Central and Eastern Europe than in Western liberal democracies. The reason is that not only the political systems but even what counted as 'political activity' and 'political attitudes' were constructed differently from those in the West.

In the rest of this chapter I analyse the symbolic aspects of the first public demonstrations against communist rule in Czechoslovakia. I try to explain why the Czech authorities responded to them not only with force (on which the attention of international media concentrated) but also with considerable symbolic manipulation. In concentrating on the symbols invoked during the demonstrations I want not only to elucidate their significance for the political process in Czechoslovakia but, in the next chapter, to suggest how they articulated the culturally specific Czech conceptualisation of the relations between the individual, the nation, and the state.

The venues of the demonstrations

The setting of demonstrations is crucial to their impact. The demonstrations in Prague took place not in centres of political power such as the party secretariat, the cabinet office, or police headquarters but, like all demonstrations everywhere, in symbolic centres (Berger 1968). Because these centres were given, the demonstrators knew beforehand where to assemble, and the demonstrations could develop spontaneously without any previous planning or organisation. Knowledge of the symbolic map was of course also an advantage for the riot police, who knew exactly what positions to take to disperse the demonstrators. Their skill improved with practice, and the demonstration in Prague on 28 October 1989 was dispersed more quickly and effectively (i.e., with less use of force) than the previous ones.

All the demonstrations started in Wenceslas Square, with the participants assembling near the equestrian statue of St Wenceslas and attempting to march from there to the Old Town Square, with its monument to Jan Hus. The final destination was Hradčany Castle across the river, but no demonstration managed to reach it. All these standard venues are redolent with nationalist connotations.

Although the street protest was limited to Prague, this did not diminish its nationwide significance, for Prague is itself a powerful symbol of the country and shares with it the appellation 'mother' (usually in its diminutive form): Prague is the 'mother of a hundred spires', the 'mother of cities', or simply 'mother Prague'. The symbol of Prague was skilfully exploited by Dubček in 1968. Soon after becoming general secretary of the Communist Party, he delivered a speech to the citizens of Prague at a mass rally on the anniversary of its assumption of power in February 1948. In the context of Czechoslovak politics, his speech was unusual in that it was free of any of the standard political and ideological references customarily expected from the general secretary on this occasion. Instead, Dubček concentrated on praising Prague's beauty and its glorious past. By openly acknowledging this powerful symbol of Czech nationalism, he firmly established his own patriotic credentials. He spoke in Slovak to his Czech audience about how important Prague was to the Slovaks, who also looked upon it as to the capital of their country. Although this was contrary to the political aims of his regime (one of which was redressing the balance of power between the Czech and Slovak nations through the creation of a federal system), through the deft use of the symbolic he created a feeling of Czechoslovak unity, reminiscent of the pre-war Czechoslovak Republic.

Wenceslas Square is the symbolic heart of the country. During the nineteenth century it was so closely associated with nationalist demonstrations that the Prague Germans nicknamed it 'Kravalenplatz' (Ructions Square) (Vlček 1986: 77). This is the reason it was chosen as the site for the Czech National Museum, the founding of which was an important moment in the Czech nationalist struggle against Austro-Hungarian rule, and the reason a statue of St Wenceslas – the patron saint of Bohemia – was erected there. The image of German troops or Soviet tanks in Wenceslas Square is more heavily loaded emotionally than that of German or Soviet troops anywhere else in the country.

The statue of St Wenceslas became the rallying point for all the demonstrations. Wenceslas, born in 907 or 908, was a son of Vratislav, the paramount chief of the Czech tribe which occupied the western part of central Bohemia, and succeeded him probably in 922 or 924 after a short period during which his mother ruled as regent. From their castle in Prague the Czechs already dominated about half of some fifteen closely related Slavonic tribes in Bohemia, and Wenceslas augmented their political dominance. The historical facts about him have to be sifted from numerous legends about his life, the first of which was already current during the rule of his successor Boleslav I (ruled 929 or 935 to 972). These legends stress Wenceslas's Christian learning and piety as befits a martyr who died in witness of Christ's truth. Wenceslas was literate when literacy was still the prerogative of priests. His scholarly tendencies and his close association with priests were probably the main reason he was murdered in 929 or 935 by the brother who succeeded him; his bookishness may well have been seen as standing in the way of the martial prowess expected of a leader.

The murder of a pious and just ruler by his own brother was almost immediately seen as martyrdom, and the significance and glory of the Czech martyr began to be systematically cultivated after the establishment of the Prague bishopric in the 970s. The day of Wenceslas's death – 28 September – was already being celebrated as a holiday in Bohemia by the end of the tenth century, and probably by that time his name was included among the saints of the diocese of Regensburg, to which the church in Bohemia belonged before a bishopric was established in Prague. Wenceslas became the patron saint of Bohemia (Pitha 1992: 12–8; Obrazová and Vlk 1994; Pynsent 1994: 196–8). According to Czech legend, St Wenceslas is one of the Czech knights who lie sleeping beneath Blaník Mountain in central Bohemia awaiting the moment when they will rise and, under his leadership, return to free the nation of its enemies. During the anti-government demonstrations in November 1989, the statue of St Wenceslas became a veritable shrine in which a number of nationalist symbols were fused. When the jubilant crowd danced in Wenceslas Square on the night the resignation of the general secretary was announced, some of them were chanting, 'The knights of Blaník have arrived.'

The next rallying point for the demonstrations was the statue of Jan Hus in the Old Town Square. Jan Hus (born around 1372) became a master of liberal arts at the University of Prague in 1396 and eventually its rector (vice-chancellor). Influenced by the philosophical and theological views of John Wycliffe, Hus led a reform movement aimed at eliminating the abuses of the church, the most notorious of which was the sale of indulgences. The papal schism led Hus to recognise only Christ as the head of the church and his followers later renewed the original Christian practice of receiving communion in both kinds, i.e., in the form of wine and bread rather than in the form of the host. The university at which these theological views were promulgated and disputed had been founded in 1348 by the Czech and Roman king Charles IV as a centre of learning and education for the whole of Central Europe. Each of the four 'university nations' – Czech, Polish, Bavarian, and Saxon – had one vote in the university council. In 1403 and again in 1408 the university denounced the doctrine which Hus was defending. The Czech king Wenceslas IV needed the university on his side in his support of the Council of Pisa, which was to end the papal schism and recognise him as Roman king. Because his policy was supported by the Czechs at the university but opposed by the other university nations, he changed the voting system in 1409 to give three votes to the Czechs and one vote to the others. The foreign masters and students left the university in protest, and it became an exclusively Czech institution. In popular historical knowledge, fostered mainly by the propagandistically oriented teaching of history in schools and by the historical novels of the patriotic Czech writer Alois Jirásek (1851–1930), this change is seen as one of Hus's achievements. Hus's views met with strong opposition from the archbishop of Prague and from the pope. He was banned from preaching in Prague and eventually summoned to the council in Konstanz to defend his views. When he refused to abandon them, he was burned as a heretic on 6 June 1415 (Pynsent 1994: 198–201). Much of the Czech nobility protested to the council, and Prague University testified to Hus's pious life and to the truth of his teaching and issued a decree supporting communion in both kinds. The defenestration at Prague Town Hall which followed the demands to release the imprisoned supporters of Hus marked the beginning of the Hussite movement (or revolution, as the official communist historiography preferred to call it) in 1419.

The cultural significance of historical figures like St Wenceslas and Jan Hus derives not from what they did, but from what they came to stand for. Their significance lies in that they become symbols. In their symbolic significance, St Wenceslas and Hus differ. Although full administrative and political domination of other tribes in Bohemia was probably achieved only in the second half of the tenth century, folk history sees Wenceslas as the founder of the Czech state, who unified the Bohemian tribes under his rule (see Škutina 1990: 89). His crown, kept in St Wenceslas's Chapel in Prague Cathedral, where he is buried, is the most important relic signifying the antiquity of the Czech state – the Bohemian kingdom, which consisted historically of Bohemia and Moravia and survived as a sovereign state until the beginning of the seventeenth century, when it fell under Habsburg rule. With the increasing centralisation of the Habsburg empire, the Bohemian kingdom eventually lost even its nominal recognition; the last Austrian emperor formally crowned in Prague as a Czech king was Ferdinand I in 1836.

In the nineteenth century St Wenceslas became a rallying symbol of the political struggle for the revival of a Czech state. The petition to the emperor in 1848 demanding the unification of the lands of the Czech crown into a single state within the empire was prepared by a committee which became later known as the St Wenceslas Committee. The revolution in Prague in 1848 began when the army attacked the participants in a mass being celebrated in what was then known as the Horse Market, at the stone equestrian statue of St Wenceslas which had stood there since 1680. Removed in 1879, it was replaced in 1912 by the present bronze one. In the latter part of the nineteenth century the struggle for an autonomous Czech state took the form of opposition to the dualism of the Austro-Hungarian monarchy, which came into being in 1867 and gave Hungary and Austria a degree of autonomy which the 'lands of St Wenceslas's crown' did not enjoy. The dualism was formally expressed by the coronation of the emperor Franz Josef I as king of Hungary; he was never crowned as a Czech king. The return of St Wenceslas's crown and other Czech crown jewels to Prague from Vienna, to which they had been removed during the war with Prussia, triggered one of the first important demonstrations against dualism. To avoid attracting attention, the train in which the jewels were transported travelled through Moravia and Bohemia at night, but it was greeted by crowds at all the stations through which it passed, and bonfires were lit on all the hills along the route to Prague. The royal box of the National Theatre, opened in Prague in 1881, was adorned not by the imperial crown but by St Wenceslas's.

If Wenceslas is the symbol of Czech statehood, Hus is the symbol of Czech nationhood and, more specifically, of the spiritual greatness of the Czech nation. This symbol is a product of the period of 'national revival' which began at the end of the eighteenth century with a conscious effort to revive the Czech language, by then merely the speech of peasants, and constitute it as a literary language. This 'veritable resurrection' of the nation (Gellner 1987: 131) as the bearer of its own 'high' culture peaked in the middle of the nineteenth century. In 1848 the Czech historian František Palacký published the Czech translation of the first two volumes of his *History of the Czech nation in Bohemia and Moravia*, originally published in German in 1836 and 1837. The third volume of his work, already written in Czech and published in two parts in 1850 and 1854, was devoted to the Hussite movement, which Palacký interpreted as the most glorious part of Czech history. The Hussite victories over the armies of German crusaders and Roman emperors became appropriate symbols of the greatness and spiritual and moral superiority of the Czech nation which was forming itself in opposition to the German elements in Bohemia and in the Habsburg monarchy at large. Inspired by Palacký's interpretation of history, the symbolism of Jan Hus and the Hussite movement was effectively fostered by literature, journalism, drama, visual arts, and music (Bradley 1984: 91–3). This had a greater effect on the consciousness of the masses than Palacký's work, which was probably not widely read outside intellectual, or at least educated, circles. Since the period of national revival, the Hussite movement has been seen as the most important period of Czech history, albeit for different reasons, by Czech historians of whatever ideological persuasion as well as by ordinary people, for whom the most significant fact about this historical period is that the Czech nation rose in an armed struggle 'against all', as the title of a famous novel by Alois Jirásek expressed it.

When Czechs speak of themselves as 'we', the 'we' tends to be polysemic. In different contexts it refers either to the Czech state or to the Czech nation. When efforts to have the autonomy of the Czech state recognised in the federal structure of Austria failed, Palacký uttered his famous pronouncement, 'We were here before Austria, and we shall be here after it.' Understood as a reference to the Czech state, this marked the beginning of the Czech struggle for independence rather than simply autonomy. In speaking of themselves as 'we' and leaving the referent of the personal pronoun implicit and specifiable only by context, Czechs construct what is for them (as of course for many others) the proper relationship between the nation and the state. It is a relationship wherein one can talk about the one through the other. With regard to this culturally constructed ideal, it is not the nation but the state that is problematic. I shall return to this point in greater detail later; suffice it here to say that the Czechs conceptualise their nation as a natural entity that has existed for at least a millennium. Until the beginning of the seventeenth century, the Czech nation had its own state, the Bohemian kingdom. The Battle of White Mountain on 8 November 1620 ended the uprising of the Czech nobility against the centralising and absolutist tendency of the Habsburg monarchy and effectively put an end to the sovereignty of the Czech state: the centre of political power moved to Vienna. Czechs refer to these events as the 'White Mountain tragedy' or 'injustice' because it was followed by three hundred years of 'darkness' (again the title of one of Jirásek's historical novels), 'oppression', and 'suffering' of the Czech nation – in less emotional terms, a period of forcible re-Catholicisation and gradual Germanisation.

The founding of the independent Czechoslovak state after World War I in 1918 was not the result of any sustained liberation struggle by the Czech nation, although modern Czech historiography has made an effort to create precisely this impression. It was the result of the new political arrangements in Central Europe agreed upon among the victorious allies and sanctioned by the Treaty of Versailles. It did, however, represent the liberation of the nation from three hundred years of Habsburg oppression and the fulfilment of Comenius's prophecy – issued as he was leaving Bohemia in 1627 rather than convert to Catholicism – that, after storms of anger, the Czech people would again achieve mastery of their own fate. The freedom of the nation – in the sense of its again having its own state to manage its collective destiny – was seen as the major achievement of this political change.

Catholicism was the official state religion until the end of the Austro-Hungarian Empire. The Protestant faith was 'tolerated' only after 1781, when Emperor Joseph II issued a 'tolerance patent' guaranteeing freedom of religion. This has direct bearing on the symbolism of St Wenceslas and Jan Hus. The ambivalence of these two symbols derives from the fact that they are not only the symbols of the Czech state and nation respectively but also distinctly Catholic and Protestant symbols. As long as the issue was merely the autonomy of the Czech state within federal Austria-Hungary, St Wenceslas was the symbol with which all Czechs could identify irrespective of their religion. When the idea of Czech independence began to gain prominence toward the end of the century, and particularly in the years shortly before and during the World War I, the Hussite symbols became appropriate vehicles for expressing this notion, given the official association between the Habsburg monarchy and the Catholic church. For example, the first Czech legions, which assembled deserters from the Austro-Hungarian army in Russia to fight alongside the Russian troops, bore the name of St Wenceslas. Only during the Russian revolution was the St Wenceslas legion renamed the Jan Hus (Pekař 1990: 308).

Symbols invoked in political discourse are almost never unequivocal.

Different political forces or shades of political opinion try to appropriate symbols of general significance to themselves or to endow them with particular meanings. When political symbols have distinct religious connotations as the symbols of St Wenceslas and Jan Hus do, they also become contested on religious grounds. When the National Museum in Prague was built (it was officially opened in 1881), it was decided to place plaques with the names of important men in Czech history above the windows. The Land Council of Bohemia ruled out the name of Jan Hus, the argument being that 'at the beginning of the Hussite movement there were many honourable characters among the Hussites, but soon the Hussites regrettably turned into a bunch of pillagers and arsonists' (Škutina 1990: 77). The decision of the council was eventually reversed and simultaneously a campaign was initiated to erect a monument to Hus in Prague. Symbols have their meaning in relation to other symbols, but that meaning does not simply derive from the structure of the symbolic configuration. It is created by linking new symbols to old ones and other forms of symbolic manipulation. The Old Town Square had symbolic significance for Czech nationalism because it was the place where twenty-seven Czech Protestant noblemen, knights, and burghers who had led the 1620 uprising against the Habsburgs were executed. The erection of Hus's monument there in 1915 was a tangible expression of the Czechs' longing for their own state.

After the declaration of Czechoslovak independence in 1918, the jubilant crowd pulled down St Mary's pillar, which had also stood in the Old Town Square and as a Catholic monument was seen as a symbol of Habsburg oppression. The founding of independent Czechoslovakia was followed by a massive renunciation of Catholicism under the banner of 'freedom from Rome' (Leff 1988: 22). It is estimated that about a million people and some three hundred priests left the Catholic church (Mali 1983: 53). Although the majority of Czechs still remained nominally Catholic, the state ideology and symbolism acquired distinct Hussite overtones. Hus's words 'Seek the truth, hear the truth, learn the truth, love the truth, speak the truth, hold the truth, and defend the truth until death' gave rise to the motto 'The truth prevails', which became part of the new republic's coat of arms. Today they are echoed in Havel's notion of 'life in truth' (see Pynsent 1994: 19), which is what the new post-communist society is to be all about, and in his campaign slogan 'Love and truth conquer lies and hatred.' In pre-war Czechoslovakia, the anniversary of Hus's death on 6 July was celebrated as a national holiday, and bonfires were lit on the eve of the holiday in every village; in the Czech Republic 6 July is once again a state holiday.

The new Czechoslovak state was short-lived. In 1939 Slovakia became an independent fascist state, and the lands of the Czech crown were occupied by Germany and became a German protectorate until 1945. In 1948 the Communists seized power in Czechoslovakia. As the spontaneous demonstrations of 1989 against communist rule indicated, the communist coup d'état was seen as yet another loss of sovereignty for the Czech state. Although this view was not explicitly stated during the demonstrations, the symbols through which people made sense of the political process played a major role in fostering it. The Communist Party systematically employed political rituals and symbols imported directly from the Soviet Union, and the party's own symbolic creativity was combined with an attack on all the symbols of the pre-war republic. It is no wonder that in the spring of 1980 the rumour was widely circulated in Prague that Czechoslovakia was to be fully incorporated into the Soviet Union as one of its republics (Gellner 1987: 126). And it is also no wonder that the communist system – and indeed socialism itself – was widely seen as alien to the national interest.

Although the majority of Czechs are nominally Catholic, Czech nationalism is expressed through Protestant religious symbols. This is because the period following the loss of Czech state sovereignty was the period of re-Catholicisation and therefore foreign and Catholic elements were symbolically fused. After Czechoslovak independence, state ideology and symbolism acquired distinct Protestant overtones which gave rise to a subtle and complex manipulation of nationalist and religious symbols. For example, the millennium of St Wenceslas's death in 1929 was a carefully staged affair in which the two meanings of St Wenceslas – as a state symbol and a religious symbol – were consciously separated. The church celebration in Prague Cathedral (the building of which was completed to mark the anniversary) took part without any participation of the representatives of the state; the state celebration was held separately in Wenceslas Square.

With their monuments to St Wenceslas and Jan Hus, the two main Prague squares represent spatially the religious divide within the Czech nation. The regular spillover of spontaneous demonstrations from one square to the other can thus be seen as a symbolic expression of the nation's acknowledgement of its unity of purpose in spite of its division along religious lines.

The final destination of the demonstrations was Hradčany Castle. Its symbolism is straightforward. It was the seat of the Czech kings, and the fact that it has also been the seat of all Czechoslovak presidents since 1918 is in itself a powerful symbolic acknowledgement of the independent Czechoslovak state as the continuation of the once-sovereign Bohemian kingdom. Hradčany Castle is the most tangible symbol of Czech nationhood and it is the most visited place of national symbolic importance. The political and religious symbols of Czech nationhood are fused in it, for the national cathedral itself stands within the castle precinct. It contains St Wenceslas's Chapel and the saint's burial chamber and is the burial place of St Vojtěch and St Jan Nepomucký, the two other most important Czech saints (see Piťha 1992; on Nepomucký, see pp. 131–2). It was until Rudolf II (ruled 1576–1611) the place where Czech kings were crowned and buried, and the crown jewels are housed there today.

The timing of the demonstrations

Just as the venues of the demonstrations were determined by their symbolic significance, so was their timing. The demonstrators knew without being told not only where to assemble but also when. Needless to say, this also facilitated counteraction by the authorities, whose favourite ploy was to detain known dissidents before the date on which a demonstration was expected to take place. The demonstrations erupted not in response to any specific unpopular government action but on the anniversaries of important events in recent Czechoslovak history: 28 October, the anniversary of the founding of the independent Czechoslovak state in 1918; 21 August, the anniversary of the Warsaw Pact armies' invasion of Czechoslovakia in 1968 which ended the Prague Spring; 19 January, the anniversary of the death of the Czech student Jan Palach in 1969; 17 November, the anniversary of the closing of the Czech universities, the execution of nine students, and the internment of some twelve hundred students in concentration camps in reprisal for the student demonstrations against the Nazi occupation in 1939. These demonstrations took place during the funeral of Jan Opletal, a student shot dead by the Germans during the pro-Czechoslovak demonstration on 28 October 1939.

Certain historical events are of course of particular symbolic significance to any nation and state, and their anniversaries are celebrated as national or state holidays. The meaning imposed on these events serves as a mythological charter for the current political system. It enables governments and holders of political office to be perceived as the legitimate custodians of the ideals which inspired these events or arose in the course of them. Like all symbols, these historical events are condensed, multivocal, and ultimately ambiguous. They are always open to potential reinterpretation in an effort to solicit support for new policies or new leaders (see, e.g.,

Wright 1985 on the manipulation of the meaning of Remembrance Day in British politics). Such support may be achieved by the imposition of new meanings upon contested symbols, but it ultimately comes to be channelled through institutional structures such as political parties, parliament, and general elections.

In socialist countries, institutionalised political processes did not provide room for the formulation and expression of political alternatives, and this endowed symbols and symbolic actions with a potency they lack in a liberal democracy. This difference between the two systems manifests itself in the relative importance which the imposition of new meanings on the events of particular symbolic significance played in the politics of socialist countries. The imposition of a specific meaning on the secret protocols of the Ribbentrop–Molotov pact became a major issue in the struggle of the Baltic states to gain their political independence from the Soviet Union, and the reinterpretation of the Hungarian 'counterrevolution' of 1956 as a 'popular uprising' became a political act with far-reaching consequences in the struggle for the change of the whole political system in Hungary. The main political divide in post-1968 Czechoslovakia was between those who imposed one meaning on the events of 1968 and those who imposed another. The power of the Ribbentrop–Molotov pact, the Hungarian revolt of 1956, and the Prague Spring and its crushing by the Warsaw Pact armies as symbols derives not only from their shaping of past political processes and the understanding of present ones but also from their determination of what count as important political issues.

Changing the symbolic system (either by creating new symbols or by reinterpreting existing ones) makes people conscious of the reality which the symbolic system reflects or represents. The aim of this process is to raise people's consciousness of reality by making this reality transparent. Promulgating new symbols makes people aware of the fact that things are not what they could or should be – that they suffer discrimination, deprivation, or oppression. In brief, the aim is to politicise them as a precondition for causing them to formulate a new political objective, whether this be political independence, institutionalisation of a pluralistic political structure, or the creation of democratic political processes. Typically, in situations of tangible deprivation (such as shortages of food or material goods and wages inadequate for the procurement of basic necessities or what is perceived as a decent standard of living), the symbolic component is not pronounced, and the action takes the form of direct political action in the narrow sense of the term. Demands are directly and openly formulated and usually accompanied by a threat of withdrawal of support if not met. The strike of Soviet miners in 1990 for better material conditions is a typical example; it was a direct instrumental action with hardly any symbolic overtones. The Solidarity movement in Poland was different; invocation of emotionally loaded nationalist and religious symbols was its characteristic feature because it was aiming at more than simply tangible material benefits. The events which preceded the political change in Czechoslovakia in November 1989 were also characterised by conspicuous symbolic manipulation. This manipulation was of course itself made possible by the fact that those involved in the events, whatever their motives (see Devereux 1978: 113–35), shared a single culture.

All the dates on which the public street demonstrations in Prague took place have strong nationalist connotations: the founding of the Czechoslovak Republic in 1918 was seen as the renewal of the Czech nation-state after three hundred years of foreign domination, and the Prague Spring was seen as the time when Czechoslovakia again achieved the national sovereignty which it had lacked until Dubček came to power. The symbolic significance of Palach's death requires a brief comment. In order to rouse people from the lethargy which was gradually setting in after the Prague Spring had been crushed and to inspire them to continue in active resistance against the government, in which the reformers of the Prague Spring were gradually losing power to conservative politicians supported by the Soviets, on 16 January 1969, while the Central Committee of the Communist Party was in session at Hradčany Castle, Jan Palach doused himself with petrol and set himself on fire in front of the National Museum in Wenceslas Square. He died in hospital three days later. Before his action he had sent letters to the government, journalists, various organisations, and friends, demanding freedom of the press, referring to himself as a 'torch', and warning that if his demands were not met within five days or if the nation did not embark on an indefinite general strike other torches would be set alight. He thus implied the existence of a group of volunteers willing to sacrifice themselves for what he called 'our cause'. Although Palach's demands were not met and there was no general strike, his act was not repeated, and the police were unable to uncover any evidence of a group of volunteers.

Palach's intentions and reasons, clearly stated by himself, made the meaning of his action transparent. By setting himself alight he was attempting metaphorically to set fire to the nation. By making the ultimate sacrifice he was trying to move people to make a lesser sacrifice for the common cause. However, the full symbolic significance of Palach's act is not by any means exhausted at this level of meaning.

The power of a symbol depends on its cognitive fit with other symbols of the symbolic system. Soon after Palach's act, official propaganda tried to reduce its symbolic significance by arguing that he was emotionally unbalanced and that his desperate act was inspired by his interest in Buddhist philosophy – the proof of which was that a book on Buddhism was found on his bookshelf. In his quest for martyrdom he emulated the Buddhist monks setting themselves on fire. The symbolic significance of Palach's act was thus to be devalued by being construed as something totally alien to Czech and, indeed, European culture. There may even be some truth in this construction of Palach's motivation, for one thing he said on his deathbed was, 'It helped in Vietnam' (Kantůrková 1989: 363).

Ultimately, however, it does not matter what Palach's inner motivation might have been, which is also the reason the government's attempt to reduce the symbolic significance of his act was ineffective. An important thing about symbols is that they 'neither arise spontaneously, nor is the continuing process of redefinition of the symbolic universe a matter of chance' (Kertzer 1988: 4). New symbols become established when people are confronted with new circumstances to which they have to react, but their creation is not haphazard. They are largely drawn from the store of existing symbols, and it is precisely this process which ultimately lends them their condensation and multivocality. In the context of Czech culture it was not the symbol of Buddhist monks burning themselves to death which endowed Palach's act with its meaning but the symbol of Jan Hus, burned to death as a heretic in 1415. If, in this context, Palach's death was bound to evoke the death of Jan Hus (Pynsent 1994: 209), it was also bound to evoke what Hus's death symbolised: his betrayal by foreigners and the inspiration of a movement in which the Czechs played their most significant role in Europe ever. It was these two particular connotations of Hus's death which gave a particular meaning to Palach's death and made him a symbol of resistance to the post-1968 regime.[15]

Proof of the power of this particular symbol is the fact that Palach's grave in a Prague cemetery became a shrine. Having failed in its attempt to impose its own meaning on Palach's act and thus to defuse its impact, the government subsequently tried to achieve this aim by removing his shrine. Palach's body was exhumed and cremated one night in 1973 by the police, and the ashes were interred in the cemetery in his native village. Needless to say, this did not stop candles and flowers from appearing at the empty grave, and if anything the police action resulted in the creation of two shrines instead of one. After the successful general strike in November 1989, the square in front of the Faculty of Arts in Prague, where Palach had studied, was immediately renamed after him without waiting for the official approval of the city council; the names of other streets in Prague were gradually changed later by official decree. And one of the first acts of the new regime was to move Palach's ashes to the grave in Prague in which his body had originally been buried.

In spite of the spontaneous character of the demonstrations, official propaganda portrayed them as organised by illegal groups backed by foreign elements hostile to socialism. Arresting foreign journalists alongside the Czech demonstrators was an attempt to make this foreign involvement visible. Given the nationalist symbols which the demonstrations invoked, to suggest that they were inspired by and served foreign interests was an obvious way of debunking them. We are dealing here with the same process of contesting symbols which was employed by the authorities in their attempt to diminish the significance of Palach's death. In any case, very few people took the suggestion of foreign involvement seriously, and the role of the various independent groups in organising the demonstrations was indirect at most.

The first demonstration took place on 21 August 1988, the twentieth anniversary of the crushing of the Prague Spring by the Warsaw Pact armies. Charter 77 had been issuing proclamations on each anniversary of 21 August pointing out the economic and cultural stagnation into which the country had sunk after the defeat of the reform movement and calling for economic reform and the democratisation of the political system – active participation of all citizens in the political life of the country, an end to police repression, and a guarantee of basic human rights for all. Charter 77 always made a point of operating openly in a way formally guaranteed by the Czechoslovak constitution. It elected its spokespersons and made their names and addresses known through its publications, the contents of which were broadcast back to Czechoslovakia by Radio Free Europe, the Voice of America, the BBC, and other stations. These spokespersons guaranteed the veracity of all the signatures on the various petitions submitted to government organs. In line with this open policy, the Charter also announced beforehand all its intended actions, one of which was placing flowers at the statue of St Wenceslas in the afternoon of 21 August 1988. At the appointed time, a few people gathered at the statue, some of them with flowers, others eager to see what was going to happen. The Charter's spokesman was detained by the police before he was able to reach Wenceslas Square, and when it became obvious that he was not going to arrive those present started to throw flowers over the heads of the police, who cordoned off the statue and threw the flowers back. The assembled people sang the national anthem, and the whole action ended after the police had taken down the names of those identified as its organisers.

In the early evening of the same day, a crowd of mostly young people began gathering at the statue and later started to march to the Old Town Square and from there to the castle. Four thousand people, according to the Czechoslovak News Agency, or ten to twenty thousand according to the underground press, took part in the demonstration. It seemed rather to have been hijacked by the independent groups than organised by them. When the demonstrators stopped at the statue of Jan Hus in the Old Town Square, a representative of the Independent Peace Association read a resolution demanding the withdrawal of Soviet troops from Czechoslovakia and greater freedom.

The demonstration on 28 October 1988 was the only one which was planned beforehand. An official rally organised by the party and the government was held in Wenceslas Square on 27 October to celebrate the sixtieth anniversary of the founding of the Czechoslovak Republic. Six independent groups applied for permission to hold their own demonstration there in the afternoon of the following day. When the application was turned down by the city council, the groups appealed to the people to exercise their constitutional right to free assembly by celebrating the anniversary in Wenceslas Square, and a demonstration took place. A year later, another demonstration evolved spontaneously after an official rally in Wenceslas Square, access to which was by ticket only. In this case the demonstration seems to have been a response to the restriction of attendance rather than the result of any effort of opposition groups to organise a street protest.

On 16 January 1989, the representatives of several independent groups planned to lay flowers at the statue of St Wenceslas to commemorate the twentieth anniversary of Palach's death. They did not ask citizens to join them, but a spontaneous demonstration erupted when the police tried to prevent people from doing so. This was in fact the second demonstration to take place commemorating the anniversary of Palach's death; the first had occurred the day before, when a few ordinary citizens acting on their own had attempted to lay flowers at the statue and had been prevented from doing so by the police who cordoned off the square ostensibly in response to an anonymous threat that a new human torch would be set alight. These two demonstrations were the ones most widely reported in the Western media not only because of the disproportionate police brutality with which they were suppressed but also because they led to the arrest of Václav Havel and his later sentencing to eight months' imprisonment for 'hooliganism' and 'incitement'.

The demonstrators' demands

The link between the demonstrations and the various independent initiatives, although not altogether absent, was at best only very tenuous (Wheaton and Kavan 1992: 25–9). Instead of organising the demonstrations in support of specific political demands, these groups took advantage of them to make their own demands publicly known. Independent initiatives normally formulated their particular demands in their various petitions. For example, in August 1988 the Independent Peace Association was calling for the withdrawal of Soviet troops from Czechoslovakia, free elections with multiple candidates, the abolition of censorship, the observance of basic human rights in accordance with international agreements signed by the Czechoslovak government, and the release of all political prisoners. The demonstrations articulated none of these specific demands, nor did they call for the legalisation of any of the independent groups. Instead they concentrated heavily on the display of nationalist symbols. The choice of venues and the timing of the demonstrations both had strong nationalist connotations; in addition, the participants sang the national anthem, carried national flags, and wore ribbons in the national colours. They chanted 'Masaryk', 'Dubček', 'Freedom', and 'Give us freedom'. En route from the Old Town Square to Hradčany Castle, they encouraged bystanders to join them by shouting, 'Czechs, come with us!' The police were greeted with shouts of 'Fascists!' and 'Gestapo!' A commentator missed the point when he suggested in an underground newspaper that the demonstrators might as well have shouted 'Communists!' because beating up opponents was an integral part of communist political culture (*Listy* 19 (1989), no. 2: 16). A different meaning of the abuse directed at the police was expressed by a participant in one of the demonstrations, who described it euphemistically as making it clear to the police that they were not Czechs (*Listy* 19 (1989), no. 1: 44).

In Czechoslovakia, as in most countries of Central and Eastern Europe, the demise of communism was accompanied by an upsurge of national sentiment. This rise of nationalist feelings creates the perception of the post-communist transformation as the replacement of one collectivist ideology, communism, by another, nationalism. What this perception fails to grasp is that nationalism did not simply replace communism as an alternative ideology, but was itself the basis for the opposition to communism which culminated in its overthrow. The people who opposed the communist regime in demonstrations styled themselves not citizens, democrats, or workers but Czechs. Why this should be so is a question which some Czech sociologists have asked themselves in the context of the resurgence of nationalism in the post-communist states of Central and Eastern Europe. Jiřina Šiklová has argued that under communism people's property, educational status, or social standing depended on cooperation with or at least accommodation to the communist regime, and, recognising this, they realised that all they could proclaim without shame was their ascribed status: age, gender, membership of a generational cohort, race, and ethnicity: 'There the question of "how and in exchange for what you have acquired it" does not arise.' Nationality is the most convenient form of self-identification, for 'if I say that I am a Slovak, a Czech, a Hungarian, or a German, I identify myself at the same time with people of the same fate' (*Přítomnost* 2 (1991), no. 3: 32). This, in my view, is a rather convoluted explanation which resorts to well-rehearsed analytical concepts such as ascribed and achieved status, and overlooks the specific cultural meaning of being a Czech.

We can begin to understand why communism was opposed in the name of the nation once we realise that two opposed models of the nation underlie the notion of national identity. Historically, these models can be traced to different developments in France and Germany in the second half of the eighteenth and the beginning of the nineteenth century. One of them, which arose from the French Revolution of 1789, is a model of a unified and indivisible collectivity which crystallised in a struggle aimed at overcoming the previous divisions of class, religion, and regional and ethnic differences. A different model, building on the ideas of Rousseau and Herder, emerged in Germany, particularly in the context of the Napoleonic wars of 1806–15. It was consciously formulated in opposition to the French model and conceptualised the nation as a linguistic and cultural rather than a political entity. The two conceptions grew out of the different historical conditions of a unified French nation-state, on the one hand, and a politically fragmented German-speaking population, on the other. The German historian Friedrich Meinecke (1907) characterised them as *Staatsnation* (state nation) and *Kulturnation* (cultural nation). Kohn (1955, 1967) similarly differentiated between the Western concept of the nation as an association of people living in a common territory under the same government and laws and the Eastern concept of the nation as an organic, ethnically based community. In his view, the Western model was the product of the middle classes which came to power particularly in France, Britain, and the United States at the end of the eighteenth century, and the Eastern model was the product of the intellectuals who led the resistance to Napoleon in the countries east of the Rhine.

Smith characterises the 'Western' civic-territorial model of the nation as 'historic territory, legal-political community, legal-political equality of members, and civic culture and ideology' (1991: 11; see also 1986: 134–7). Historically, this model emerged as a 'consequence of prior economic, social, cultural and political developments. Unity defined in terms of the nation followed facts established by firm administrative, legal, and cultural institutions' (Csepeli 1992: 235). Given the importance of the legal-political component of this conceptualisation of the nation, the national ideology which it produced could be said to be 'centered around the idea of the nation defined in terms of *state*' (Csepeli 1992: 235). The distinguishing features of the 'Eastern' ethnic-genealogical model are 'its emphasis on a community of birth and native culture', and its elements are 'genealogy and presumed descent ties, popular mobilization, vernacular languages, customs and traditions' (Smith 1991: 12; see also 1986: 137–8). The national ideology which this model produced could be said to be 'centered around the idea of the nation defined in terms of *culture*' (Csepeli 1992: 235). Historically, this model emerged as a result of the formulation of national unity in the absence of 'adequate economic, social, political and cultural foundations. Here the notion of the nation came before the establishment of the relevant national institutions; the emerging national ideology had to refer more actively to such elements of the ethnocentric heritage as descent, cultural values, and norms' (Csepeli 1992: 235).

Although the two models of the nation and the ensuing types of nationalism played their roles in different historical periods in Western and Eastern Europe, particular national ideologies differ in the extent to which they follow one or other ideal type. The civic-territorial conceptualisation of the nation was not altogether absent among the Czech intellectuals of the nineteenth century (Kořalka 1988: 30), but the conscious building of the modern Czech nation during the national revival was informed by the ethnic-cultural model. Since then this conceptualisation of the nation has been perpetuated through the teaching of history in schools and through literature, art, and the popularisation of such disciplines as ethnography, history, art history, literary criticism, and linguistics, which investigate and thus in fact create (Smith 1986: 148, 200–8) national culture and traditions. Whilst the civic-territorial model of the nation conceptually subsumes the state, in the ethnic-cultural model the nation and the state are conceptually separated. The Czech nation has been construed as having existed without its own state, and the political goal of Czech nationalism, which gradually came to the fore in the second half of the nineteenth century, was at first the revival of Czech statehood within the federated Habsburg empire and later the creation of an independent Czech nation-state. The two opposed models of the nation give rise not only to different types of nationalism (Smith 1991: 82–3) but also to different conceptualisations of the main functions of the state. The argument of the Czech political nationalism of the nineteenth century was that the nation's language and culture could be preserved only if it had its own state. The main function of the state was thus defined as the protection of the nation's vital interests and its continuous existence as a distinct cultural entity.

The rise of nationalist sentiments which accompanied the collapse of the communist system stemmed precisely from this conceptualisation of the role of the state. The reason that the demonstrators opposed the communist system as Czechs rather than as citizens or democrats derived from their perception of the communist system as yet another form of foreign domination which served first of all foreign – specifically Soviet – rather than Czech interests and, moreover, was alien to what the Czechs perceived as their national traditions. Because it was the state which imposed this alien system on the Czech nation, the opposition to communism pitted the nation against the state, and the overthrow of the communist regime was seen as yet another national liberation.

What the demonstrators articulated, first of all, was a specific meaning ascribed to being a Czech – a meaning resulting from two competing constructions of the relationship between individuals and the nation. In one of these constructions, most clearly formulated in the ideology of Czech nationalism, individuals exist only as parts of the nation. In the other, formulated in the ideology of Western individualism, individuals are imagined as distinct and as endowed with agency not only as members of a collectivity but as persons in their own right. The meaning of being a Czech can be seen as being negotiated in simultaneous discourses on nationalism and individualism. On the one hand, these two discourses are in competition with each other; on the other, they draw upon and are occasionally collapsed into each other. We can unpack the meaning of being a Czech by considering the demands the demonstrators articulated and the specific symbols through which they expressed them.

In none of the pre-November demonstrations were there calls for the government's resignation, a change in the party's leadership, the relinquishing by the party of its monopoly of power, or a change in the political system as a whole. If no specific political demands were the *raison d'être* for the demonstrations, it seems simplistic to view them merely as instrumental acts aimed at toppling the government of the day, as most political commentators and analysts did. It is necessary to view them also as expressive acts, to analyse what they were attempting to express, and to explain why they took the form they did. The idea that the main point of the demonstrations was not to bring about any particular change in the political system but to express more general and enduring values was shared by the demonstrators themselves. In a reported discussion between two participants in the demonstration of 21 August 1988, this view was stated in the following way: 'As you well know, nothing much is really the matter; what matters is just a principle – to show the world that we are not monkeys' (*Listy* 18 (1988), no. 6: 19). The image of a monkey is not merely that of an animal which in some respects resembles humans but in other respects is fundamentally different from them. For Czechs, most of whom have seen monkeys either in a zoo or a circus, it is the image of a caged animal or an animal conditioned to perform tricks at the whim of its master – the opposite of what a person is or should be: a free agent, certainly not caged and not reduced to a performing circus animal.

The demands explicitly expressed by the demonstrators were for freedom. These demands were the most visible signs of a new discourse opposed to the discourse of the Communist Party, in which 'freedom' was defined explicitly as freedom from exploitation and unemployment. In the emerging discourse, the meaning of freedom was redefined. The demonstrators did not demand specific freedoms such as freedom of the press, freedom of assembly, freedom to travel (which had become a powerful symbol for example in the German Democratic Republic), or freedom to choose one's own political representatives but freedom in the most diffuse sense – which, as one of my informants expressed it, is 'a prerequisite of one's identity and of the preservation of one's self'. In general terms, freedom so understood implies the possibility of free expression while respecting the generally accepted ethical norms and the freedom of others. Most of my informants contrasted freedom with the pressure to follow the officially prescribed way of thinking and acting and mostly defined it as the possibility of saying, thinking, and doing what one feels like saying, thinking, and doing without any fear of punishment or repression. Specifically, it includes the freedom to choose with whom to associate, what to believe, what music to play (one of the independent organisations was the persecuted Jazz Section, a group which could hardly play a direct political role in a liberal democracy), what books to read (censorship determined not only what books might be published but also what books might be stored in libraries), etc. In brief, what the demonstrators demanded was that freedom which is the basic attribute of a person and a condition of one's humanity.

Discourse analysts have argued that words take on meaning only in conflicting discourses (Pecheux 1982: 111; Macdonell 1986: 12, 54; Seidel 1989: 223). Some linguists have recently taken exception to this view, suggesting that it is precisely because of the linguistic rules and invariant meanings of a language system that particular words are employed in particular discourses which draw upon the substratum of their meaning embedded in the language (Hervey 1992). A discourse may, of course, alter the meaning of particular words by contextualising them differently. Any discourse modifies the meanings of words, but it does so only because some trace of their earlier meanings lingers and makes it possible to utilise a particular word in a new discourse in the first place. Austin described this process as 'trailing clouds of etymology' (1971: 99–100). By seizing upon a particular word, a discourse expresses or embodies the experience of those it addresses so that they can see their interests reflected in what the discourse proposes. The demonstrators' discourse did so by taking advantage of the commonality of the meaning of 'freedom' as a preexisting sign in the Czech language and giving it a new twist by articulating freedom not merely as absence of exploitation and unemployment but as the basic attribute of a person and the basic condition of human existence. It was precisely in its capacity to give a new twist to this existing sign – to emphasise by its use in a new and broader context something that had not been emphasised before – that the discourse became effective.

However, the demand for freedom was expressed in the context of strong nationalist sentiment and was understood by the demonstrators and the government alike as an anti-government protest. Nationalism, government, and personhood are thus intertwined and draw upon one another. As one participant in the demonstration of 21 August 1988 put it, 'We look at one another and I have an intense feeling that we are united in something which I cannot describe in a word. I suggest the following alternatives and let everyone choose according to their taste: solidarity, patriotism, the longing for freedom' (*Listy* 18 (1988), no. 6: 19). The popular opposition to the communist regime in Czechoslovakia, which the demonstrations of 1988 and 1989 openly expressed for the first time, was neither triggered by a sense of material deprivation nor carried out in the name of democracy and the free market, which gradually acquired a prominent place in political discourse only after the collapse of the communist system. It was carried out in the name of the freedom of individuals and the freedom of the nation. The demonstrations were of course political acts in the narrow sense of the term. However, in the symbols they invoked and manipulated, they expressed much more than limited political demands. If we take them to be primarily expressive acts, what they ultimately expressed was a specifically Czech cultural construction of the relations between the person, the nation, and the state. In the next chapter I shall first consider the symbols through which these relationships were expressed before sketching the relationships themselves.

2

Freedom, nation, and personhood

The demonstrations in Prague in 1988 and 1989 primarily expressed people's strong nationalist sentiments, but the official propaganda was built around their construction as not only anti-socialist but also anti-state actions which the government was obliged to suppress by force. The reason for this was that if the street protests were allowed to continue, nationalist sentiments might evolve into specific political demands which challenged the existing monopoly of power – and this, indeed, is what happened. On 28 October 1989 the demonstrators were already chanting 'We want another government' and 'We want free elections' and shouting support for Charter 77 and Václav Havel. Many more specific political demands were articulated in the students' demonstration on 17 November. The exceptionally brutal way in which it was suppressed by the police led directly to the continuous mass demonstrations all over Czechoslovakia during which opposition to communist rule crystallised, eventually to bring about sweeping political change. But apart from this politically pragmatic reason, another reason both the demonstrators and the government saw the demonstrations as anti-state acts was that those who represented the state and those who were demonstrating against it shared a single symbolic system.

The central ideological construct or core symbol of a nation enclosed within its own state is 'freedom'. The calls for freedom were not only calls for the right to express individuality as the basic attribute of a person but also – at least to a certain extent – an invocation of this core symbol. It is a symbol logically related to the other overtly nationalist symbols which the demonstrators manipulated, and one of its implications is that the nation is free not simply when it has its own state but when the state is the instrument for the management and channelling of its interests. This is the reason the freeing of the nation was seen as the major achievement of the establishment of the Czechoslovak Republic at the end of World War I. The newly created state gave political expression to the nation, and its bureaucracy and organs of government became the instruments for managing the nation's destiny. The ultimate interest of the nation is of course its continued independent existence. All this is contained in the notion that the Czech nation existed throughout the centuries of darkness and oppression but was not free because it lacked a state as an organisation for managing its interests. To understand fully why Czechs did not feel free in the pre-November days in spite of having their own state or, rather, did not see the existing state as their own, we have to unpack the other symbols invoked during the demonstrations: Masaryk and Dubček.

Masaryk and Dubček

The chants of 'Dubček' were seized upon by party propaganda in its effort to construe the demonstrations as anti-socialist and anti-state. They were interpreted as a demand for the reinstatement of Dubček and a return under his leadership to the policies of 1968, a period of crisis for the party during which the counterrevolutionary forces had attempted to stop socialist development in Czechoslovakia and restore capitalism. It cannot be denied of course that some of the demonstrators would indeed have liked to see Dubček installed in Hradčany Castle, but the fact that 'Masaryk' and 'Dubček' were chanted together and that Masaryk, who died in 1937, obviously could not be reinstated suggests that for the majority of the demonstrators 'Dubček' was something other than the name of a desired future leader. The fact that these two names and 'freedom' virtually formed a single slogan chanted in unison indicates that they were symbols mutually interrelated with all the other symbols with strong nationalist connotations. This became apparent during the events of November, when all the nationalist symbols were fused at the equestrian statue of St Wenceslas: a Czechoslovak flag was tied to the leg of the horse, pictures of Masaryk and Dubček were displayed beneath it, and its plinth was covered with posters demanding freedom.

Masaryk is the symbol *par excellence* of pre-war Czechoslovakia, its establishment being construed by much Czechoslovak historiography as principally the result of his diplomatic efforts in the United States during World War I. When the provisional Czechoslovak government was founded in exile in September 1918, Masaryk was appointed president of the future independent Czechoslovak Republic. The provisional government was gradually recognised by France, Great Britain, Serbia, and Italy, and when Masaryk returned to Czechoslovakia in December 1918 he was welcomed as the nation's liberator. To the people he was a father figure who had given his children, the nation, the most precious gift imaginable – freedom. Although the pre-war Czechoslovak Republic was a multiethnic state, Czechs clearly saw it as an instrument for the pursuit of Czech interests, and its actual ethnic policy gave full credence to this view. Czechs as a nation in fact had reason to feel free, for they were now doing to others what others had done to them. The others were the Slovaks, whose separate national identity was denied through the concept of a Czechoslovak nation and a Czechoslovak language, and the Germans. The uncompromising Czech domination of other ethnic groups eventually led to the collapse of the first republic (Svitak 1990, vol. I: 27–8, 31–2).

It may seem ironic that Dubček, the other symbol of a free Czech nation, and during the 1980s perceived as equal to Masaryk in importance, was a Slovak. It does not matter, however, who Masaryk and Dubček were in terms of ethnic classification. Masaryk, after all, was himself at best a marginal Czech: he was born in a Moravian–Slovak borderland, and his roots were in a local and regional culture which is distinctly Slovak (Szporluk 1981: 20). What matters is what they stand for as symbols. Dubček is first and foremost the symbol of the Prague Spring – the brief period of liberalisation in which the Czech nation again felt free because the state was once more seen as an instrument of national interests rather than foreign (i.e., Soviet) ones. What the actual policies of this or that particular regime were mattered less than the symbols through which these policies were perceived.

The political rituals and symbols employed by the Communist Party in the 1950s and 1960s could hardly have engendered a perception of the Czechoslovak state as an organisation for the pursuit of national interests. The two most important slogans, which could be seen all over the country, were 'The Soviet Union – our example' and 'With the Soviet Union forever' (the popular attitude was expressed in a widely circulated joke: 'With the Soviet Union forever but not a day longer'). The playing of the national anthem was routinely followed by the playing of the Soviet anthem, even during events that were exclusively of Czech national significance. Soviet flags were hoisted alongside the Czechoslovak ones on holidays. Russian was the first foreign language taught in schools, as a result of which very few Czechs are fluent in it. The Czechoslovak army's insignia were replaced by those of the Soviet army (ironic in view of the fact that Soviet army had kept the old tsarist insignia), and in the early 1950s a huge granite statue of Stalin, proudly proclaimed to be the largest in the world, was erected in Prague and together with Hradčany Castle dominated the city for several years. The Czech names of occupations such as station-master or postman and of institutions such as the fire-brigade or the police were replaced by names derived from Russian which to the Czechs sounded distinctly odd. Newly created institutions modelled on their Soviet counterparts were called by names which were direct translations from Russian.

The Communist Party's own symbolic creativity was combined with an attack on all the symbols of the pre-war republic. Czechoslovak historiography busied itself with interpreting the founding of the Czechoslovak Republic after World War I as the direct result of the struggle of the Czech and Slovak working class inspired by the ideals of the October Revolution. For good measure, 28 October was demoted from the main state holiday to just one of a number of minor anniversaries; instead of celebrating the foundation of the state in 1918, it became Nationalisation Day, commemorating the nationalisation of key industries, banks, and financial institutions in 1945 and timed to coincide with the anniversary of the founding of the first Czechoslovak state. The new state holiday became 9 May, the day of the liberation of Prague by the Soviet army in 1945. The Masaryk legend was at first contested and the 'nation's liberator' reinterpreted as the representative of the interests of the bourgeoisie and multinational capitalism opposed to the interests of the people. Gradually, his name disappeared completely from history textbooks; his books were removed from all libraries; hundreds of statues of him which had survived the Nazi occupation were melted down; the Masaryk Streets, Masaryk Squares, and Masaryk Avenues of almost every town in the country became streets, squares, and avenues of Peace, the Heroic Soviet Army, Victorious February, 9 May, People's Militias, etc. Even the double-tailed lion – the emblem first of the Czech kings and then of the republic – had its crown replaced by a red star.

The Party's symbolic creativity continued unabated even when it should already have been clear to its authors that it was at least politically inopportune. A new hundred-crown banknote issued in 1989 bore a picture of Gottwald, the first Communist ruler of Czechoslovakia and a hardline Stalinist. A student interviewed after the demonstration on 17 November pointedly asked whether this was intended as a provocation. During the mass demonstrations in November, one of the posters which appeared on the streets of Prague was a new hundred-crown banknote bearing a portrait of Masaryk instead of Gottwald. All these are just a few examples of the grandiose symbolic restructuring which made it barely possible for the state to be perceived as the structure for representing and defending the nation's interests.

Dubček stands alongside Masaryk as a powerful symbol of a free nation because under his leadership – after more than twenty years of intense feeling that Czechoslovakia was nothing more than a province of the Soviet empire – the nation, although led by the Communist Party, became once again the master of its own destiny in its search for its own specifically Czechoslovak road to socialism. The feeling that national sovereignty had been achieved once more was strongly reinforced by the fact that with the resurgence of a free press the nationalist myths of the pre-war republic (the role of Masaryk and the Czechoslovak legions during World War I) were again widely discussed, various organisations which had existed in pre-war Czechoslovakia and had been banned by the Communists were revived, nationalist symbols were again openly acknowledged (the veterans appeared in their legionnaires' uniforms on national holidays), and the Communist Party's own myths (e.g., about the events which led to the party's assumption of power in February 1948) were openly contested.

The pre-November government was perceived as the government of those who came to power after the nationalist resurgence had been crushed by the Soviets and in consequence as perpetuating foreign interests even though these interests were already dead in the country in which they originated. This perception was reinforced by the particular kind of symbolic manipulation in which the government was engaged. The opposition, represented by a handful of intellectuals, was poorly organised and lacked any coherent political programme, recognisable leaders, or tangible support from the working class. Nevertheless, during the last few years before November 1989, change had been taking place. It was manifest not in the formulation of alternative political programmes, much less of alternative political structures, but in the invocation of new symbols. The demonstrations were an attempt to contest some symbols and advance others. The power of these symbols in creating a new political reality was indicated by the severity with which the government dealt with the actions in which they were invoked. Rather than relying solely on force, however, the government undertook its own symbolic manipulation, and that it was forced to do so indicated the real strength of the political opposition. In this symbolic struggle the opposition set the agenda. Much of the party's ideological and propagandistic work was confined to challenging the meanings of the symbols invoked in the course of the political process. Politics in pre-November Czechoslovakia became semiotics on a grand scale.

The party's and the government's challenge to the opposition's symbols was twofold: they tried to appropriate some and contested others. Among the former was 28 October, which in 1988 was once more declared a national holiday to coincide with the sixtieth anniversary of the founding of the Czechoslovak Republic. In 1988, representatives of the communist government laid a wreath at Masaryk's grave for the first time. I have already mentioned how official propaganda contested the meaning of Palach's death. The most bitterly contested symbol of all was, however, the Prague Spring and its infamous end, since it posed the question of the legitimacy of the government which had come to power as the direct result of the Soviet military intervention. Charter 77 had consistently called for the reappraisal of the official interpretation of the events of 1968 and for an open discussion of the Prague Spring. The official line of the Communist Party was that the Prague Spring was the period of political crisis when the very existence of socialism was threatened by counterrevolutionary forces whose organisation was made possible by Dubček's weak leadership. Calls for a re-evaluation of the events of 1968 were dismissed as the anti-socialist propaganda of illegal groups. These events were 'correctly' appraised in a party document called 'Lessons from the Development of the Crisis'. Letters to the party newspaper *Rudé právo* in which various citizens condemned the activities of forces hostile to socialism consistently pointed to the validity of the 'Lessons'. Although any kind of discussion of the Prague Spring was ruled out of bounds, the party was quite clearly aware of the importance of this symbol and of the necessity of advancing its own interpretation of its meaning. For example, the Central Committee's May 1988 report to party members on the activities of forces hostile to socialism stressed the importance of an active propaganda for the Marxist-Leninist interpretation of the country's past, particularly of the crisis years of 1968–9 (*Studie*, 1988, no. 118–19: 387).

In November 1989 the political demands to which the government yielded went far beyond the limited reforms of 1968. Dubček openly addressed a demonstration in Bratislava and two mass rallies in Prague which were televised nationwide, and the hardliners in the Politburo, who had come to power after the Soviet intervention in Czechoslovakia, resigned. What had happened in 1968 was undone at a stroke. The political changes, however, still had to be symbolically expressed, and the meaning imposed on the Prague Spring by the opposition had to be publicly acknowledged. The Civic Forum sent a letter to the Central Committee of the Soviet Communist Party requesting it to condemn the Soviet-led invasion of Czechoslovakia in 1968, and under pressure from the Civic Forum the Czechoslovak government formally renounced its previous interpretation of the Prague Spring. The importance of symbolic action in the politics of socialist countries could not have been made more obvious. Whereas in Hungary political change followed the reinterpretation of the meaning of the 1956 revolt, in Czechoslovakia it preceded the reinterpretation of the country's past, but it too was seen as incomplete without the imposition of new meaning on symbolically important past events.

The nation and the individual

The relationship between the individual and the collectivity – society or nation – can be conceptualised in two ways. One way is to imagine collectivities as made up of heterogeneous individuals. The collectivity can thus be conceptualised as 'a plurality of particulars' or 'a collection of individuals' (Strathern 1992: 26). The emphasis in this conceptualisation is on personal autonomy, and what is valued is individualism. Complete personal autonomy is of course limited by the necessity of maintaining culturally meaningful communication with significant others – the members of one's local community, region, class, and so on. But in the same way as individualism is valued, so is the individuality of all these aggregates, whether they be local communities, regions, or classes. The result is the acknowledged heterogeneity of the lifestyles and cultures of communities, regions, and classes through which the autonomy and individualism of particular persons are channelled. This conceptualisation of the relationship between the individual and the collectivity was expressed in the pre-November demonstrations in the desire for freedom as the basic attribute of a person and the basic condition of human existence.

The second way of conceptualising the relationship between the individual and the collectivity is to define individuals 'in reference to the whole' (Strathern 1992: 26). If individuals exist only as part of a whole – the nation – their essence is the sharing with others of this transcendent whole. In essence, individuals are replicas of one another. This, I would suggest, is the way in which the relationship is construed in the ideology of nationalism, and in the pre-November demonstrations it was expressed in the desire for freedom in the sense that the state should pursue the nation's interests. In this construction of the relationship between the individual and the nation, the freedom of individuals and the freedom of the nation are conceptually collapsed or, rather, freedom as an attribute of a person is conceived as deriving from that person's membership of a collectivity which is free when it is the master of its own destiny.

The two senses of freedom derive from two competing discourses, one on individualism and one on nationalism. The former takes for granted the nation as a natural and self-evident unit and its continued existence, whether as a politically autonomous entity or not; it problematises individualism and personal autonomy. The latter takes for granted the individual as an autonomous entity in nature and the existence of personal individuality; it problematises the conceptualisation of the whole – the nation.

I would suggest that it was the multivocality of the symbol of freedom which made it possible to collapse the two competing discourses into one everyday discourse during the pre-November demonstrations and the events of November 1989. Outside these politically charged situations in which the specifically Czech nationalist ideology can be reconciled with the universal Western ideology of individualism, the two ideologies are in competition with each other. Before I analyse the debate surrounding the question of emigration as an instance of this competition in particular everyday discourses, I want to describe the relationship between the individual and the nation as it is constructed in Czech nationalism and the way in which this construction shapes the particularities of Czech culture.

An individual member of the nation is spoken of not simply as a Czech but more often as *malý český člověk*, 'the little Czech man' – a character so popular that he[1] has acquired his own acronym, MČČ. The little Czech is not motivated by great ideals. His lifeworld is delineated by his family, work, and close friends, and he approaches anything that lies outside it with caution and mistrust. His attitude is down-to-earth, and he is certainly no hero: hence the popularity of the Good Soldier Schweik, the epitome of the little Czech. The little Czech as the ideal member of the nation has roots in national mythology. The Czech nation survived three hundred years of oppression not because of its heroes but because of the little Czechs who were the nation. The obverse of conceptualising a typical member of the Czech nation as the little Czech is the construction of the Czech nation as a nation of common, ordinary, and unexceptional people which generates a strong feeling of egalitarianism. The little Czech, the representative of the everyday and the ordinary, is the role model, and what is important about him as a role model is that he lacks individuation.

A person's name provides no clue to the person's status, occupation, level of income, or class, and in consequence it is a means to individuation. The reluctance to individuate persons is manifest in the Czech custom of addressing people by their occupational roles. It is not only people whose roles are much more important in a given encounter than their individual identities, such as doctors, nurses, or policemen, who are addressed in this manner, but almost everyone. To address someone as Mr or Mrs Editor, Writer, Accountant, Shop Assistant, Director, Conductor, Gardener, and so on, is common. It is as if one could manage without needing to know anyone's name at all.[2] What this usage emphasises, however, is not one's role in the complex division of labour but the denial of individuation and the stress on identity deriving from category membership. It is an expression of the importance of the collective (in this case categorical) identity over the personal one. The same was expressed in the ritual listing of the full titles of party and government representatives in all official statements. During the rallies in November 1989, when Václav Havel referred to the general secretary of the Communist Party as 'Mr Jakeš', his audience understood it as a denial of Jakeš's position in the existing power structure. The message was clear: 'We have nothing to fear, as we are no longer confronting the once all-powerful Communist Party. We are no longer dealing with the once most powerful man in the country, the general secretary of the Communist Party; we are dealing with one ordinary individual, a Mr Jakeš.' Through this simple rhetorical device, Havel's audience was made aware that the general secretary had been effectively stripped of his power and was no longer an adversary to be feared.

In examining how Czechs represent the nation to themselves and what images they employ to make the relations between the nation and its individual members apparent to themselves, one can usefully look at the gymnastic association called Sokol. Sokol was founded in Prague in 1862 and soon had branches in towns and villages throughout the country. The Czech word *sokol* means 'falcon' and this image of a free bird resonated with the association's overtly nationalist role. After Czechoslovak independence, the pan-Sokol gatherings held in Prague every four years and stretching over three weekends became regular mass festivals in which the nation celebrated itself. Sokol contingents from Vienna and the United States always received a prominent welcome in appreciation of their nurturance of national ties. The main events of these gatherings were mass gymnastic displays in which tens of thousands participated. The image of a large number of bodies attired in the same garb, each body an exact replica of the others and all moving in unison as a single collectivity, was more than anything else the image through which people made their nation apparent to themselves. In this image the nation was not a collectivity arising out of diversity but a collectivity of ideally homogeneous units.

This emphasis on collectivity correlates well with the view of individuality as undesirable. Individuality interferes with the possibility of unified action; it leads one in one's own direction away from the direction taken by the collectivity; it is potentially dangerous to the collectivity and disrupts it (Strathern 1992). The devaluation of individualism is manifest in the often-heard saying 'We all have the same stomach', which expresses the assumption that we all have the same needs, desires, and aspirations. At the level of social action, this expectation is realised in the striking homogeneity of people's appearance, lifestyle, and conduct. This is the result not only of an economically imposed limit on available alternatives during socialism but of a positive tendency and pressure to conform and a readily expressed intolerance of any deviation from the collective norm. This intolerance of individual difference and personal autonomy springs from an ideal of unity in homogeneity (or at least similarity) or consensus. The invocation of common Czech identity is an appeal to unity: 'Let us not quarrel, aren't we all Czechs?' Although this sentence is often used jokingly, it is more than a joke; it is an ironic comment on a deeply shared assumption.

Kohn defined nationalism as 'a state of mind in which the supreme loyalty of the individual is felt to be due to the nation-state' (1955: 9). Nationalism understood in this sense inevitably engenders the conceptualisation of national identity as the individual's primary identity. For Czechs, national identity differs qualitatively from the identities which individuals assume on the basis of their achieved statuses. It is 'superordinate to most other statuses, and defines the permissible constellation of statuses, or social personalities, which an individual with that identity may assume'. It is an imperative identity 'in that it cannot be disregarded or temporarily set aside by other definitions of the situation' (Barth 1969: 17). It resembles gender identity or identity determined by one's age in that it too is seen as something naturally given.

When talking about the sense of Czechness, on the whole, people mentioned three criteria: having been born in the Czech lands, speaking Czech as one's mother tongue, and having been born of Czech parents. Whilst some of them mentioned all three criteria, most were of the opinion that having been born in the Czech lands and speaking Czech were not enough to make one a Czech. Hardly anyone thought that those gypsies or Jews who were born in the Czech lands, and who sometimes spoke only Czech, were Czechs, and most people asserted quite strongly that 'someone who speaks Czech is not necessarily a Czech: a Czech-speaking gypsy is not a Czech'. Many people spoke of 'Czech gypsies' or 'Czech Jews', but particularly as far as gypsies were concerned they vehemently denied the possibility that they could become Czechs: 'A gypsy will always remain a gypsy' was a phrase I heard many times. Some argued that national identity was 'in one's blood' and that 'gypsies cannot change their blood', but most suggested that gypsies or Jews could never become Czechs because they had different customs and traditions. Many informants also pointed out their racial difference. Virtually all agreed that to be a Czech one had to have Czech ancestors or at least be born of Czech parents; some stated bluntly that Czechness was established through birth. Few people maintained that it was transmitted genetically and that a newborn baby already had a nationality ('it is in the blood'); most argued that if one was born of Czech parents, one would be brought up as a Czech through the socialisation process beginning in the family and continuing through formal school education and living in a Czech environment. Many informants stressed the role of the mother in the process of acquiring national identity. One learned from one's mother to speak Czech, and from one's parents one gradually picked up Czech customs, learned about Czech traditions, acquired love for one's country, and thus became a 'true Czech'.

For Czechs, their country is particular: it is their *vlast*, 'homeland'. At least in one of its original meanings, the word *vlast* is etymologically connected with the word *vlastní*, 'own', and *vlastniti*, 'to own', and this makes it different from all other countries (*země*, 'lands'). Unlike the terms 'fatherland' and 'motherland', the term *vlast* has no semantic association with parenthood. Its parental role is, however, made explicit by reference to it as *matka vlast* (*matka*, 'mother'). Through this metaphor the homeland is construed as a life-engendering entity; it is a mother to every individual Czech, and all Czechs are its children (building upon this metaphor, one of the independent initiatives called itself the Czech Children). Just as one is born into a family and one's personal identity – signified by one's name – is established at birth, one is also born into a nation. Like personal identity, one's national identity is primary, and just as one's personal identity derives from being part of a family, one's national identity derives from being part of a nation. Like one's family, one's nation too is a precondition of existence. Just as a family is made up not of autonomous individuals but of individuals brought into being as parts of families, a nation too is made up not of autonomous individuals but of individuals brought into being only as parts of a nation.

Through the metaphor of the mother country Czechs remind themselves that each individual has two mothers: as a member of a family one has a biological genetrix, and as a member of a nation one has a symbolic one. Karel Čapek's play *Mother* is about the competing claims of a man's two mothers – the contradiction between one's personal and national identity. In the nationalist discourse the contradiction is resolved in favour of the symbolic mother; national identity overrides personal identity. Čapek's play makes obvious sense to a Czech audience because it resonates with their understanding of the relationship between the individual and the nation as it is constructed in this discourse.

As I have already suggested, the construction of the relationship between the individual and the nation in the nationalist discourse contradicts the construction of this relationship in the universalist Western discourse, which valorises individualism and personal autonomy. This unresolved contradiction gives rise to the Czech debate on emigration, leads to the conceptualisation of emigration as a problem, and ultimately fosters ambivalence toward it.

Nationalism and emigration

In the ideology of Western liberalism, in line with its emphasis on individualism and personal autonomy, emigration is a private matter and no concern of the collectivity. In an ideology which emphasises collectivism, it is the opposite. Both socialist and nationalist ideologies are collectivist, and, therefore, emigration was construed as a moral problem by both the pre-November 1989 communist government and its opponents. The government's attitude to emigration was straightforward: it was a betrayal of the country, the nation, or socialism. Although people may not have always agreed with what the Party construed as being betrayed (particularly if it was socialism), the notion of betrayal was not culturally alien to them. It was an appropriate gloss for abandoning the whole of which one was inherently a part – a morally despicable act paralleling the violation of the Christian Fifth Commandment: 'Honour thy father and mother.' This notion was not foreign to the dissidents' thought, but in their case it conflicted with their support for individual human rights, one of them being the right to emigrate. The anguish which surrounded the 'problem of emigration' in dissident circles in Czechoslovakia, among Czech emigrants, and in the discussion between these two groups (see, e.g., Filip 1989: 79–81) and the persistence of the problem – clearly perceived as a moral one – were the result of the contradiction between transcultural human rights and the specific notions of Czech nationalism simultaneously embraced.

This ambivalence toward emigration did not disappear after November 1989. Because emigrants could now return to Czechoslovakia and because they had been openly mentioned in the press and could be seen on television, they became more visible. In consequence, discussion of the problem of emigration ceased to be the preserve of a small circle of former dissidents and became part of national discourse. On the one hand, emigrants are a source of national pride in that they demonstrate that Czechs can become successful even in the competitive West. Czechs point out with distinct satisfaction that people like Tomáš Baťa, Miloš Forman, and Robert Maxwell are or were once Czechs and that in the 1930s Chicago had a Czech mayor. On the other hand, any comparison of the situation in their old homeland with their experiences in the West, which often implies criticism of many practices which Czechs at home take for granted, is detested. Emigrants are expected to display supreme loyalty to the nation.

When legislation about the restitution of property to its original owners or their heirs was passed in 1991, it included only Czechoslovak citizens with permanent residence in Czechoslovakia. Czech emigrants in the United States, who were thus deprived of the possibility of recovering their former property in Czechoslovakia, accused the Czechoslovak government of violating the UN Charter of Human Rights. By lobbying their congressional representatives and publicising their discrimination in the US press, they tried to move the US government to exert pressure on the Czechoslovak government. In numerous letters to Czech newspapers and in interviews with the Czech press, radio, and television, they pointed to the negative consequences of the legislation for the Czechoslovak economy, the most important of which was that, in contrast to Hungary and Poland, Czechoslovakia would miss the opportunity of creating a Czech lobby in the West for needed foreign investment and markets for Czechoslovak goods. One such interview was given by Arnošt Lustig, a Czech writer living in Canada (*Nedělní Lidové noviny*, 11 January 1992). A reader responded to it in the following way:

An emigrant who has lost his holiday cabin in Czechoslovakia is able to deprive his suffering former countrymen of, let us say, the profitable export of nails . . . I think that the emigrants could occasionally be more magnanimous. And as far as those who ruin our trade in nails and influence American opinion against us because of a cabin in the Czech woods are concerned, I suggest that we tighten our belts even more instead of trading with them.   *(Lidové noviny, 3 February 1992)*

The first emigrants to visit Czechoslovakia after November 1989 (among them the conductor Rafael Kubelík, the industrialist Tomáš Baťa, the pop singer Waldemar Matuška, the actor Jan Tříska, and the writer Josef Škvorecký) received a hero's welcome. They were interviewed by journalists; they appeared on television and staged concerts and performances. It was generally expected that they would show the utmost happiness at being home again and resettle in Czechoslovakia for good (see, e.g., Smetana 1991: 112). All were asked whether they would indeed be returning for good and there was a certain disappointment when they made it clear that they did not intend to do so because of their commitments in their adoptive countries.

Such replies went against the grain of the Czech notion of national identity as the primary one and the expectation that logically follows from this particular construction of the relationship between the individual and the nation: that of unswerving loyalty to the nation to which any other loyalty and commitment must be subordinated. These emigrants had turned renegades – an idea rendered in Czech by the verb *odroditi se*. The nearest English equivalent is 'to renounce one's birth' but the Czech verb refers not to something people do but to something that happens to them and in this sense is precisely opposite to *naroditi se*, 'to be born'. The verb with which the loss of national identity is described indicates again that Czechs conceptualise national identity not as culturally constructed but as naturally given. The key to the Czech cultural construction of national identity, of the relationship between the individual and the nation, and of the nation as a natural entity is the metaphor of birth. The process of national revival is referred to as *národní obrození*, 'the rebirth of the nation'. From the key metaphor of birth follow further metaphorical elaborations, such as that their homeland is the mother of all Czechs. Admittedly, although it would nowadays be considered rather stilted and distinctly poetic, the homeland can be spoken of as having a womb (*lůno*). As one originates from it or, rather, permanently exists within it, one can also return to it.

Aware of the implications of not returning to the womb of his country (*lůno vlasti*) when given the chance, Škvorecký, now living in Canada, handled the question about the chances of his permanent return in the following way:

They asked me if we would return. That has always been a slightly uncomfortable question, for it is difficult to explain to people who have lived there all the time that one feels at home somewhere else without casting on oneself the unpleasant shadow of having 'renounced one's birth'. One has not really renounced one's birth, but simply – we live in Canada.   *(quoted in Smetana 1991: 113)*

If emigrants show divided loyalties or criticise Czech attitudes and practices too strongly (particularly if their criticism does not tally with that expressed by Czechs themselves or goes beyond it), their Czechness becomes suspect. Jan Tříska is a case in point. He was the most promising young actor in Czechoslovakia before he left in 1977 for North America. The films and television plays in which he performed were no longer screened in Czechoslovakia after he had emigrated. When he visited

Prague in 1990, like many other prominent emigrants he was welcomed back as a returning hero. His visit coincided with the new showing of one of his films, and while in Prague, he appeared in a performance of Debussy's *Le Martyre de Saint-Sébastien*. He gave numerous interviews and was featured in a special documentary on Czechoslovak television. Although he expressed his delight at being back in Prague where his career had begun, he also made it clear that he preferred to be a small fish in a big pond rather than a big one in a small pond and that he intended to continue his successful career as an actor in North America. Comparing life in Czechoslovakia to life in a zoo and life in North America to life in a jungle, he expressed his preference for the latter: 'In a zoo, you have to accept what you are given. In a jungle you can have delicacies – provided you know how to hunt' (quoted in Smetana 1991: 86).

The critics were disappointed with Tříska's appearance in the television documentary. He was found to be more American than the Americans and was criticised for his explicit lack of interest in the past, which was taken as his renunciation of Czech traditions. His once beautiful Czech was found to have been corrupted. He was considered to have succeeded in North America at the cost of the unforgivable loss of Czech cultural consciousness (Vladimír Just in *Literární noviny*, 19 July 1990, quoted in Smetana 1991: 92). A journalist who interviewed him found him no longer Czech at all: 'I do not say it as a reprimand, I only want to say that he is an American through and through – to the extent that I was not sure at times whether I was talking to Jan Tříska or John Splinter' (the English translation of Tříska's name) (Jana Kolářová in *Forum*, 1990, no. 14, quoted in Smetana 1991: 87). The reaction of ordinary viewers to the television documentary was similar: they thought that he was showing off by using English words and were critical of the fact that his daughters – who left Czechoslovakia when they were four and six years old and went to school in Canada and the United States – did not speak Czech well. Tříska was judged to have 'renounced his birth'.

Milan Kundera, the best-known Czech writer now living abroad, is in a similar situation. He returned to Czechoslovakia incognito, shunning all publicity, and from the Prague airport went straight to Moravia, where he spent a week with his mother before returning home to Paris. His name is only rarely mentioned among the Czech writers who live abroad and who, like him, also write and publish in the languages of their adoptive countries. Kundera too seems to be seen as 'having renounced his birth' by not publicly proclaiming the expected loyalty to the Czech nation.

Nationalism, democracy, and egalitarianism

As an ideology, nationalism is totalising in stressing the collectivity united in a common purpose; democratic ideology is pluralistic. Throughout Czech history, the state has always had the firm support of the nation when it was perceived as fighting for or defending the nation's interest – the continued existence of the nation as a self-governing entity. Such was the case during the first republic, to which the Czechs look with pride, for their state was at that time the only liberal democracy in Central Europe. But such was also the case in 1968, when Dubček enjoyed wide popular support in spite of the fact that he was not a democratically elected leader of the country, but the general secretary of the Communist Party who assumed his leadership by the decision of the Politburo and not as a result of universal suffrage.

During the last years of communist rule in Czechoslovakia, the tension between totalising nationalism and the pluralism embodied in the democratic ideology was resolved in favour of nationalism. This, I would suggest, is the reason the pre-November demonstrations, the main demand of which was freedom, were distinctly nationalist and not at all concerned with articulating specific political means and structures for the achievement of freedom. Whether the party should be reformed or whether its monopoly of power should be abolished and replaced by a new political structure was not at all the issue before November 1989. Demands for such reform were clearly articulated for the first time by the intellectual leaders of the 'velvet revolution'. Thus they came on the coat tails of strong nationalist feeling. They were nevertheless embraced by the people for the majority of whom democracy was not a particular type of political arrangement but a system which guarantees that people can freely express their opinions and beliefs and choose how they want to conduct themselves. For most Czechs, democracy is first of all coterminous with freedom; as one of my informants formulated it, it is 'a system which guarantees the freedom of every individual'. The demands for democracy were accepted by those who revolted against the communist state, which they saw as limiting their freedom, for democracy was the means for achieving their main objective: an end to the hated state. Why this should have been people's main objective brings me back to the problem of individual freedom.

If the individual is construed not as an autonomous entity in nature but as a part of the nation and if the state is the political instrument of the nation's freedom, the state has to guarantee both the freedom of the nation as a whole and the freedom of all its constituent parts. The freedom of the nation and the freedom of individuals become synonymous. A nation-state cannot be repressive and still serve the nation's interest. In this context it is logical that the demand for freedom was expressed in overtly nationalistic terms and eventually pitted the nation against the state. Since the police are the visible instrument of the state's repression, the police were of course seen as standing outside and against the nation. This view was strongly reinforced whenever they repressed demonstrators waving national flags, singing the national anthem, and invoking other nationalist symbols. When on 17 November police brutality became all too clearly visible, the tension between the nation and the state escalated into an open revolt of the people against the state.

The 'velvet revolution' can be seen as an effort to bring the existing relations between the state, the nation, and the individual in line with the culturally constituted ideal. I would go so far as to suggest that in the context of the cultural construction of these relations, questions of the specific form the government should take were initially quite secondary. They eventually came to the forefront, for such questions ultimately have to be answered by creating tangible structures through which these relations can be expressed. What the 'velvet revolution' and the demonstrations which preceded it expressed was something deeper than political dissatisfaction – a dissatisfaction with the definition of the relationship between the nation and the state in such a way that one could not talk about the one through the other. The 'political' crisis was precipitated by the adoption of a culturally unacceptable conceptualisation of this relationship.

3

Self-stereotypes and national traditions

The most obvious expression of the search for the essence of national identity is the images people have of themselves and of other nations. When reflecting on themselves as a nation, Czechs refer either to certain national qualities or dispositions or to what they consider to be their national traditions. The self-images expressed through the characteristics which they ascribe to themselves and through the traditions which they claim as their own differ considerably. This raises the questions of why this should be so and how it can be cognitively tolerated and managed.

The ultimate source of the Czech egalitarian ethos is the belief in the equality of individuals in nature. It is acceptable to ascribe an individual's failure to a lack of effort or hard work but bad form to ascribe it to a lack of intelligence, for this would amount to the admission of inherent inequality, which is culturally denied. We may not all be good at everything, but each of us is good at something, which proves our natural equality. I do not think that anyone was sorry when IQ tests disappeared in communist Czechoslovakia, having been declared an invention of bourgeois pseudo-science; the illusion of equality in nature could thereafter be maintained without being openly challenged.

The little Czech as the typical representative of the Czech nation is the embodiment of ordinariness and healthy common sense. Whatever else he may lack, he does not lack intelligence. Hence the unresolved problem which has not ceased to occupy the imagination of literary critics and the population at large: was the Good Soldier Schweik actually a simpleton, or was he an intelligent man? Did he really believe in what he was doing, or did he only pretend to believe (a sign of his shrewdness and natural intelligence)? However tenuous, tortuous, and unconvincing the proofs may be, the consensus tends to be that Schweik was an intelligent man who simply put up a great show. It could hardly be otherwise: Schweik was a Czech and therefore he must have been intelligent. Those who say otherwise virtually brand themselves as national traitors.

The little Czech has 'golden Czech hands' – an expression one continually hears uttered with pride – that manage to cope with everything they touch: he is talented, skilful, and ingenious. The ascription of stupidity is the main device for constructing the Other. The stereotype of the Slovak is of a dim-witted shepherd, and the most popular jokes circulating in pre-November Czechoslovakia portrayed policemen – admittedly the representatives of the state but certainly standing outside the nation – as idiots.

The generalisations about national character which widely exercised the imagination of nineteenth-century scholars have long since ceased to be seen as a legitimate topic of academic concern, but they remain a part of the popular discourse of every nation and, indeed, of any group which sees itself as different from others. Czechs are no exception in this respect. They too have more or less clearly formulated ideas about their characteristic traits, which often compare unfavourably with the traits which they ascribe to others. Such comparisons have re-emerged since the overthrow of the communist regime, when encounters with foreigners from Western Europe, of whom most ordinary Czechs had had no prior personal knowledge, became part of their experience. The renewed contemplation of national characteristics was, however, the result not only of this new personal experience of individuals but also of the change in political culture and ideology. The official communist ideology emphasised the socialist character of Czechoslovak society. Any characteristics which might have been perceived as typical of Czechs were seen as unimportant; what were emphasised were the characteristics of the new socialist man, which Czechs were not only encouraged to embrace but presumed to share with people everywhere who were building socialism. International sport remained the only possible field in which nationalist feelings could be expressed, and it is significant that the last major anti-Soviet demonstration after the suppression of the Prague Spring by Soviet troops broke out spontaneously in Prague in April 1969 after the Czechoslovak national ice hockey team defeated the Soviet team.

Apart from commenting incessantly on the rude behaviour of officials, waiters, shop assistants, nurses, and anyone else who is ostensibly employed to serve the public (see, e.g., *Lidové noviny* 28 December 1990; 14 March 1991) and comparing the politeness which permeates the public sphere of life in the West with the rudeness and haughtiness typical of Czechs in public (see, e.g., *Vlasta* 45 (1991), no. 43: 12), the Czech press provides numerous other insights into the way in which Czechs see themselves. The images which emerge are quite distinct from the Czech intelligence, talent, skill, and ingenuity that are emphasised when Czechs construct the boundary between themselves and others:

The Czechs are envious and grudging beyond belief; they are capable of envying others even their chastity . . . We are our own enemies in our discord.

(Forum, 1990, no. 35: 3)

The other day I was watching the television discussion group *Netopýr* on the phenomenon called Czech national character – our national subaltern tutorship, our regional and intellectual inferiority, our magnificently justified mediocrity, our shrewdly circumvented off-the-peg morality and lack of any high vision, and everything that has made us (and, although we do not like to admit it, still makes us) 'an open-air museum of idiots in the heart of Europe'.   *(Tvorba, 1990, no. 42)*

Everybody here is almost neurotically dissatisfied with everything. (I sometimes suspect that this characteristic of ours is pretence; I wonder if it does not mask the fact that people are in fact content but do not want to admit it lest someone should envy them. Maybe our people would be missing something in life if they did not envy and grumble. This masking of the real state of affairs is also our second nature, conditioned by a disconsolate history.) And moreover: dissatisfaction also suggests that we are people of great wants and not easily satisfied with just anything. Dissatisfaction is part of our national *bon ton* and apparently also the origin of the Czech critical attitude, which undoubtedly has its intellectual advantages. It usefully dissolves anything stagnant and laughs at it satirically; however, it mostly manages to dissolve even itself and probably contributes to the fact that our development is always bumpy, full of discord and quarrels.   *(Smetana 1991: 9–10)*

In contemplating the Czech attitude toward talented people, Smetana – along with many other commentators – stresses envy as the most typical trait of the Czech character:

A hero in Bohemia faces many more difficulties than anywhere else because he is confronted – sooner or later – with malicious petty-mindedness and envy.

With us, this envy is the obverse . . . of popularity. A proud, sincere, and truthful person is a thorn in the side of the people of Bohemia, whether he is a politician, an entrepreneur, or an artist. Since time immemorial, democracy with us has degenerated into a kind of egalitarianism which is intolerant of authority, rejects responsibility, and dissolves everything with doubts and slander, as if our people did not believe that greatness is indeed greatness, noble-mindeness is noble-mindedness, and truth is truth . . .

And in Czech political and social life this traditionally manifests itself as extraordinary discord, quarrelsomeness, and intolerance, selfish haggling, and all this even at times when it would be more useful to pull together in the same direction (1991: 98).

Until our hero changes into a martyr, the nation is not satisfied.   *(1991: 97)*

Similarly, Arnošt Lustig said in an interview for a Czech newspaper during one of his visits to Prague,

Škvorecký once explained some of the least pleasant traits of the Czech nature to me in the following way: when a Czech has a goat, his neighbour does not want to have one as well but rather wishes his neighbour's goat to die.

(Nedělní Lidové noviny, *11 January 1992: 3*)[1]

The above selection of quotations from the Czech press accurately represents the views of the Czech population at large. According to a sociological survey of stereotypes of Czech character conducted in January 1992, a full 76 per cent of the traits most often mentioned by Czechs as characteristic of themselves were distinctly negative ones. The most prominent among them were envy (mentioned as the most characteristic trait of Czechs by 28 per cent of respondents), excessive conformism (mentioned by 15 per cent), cunning (mentioned by 15 per cent), egoism (mentioned by 11 per cent), laziness (mentioned by 8 per cent), and, in descending order of frequency of mention cowardice, quarrelsomeness, hypocrisy, haughtiness, and devotion to pleasure and sensuous enjoyment. When it comes to positive characteristics, the respondents mentioned that Czechs were hardworking (17 per cent) and skilful (8 per cent), and had a sense of humour (8 per cent). One-third of the respondents maintained that the Czechs had no special characteristics, were unable to think of any, or argued that it was possible to ascribe characteristic traits only to particular individuals, not to the nation as a whole. A similar survey had been conducted in October 1990, and between the two surveys there emerged a distinct polarisation between the positive and negative characteristics which the Czechs ascribed to themselves. The percentage of respondents in the two surveys who considered certain traits typical is summarised in table 1.

The little Czech is an ambivalent character. On the one hand he is seen as talented, skilful, and ingenious, on the other as shunning high ideals and living his life within the small world of his home, devoting all his efforts to his own and his family's well-being. By some people he is seen as the salt of the earth, with a character that has made it possible for the Czech nation to survive its frequent and often lengthy periods of oppression and foreign domination. Many others consider him to embody all the negative Czech self-stereotypes. One of my informants aptly characterised the little Czech as 'someone on to whom all Czechs project the characteristic traits which they possess but do not want to admit it'. Some of my informants, in response to the question of who the little Czech was, said 'ninety-nine per cent of Czechs' or 'most Czechs'. Characteristically,

Table 1. *Traits ascribed by Czechs to themselves
(percentages), 1990 and 1992*

Trait	1990	1992
Negative		
Envious	12	28
Conformist	9	15
Cunning	7	15
Egoistical	10	11
Lazy	3	8
Positive		
Hard-working	4	17
Skilful	3	8
Having a sense of humour	3	8

Note: The eight traits are those most frequently
mentioned by respondents in the 1992 survey.
Percentages are those of respondents who mentioned
one of the eight traits. The replies in the 1992 survey
add up to more than 100 per cent because the
respondents could mention as many traits as they
wished.
Source: Aktuálne problémy Česko-Slovenska, January
1992: 74–6.

although all the people I spoke to could name specific others who were, in
their opinion, little Czechs, none of them considered themselves to belong
to this category. Indeed, people often said, 'I sincerely hope that I am not
one.' Czechs often see the negative self-stereotypes as typical not of the
little Czech but of the *čecháček* (a pejorative diminutive of 'Czech'). Apart
from petty-mindedness, *čecháčkovství* ('being a *čecháček*') includes intolerance to views, attitudes, and conduct which differ from one's own, envy,
and a conviction that whatever one does or thinks is best and that those
who deviate from it should be reminded in no uncertain terms of the error
of their ways. The image of the little Czech or the *čecháček* is the main
image into which can be collapsed the various negative characteristics
which Czechs consider typical of themselves. Another image is expressed
in terms of what they consider to be their national traditions.

When Czechs talk about their traditions, they do not mean presumably
time-honoured but in fact often newly invented customs (see Hobsbawm
and Ranger 1983) such as the various public ceremonies. Tradition for
them is an attitude, characteristic, or proclivity of a particular collectivity

which its members assume they share and which each generation transmits more or less unchanged to the next. Any group or category of people, from a family, a kin group, or a local community, to a state or a nation, can, and probably does, have its own traditions in this sense. When Czechs talk about their national traditions they have in mind specific historically determined proclivities and attitudes which they see as typical of themselves as a nation. The image of the Czech nation which is most frequently invoked when Czechs talk about their assumed national traditions is the image of a democratic, well-educated, and highly cultured nation, and this image is, in numerous contexts, a distinct source of national pride. In much scholarly writing it is accepted as an objective fact. In the introduction to a sociological study of social stratification in Czechoslovakia, for example, it is stated that Czechoslovakia is a 'small, relatively industrially developed Central European country with a great tradition of spiritual culture and democratic and national political movements' (Machonin *et al.* 1969: 9). Again, it has been invoked as an explanation of the Prague Spring, described as 'the manifestation of the cultural strength and democratic traditions of the Czech nation, a movement to overcome the totalitarian system by utilising its own resources, a movement which occurred even within the Communist Party' (R. Štencl in *Respekt*, 1991, no. 35: 2). A number of political analysts, both Czech and foreign, pointing out that Czechoslovakia was the only democratic country in Central Europe between the two world wars, have stressed the democratic tradition as an important part of Czech political culture.

This highly positive image of the Czech nation and the distinctly negative image of Czechs are of course contradictory. Czechs see themselves as envious, resentful, conformist, cunning, and egoistic and yet consider themselves to be members of an inherently democratic nation in which they take distinct pride. They see themselves as petty-minded, intellectually limited, and mediocre, and yet consider the Czech nation highly cultured and well educated. The coexistence of the two images poses constant dilemmas. A favourite occupation of Czech intellectuals is considering such topics as 'the greatness and pettiness of Czech history' and contemplating the nationally parochial and the cosmopolitan aspects, or the inward and outward orientations, of Czech art, literature, or music. Dvořák's music is considered by some to be inferior to Smetana's because it is too cosmopolitan and not Czech enough; Smetana's music is considered inferior to Dvořák's by others because it is too parochially Czech. Contemporary Czech newspapers again provide examples of this Czech dilemma:

Let us listen to ourselves for a while: we are wretched, unreliable, immoral, envious, vile, greedy, inept, full of complexes, resentful and full of the residues of totality . . . We compensate for feeling powerless and untalented with a ridiculously pompous and pretentious messianism: we are the navel of the world, and we have to teach the world how to do it. We are the geniuses and all others are idiots. We do not let any business in here; it would destroy our grand world culture . . . We flutter here and there, from inferiority to inflated self-importance. *(Respekt, 1990, no. 40: 3)*

Considerably helped by the mass media, we constantly persuade each other that we are not what we necessarily must be after fifty years of systematic brainwashing: a horde of lazy ignoramuses and hateful and envious cowards. Instead, we persuade ourselves with characteristic megalomania that we are hard-working and intelligent people whose 'gentle' revolution was watched with envy by all Europe.

(Forum, 1990, no. 44: 4)

We are extremely touchy on the question of national traditions and cultural heritage. Our national pride easily becomes uncritical enthusiasm – usually short-lived. When faced with difficulties and reverses, we equally quickly sink into passivity and scepticism. In this lack of steadiness and balance which moves us constantly between two extremes – between overestimating and underestimating ourselves, between enthusiasm and depression – I see the problem of our national character, formed by the constant pressure to which a small nation has been exposed in the midst of a large world.

This lack of balance – to remain with examples from the sphere of culture and arts – has its further disastrous side: we like to love and celebrate our artists subsequently, as it were *ex post facto*, when they are dead. At the time when they were creating and struggling we were deaf and blind, indifferent as hardly anywhere else in the world.   *(Smetana 1991: 34–5)*

How can these two contradictory images coexist? To answer this question we have to bear in mind that they not only differ in content but also are generalisations of different experiences, constitute different models, and have different carriers.

Self-images as generalisations of experience

The characteristic traits which Czechs attribute to themselves are generalisations of particular individuals' 'lived experience' (E. P. Thompson 1981), of the conduct of other Czechs they know, or of their perception of the differences in behaviour and attitudes between Czechs and non-Czechs. As people's experiences differ, so too do their perceptions of the typical Czech character. Although some characteristic traits are seen by most Czechs to be typical, agreement on them is far from absolute. The generalisations which particular people offer are thus individual and not necessarily universally shared. As they are individual opinions, they cannot rely on self-evidence and, when necessary, have to be demonstrated by pointing to the conduct or attitudes of particular selected individuals and declaring them typical of others, including those of whom the speaker has no personal experience. The Czech self-image expressed in terms of assumed characteristic traits does not go beyond the limits of experiential data and the deductive associations linked with them.

Czech national traditions, in contrast, are not generalisations of particular individuals' own experiences. It is true that between the two world wars Czechoslovakia was the only country in Central Europe with a democratic political system, but the democratic form of government ended in 1938 following the surrender of the Sudetenland to Nazi Germany as a result of the Munich agreement. Even many Czechs doubt to what extent the short period between the end of World War II and the Communist coup d'état in 1948 can be seen as fully democratic. In its history since 1918, Czechoslovakia has enjoyed a democratic system of government for twenty or at best twenty-three years. For more than twice as long – a full forty-six years – it has had a totalitarian form of government. But totalitarianism has not created a tradition; it is the democratic tradition which is constantly being acknowledged and invoked.

If we assume that those who actively participated in the political life of pre-war Czechoslovakia must have been at least twenty years old, it follows that nowadays only people over the age of seventy, a very small minority of the total population, have ever had any personal or 'lived' experience of a democratic form of government. This does not mean, of course, that a democratic form of government has been obliterated from the social memory of the Czechs or, as some historians and anthropologists would express it, from their experience. For example, E. P. Thompson distinguishes 'perceived experience' from 'lived experience' (1981), and, accepting this notion of experience, Collard, for example, in formulating her notion of 'social memory', suggests that '"history" can be said to work through experience' (1989: 91).

Lumping together 'lived' and 'perceived' experience not only contradicts the common-sense understanding of 'experience' but also conflates two different cognitive processes. Admittedly, there is no 'pure' experience. What we experience is determined by our culture – our system of classification and our criteria of significance and relevance. What we call our experience of the world is the result of our observation of this world through living in it and our evaluation of what we observe in terms of our culturally given criteria and their accompanying values. Two processes seem to be involved in 'lived' experience: observation of or, more precisely, witnessing (itself culturally determined) events through participating in them; and evaluation in terms of the culturally given criteria of significance. These two processes can result either in a confirmation of the observation in terms of the existing criteria or the revision of these criteria as a result of what has been observed. The latter process results in cultural change as a change 'in men's ideas and their values, argued through in their actions, choices, and beliefs' (E. P. Thompson 1978). Cultural change is tantamount to change in 'lived' experience. Minor cultural changes such as this occur all the time and we witness them whenever someone says, 'That has not been my experience.'

'Perceived' experience replaces personal participation in events with a mediated account of them. The difference between 'lived' and 'perceived' experience is the difference between life and text. If 'perceived' experience is experience at all, it is experience of stereotypes and images which, unlike 'lived' experience, lacks any basis for their redefinition. A mediated account of events certainly constitutes awareness or knowledge of them and thus makes it possible for them to become part of social or historical memory, but it is a knowledge which is cognitively distinct from the knowledge of events one has participated in or witnessed. It is of necessity impoverished, filtering out the multiplicity of meanings which events may have had for their participants and making possible a single, usually officially asserted meaning. Commonsensically, we would deny people any experience of the United States who know it only from television, films, novels, or news reporting. Although they have knowledge or awareness of the United States, they have experience only of its images. What applies in space applies in time as well. However, beliefs and attitudes can be transmitted from generation to generation even if no one has personal experience of the events and actual practices motivated by them. Personal or 'lived' experience of a phenomenon is not a necessary condition for its being seen as a tradition, and a phenomenon can be seen as constituting a tradition even if no one whose tradition it is has any personal experience of it. A tradition can be characterised as a text which is unquestionably accepted as valid and authoritative. The amount of personal experience with a democratic form of government is about the same in present-day Czech Republic as it is in Poland or Hungary, which the Czechs consider to lack democratic traditions.

Unlike generalisations about character traits, a national tradition is by definition collective, shared by all members of the nation, supraindividual, and intergenerational. However, it is not a discourse which relies on self-evidence. The validity of a tradition needs to be demonstrated, and there are standardised ways of doing so. The existence of the Czech democratic tradition is demonstrated not only by pointing out that Czechoslovakia was the only democratic country in pre-war Central Europe but also by interpreting this fact as a specific manifestation of the tradition. Tradition of course implies continuity, and only something that has always been done or has been done for a long time in a certain society constitutes that society's tradition. Thus, it makes sense to speak, for example, about a parliamentary tradition in Britain or about a tradition of neutrality in Switzerland.

Czechs too understand tradition in this sense of continuity resulting from a particular reading of Czech history. The canonical text of this reading which was accepted by most subsequent Czech historiography and thus 'made history' (Stern 1992: 36), is Palacký's *History of the Czech Nation in Bohemia and Moravia* (1836–54). Palacký's was the first history of Bohemia to be based on the study of primary sources. For Palacký, the very beginning of Czech recorded history is characterised by the 'old-Slavonic democratic spirit', standing in sharp contrast to German feudalism. What later came to be seen as his 'philosophy of Czech history' is his view of that history as the continuous realisation of the nation's libertarian, egalitarian, and democratic spirit in the constant struggle against German autocracy. The Hussite movement of the fifteenth century in particular is viewed from this perspective as the culmination of 'the unending task of the nation on behalf of humanity as a whole'. Palacký's 'philosophy of Czech history' provided the basis for Masaryk's politics and for his belief that the Czechoslovak nation should pursue the ideals of the Hussite reformation, which became the official ideology of the pre-war Czechoslovak Republic and the source of the most important state symbols.

With Masaryk's authority behind it, Palacký's view dominated the republic's official historiography (Stern 1992: 36). It also dominated the official historiography of the communist period, which found in Palacký's emphasis on the Czech–German struggle a convenient ideological validation for its presentation of German revanchism and the international imperialism of NATO (in which Germany played a prominent role) as a perpetual threat to the socialist order. Palacký's emphasis on the positive aspects of the Hussite movement was also positively evaluated in socialist historiography, which de-emphasised its religious aspect and emphasised its social, egalitarian, and revolutionary aspects. In fact, the Hussite movement became the main source of the communist regime's symbolism; for example, the heraldic shield of the state's official coat of arms was replaced by the Hussite shield, with the lion of the Bohemian kings adorned by the red star.

Part of ascertaining the continuity of the democratic tradition is not only emphasising the parliamentary democracy of the pre-war Czechoslovak Republic but, pointing to the active communal and club life characteristic of nineteenth-century Czech society, arguing that the Czechs of the time were much more democratic than any other nation of the Austro-Hungarian Empire. Critical Czech historiography has debunked these views, emphasising that the political parties of the pre-war Czechoslovak Republic were autocratically governed by their leaders (Podiven 1991: 540) and that nineteenth-century Czech society was very authoritarian. Treating the Austro-Hungarian state as a foreign imposition which they wanted nothing at all to do with, Czechs made no attempt at any democratisation of the existing political system (Podiven 1991: 134, 161).

Similarly, the tradition of high culture and education is routinely demonstrated by listing world-renowned Czech composers, musicians, writers, poets, and playwrights such as Smetana, Dvořák, Janáček, Martinů, Kubelík, Čapek, Kundera, Seifert, or Havel. Any nation can come up with such names, however, without necessarily seeing itself as exceptionally cultured, and therefore Czechs go on to invoking names of similarly outstanding individuals from the past. Constant reference to Czech history is part not only of much political commentary but also of much everyday political discourse. Czechs tell themselves who they are by projecting contemporary ideas and values onto the narrative of the past, which in turn is invoked as their legitimation. In this respect history functions as a myth which is truly a charter in Malinowski's sense. One of the important myths which the Czechs create in narrating their history is the myth of a nation whose leading personalities have always been intellectuals: the 'father of the country', King Charles IV, is remembered first of all as the founder of the oldest university north of the Alps, and the most important Czech martyr, Jan Hus, was its professor. Hus's death inspired the Hussite movement mainly because the Czech people were led by preachers with more knowledge of the scriptures than the pope himself. A tiny group of Czech intellectuals kept the Czech language alive and managed to bring the Czechs into the fold of modern European nations. Masaryk, a university professor, Beneš, a high school teacher, and Štefánik, an astronomer, were the founding fathers of the Czechoslovak Republic in 1918. The specific historical events which the Czechs invoke when telling themselves their history attest to the high standard of learning and education among Czechs in the past. Every Czech schoolchild is reminded of the seventeenth-century papal nuncio's assertion that any Czech woman knew the Bible better than many priests.

Even Petr Pithart, prime minister of the first post-November Czech government and a political scientist and historian who is otherwise highly critical of the tendency to glorify the Czech past, repeats the popular image according to which 'our ancestors had an exceptional respect for the written word, for a book. Illiteracy was eradicated relatively early, and the Czechs have become a nation of readers' (1990b: 23). He sees the problem of the Czech nation as the 'problem of a cultured nation without politicians and in fact without full-fledged politics . . . and hence as the problem of the political responsibility of intellectuals' (Pithart 1990b: 16). The tradition of the highly cultured nation, like the democratic tradition, can thus also be traced to the radical politicisation of culture in the nineteenth century (see Stern 1992: 37; Gellner 1987: 131). In general, the Czechs substantiate their image of themselves as an exceptionally cultured and well-educated nation by a specific reading of their history in which they construct a close relationship between culture and politics. A rather succinct version of this construction was offered by Eduard Goldstücker in an interview for the Czech cultural weekly *Tvorba* in 1990:

The Czechoslovak Republic was . . . a highly cultured state even before World War II. It was a rather unique case. At the beginning of the seventeenth century, the Czechs lost the leading strata of their society, their nobility and their wealthy and educated burghers. When the national revival arrived, the middle class had to be created anew; the success or failure of the national revival depended on it. Because the nation had lost its leading strata, their place had to be taken by intellectuals, who literally had to fill the gap and at the same time to play the role of national leaders. A case like this, in which the intellectuals become the leaders of the nation, does not exist anywhere else – from Palacký to Masaryk and beyond. The intellectuals gave a humanistic programme to the movement of national revival which achieved realisation in the exceptional moment of the year 1918.

In answering the question of whether contemporary culture should devote itself exclusively to politics or aim at awakening truly democratic and humanistic values among the people, Goldstücker argued that

it is impossible to separate these two things because in Bohemia, where culture has traditionally been put in a position where it has to be a representative of national interests, in other words, to take the place of the politicians, every cultural act has its political implications. Inevitably, it heightens self-awareness, a critical attitude, etc.   (*Tvorba, 1990, no. 7: 7*)

What this reading of modern Czech history indicates is that the Czechs are a cultured nation because of the political role which culture plays among them. This role of culture is also expressed in the Czech metaphor of the writer as the conscience of the nation.

Self-images as models
The characteristic traits which Czechs attribute to themselves are generalisations of particular individuals' own experiences, and their existence can be proved by simple ostension. National traditions are not generalisations of particular individuals' own experiences; they are asserted beliefs, and their existence ultimately cannot be either proved or disproved because any possible proof of a tradition presupposes the existence of that tradition. Presumed national traditions can best be seen as condensed myths. Whereas a typical mythical narrative is a sequence of images which in their totality convey the meaning of the myth, a tradition condenses the narrative into a single simple and unambiguously meaningful image. What it shares with myth is that the truth of the meaning conveyed is taken as a dogma whether or not it corresponds to experienced reality.

Because the character traits which Czechs attribute to themselves are generalisations of particular individuals' experiences of the behaviour and attitudes of themselves and others, they are seen as reflecting reality at least as it has been experienced by particular individuals at particular times. As models, these traits are, in Geertz's term, 'models of'. Most of the character traits which Czechs attribute to themselves are ascribed a negative value; they are certainly not ideals which everyone is expected to emulate.

National traditions are not generalisations of trends distilled from the totality of events constituting the nation's history. On the contrary, the events of the past which are quoted as standardised proofs of traditions are always highly selective. If anything, the actual historical events would in fact point to other traditions: one of the absence of a democratic system (at least as far as the twentieth century is concerned), of a recurrent threat to the building of democratic structures, of frustrated attempts at establishing an enduring democratic system of government, of democratic development recurrently interrupted by its collapse under the onslaught of totalitarianism. Historical periods and events which are negatively valued are not obliterated from historical memory but declared to be anomalous discontinuities in Czech history and, as such, are excluded from the construction of national traditions. Czechs certainly do not imagine themselves as a nation with, for example, a long tradition of totalitarianism (as the Russians now do) or of cheating at work. In relation to the actual course of history, the prevailing images expressed in terms of national traditions are idealisations or formulations of ideals perpetually thwarted and never permanently achieved. In Geertz's terminology, they are 'models for'. They are assigned a highly positive value and considered to shape people's attitudes to life, to guide their behaviour, and to formulate a set of shared principles and values as the basis of existence.

The carriers of self-images

The behaviour and attitudes which Czechs consider characteristic of themselves are attributable to specific individuals. They are spoken of as typical of the Czech nation when they seem so prevalent as to apply to most Czechs or at least to most Czechs that the speaker knows. Their carriers are particular individuals who if need be can be specified. The people now alive in Czechoslovakia who have had any personal or 'lived' experience of a democratic political system are too few to be effective carriers of a democratic tradition which is not only *theirs* but that of the whole nation, of which they are only a small part. Particular individuals cannot be the carriers of a democratic tradition if they have no 'lived' experience of democracy or carriers of the tradition of good education if they themselves have had only the most rudimentary education and are oblivious of the products of high culture which are a manifestation of the Czech nation's exceptional *kulturnost* (a noun derived from the adjective *kulturní*, 'cultured'). The carrier of these traditions is the nation as a whole, not any of its particular members. This means not only that the ideals which the national traditions embody can persist even if most people do not live up to them, but also that the nation can be imagined as a whole which is not divisible into its individual parts and which is more than the sum of its parts. The very notion of national traditions makes possible the imagination of the nation as a truly supraindividual entity.

This is, however, not the only effect of the assumed existence of national traditions on the process of imagining and conceptualising a nation. In the next chapter I shall return to the role of the notion of national traditions in this process. Here I want to discuss some other aspects of Czech self-images in general and of Czech national traditions in particular to which I have so far only briefly alluded.

Self-images and self-criticism

The negative character traits attributed to Czechs are always mentioned disapprovingly as something that they ought to overcome. National traditions are also invoked in the context of a critical attitude toward existing everyday practices. Because of its generality, a tradition can serve as a measure of any particular behaviour. At the same time, it provides a sense of empowerment for those who invoke it, making it possible for them temporarily to occupy the moral high ground. When the ideal embodied in the tradition is contrasted with the perceived real situation, the hollowness of the ideal is of course revealed, but the ideal is not rejected; instead, the discrepancy between it and the real situation is used to stress the urgency of a more determined effort to secure it.

It is particularly the taken-for-granted self-image of Czechs as a cultured and well-educated nation which is used in this way. According to UNESCO statistics, expenditures on education in the 1980s put Czechoslovakia into seventy-second place in the world, with Nepal in seventy-first. One of the students' slogans during the 'velvet revolution' was a pun on the well-known Czech folk prognostic: *Na nový rok o krok dál, dostanem se před Nepál* ('One step further in the New Year, we shall leave Nepal behind'). This was not a denial of what every Czech accepts as a self-evident truth – that the Czechs are a cultured and well-educated nation – but a criticism of the government for not treating such a nation as it should.

In so far as the tradition of the Czechs as a cultured nation is routinely substantiated by invoking the names of present and past Czech artists and intellectuals, culture is understood in the sense of 'high' culture (literature, drama, music, arts). Understanding culture in this sense, the Czechs can demonstrate to themselves their *kulturnost* by pointing to the number of theatres and bookshops in their country, which is certainly greater in proportion to the population than, for example, in Britain, or to the great number of books which can be found even in the households of workers and farmers. When Czechs – mostly of the educated middle class but short of foreign currency – began travelling to Vienna with the reopening of the borders after the fall of the communist system, they flocked to the museums and galleries instead of to the supermarkets as the East Germans, with newly acquired Deutschmarks in their pockets, did. This was reported with astonishment in the Austrian press and taken by the Czechs as a clear sign of their *kulturnost*. In January 1990 an actress expressed on television her approval of applying market principles to the sphere of culture by saying that now theatrical performances would at last be attended by people who understood and enjoyed the theatre instead of being 'sold out' through the trade union's distribution of free tickets to people from the country for whom a free bus ride to Prague to attend a theatrical performance was primarily a free shopping trip. Her remark inspired numerous letters protesting her denial of their authors' *kulturnost*.

But 'culture' is understood not only as 'high culture' but also as the 'culture of everyday life',[2] and the discourse in which the notion of Czech *kulturnost* is invoked plays on both its meanings. When this notion is being invoked critically in an attempt to make people live up to the ideal expressed in the national tradition, it is always the culture of everyday life which is found wanting. When the astonishment of the Austrians at the Czech passion for museums and galleries was replaced by hastily prepared notices in Czech informing the customers in Austrian supermarkets that shoplifting was a criminal offence, the articles and letters in Czech newspapers invoked the Czech national tradition critically by asking, 'Are we really a cultured nation?' In reading Czech newspapers and magazines I came across the invocation of the image of Czechs as a cultured nation in the context of a critical attitude toward such varied aspects of everyday life as cruelty to animals (*Forum*, 1990, no. 44: 3), the proliferation of pornographic magazines and intolerance of the views of others (*Rudé právo*, 13 January 1990), the defacing of the walls of underground stations with posters and notices and the renaming of streets and public places (*Rudé právo*, 9 February 1990), the rudeness of people toward each other in public, the lack of cleanliness of lavatories and the general untidiness of public places, and cheating or overcharging of customers.

The critical edge was always underpinned by the question 'Is this a sign of a cultured nation?' This critical attitude to many aspects of everyday life does not deny the existence of the national tradition of culture and education: the tradition persists in spite of repeated demonstrations that individual Czechs fall short of the ideal which it embodies. Demonstration of these shortcomings does not lead to the rejection of the tradition but forms the basis of a critical attitude toward actual behaviour. 'Are we really a cultured nation?' is a rhetorical question. As with the characteristic traits which Czechs attribute to themselves, the aim of the critical attitude toward behaviour perceived as not being consonant with a national tradition is to make it approximate the ideal. The critical attitude stresses that to achieve its full meaning this tradition needs to be realised not only in the sphere of high culture but also in the culture of everyday life. The ultimate moral of the critical attitude is that only when we change our ways will we really be what according to our national traditions we should be – a cultured nation (see, e.g., *Svobodné slovo*, 23 June 1990) which has a right to claim its place in a Europe which values cultured and civilised behaviour.

The asserted democratic tradition too is invoked, although not as frequently as that of the cultured and well-educated nation, in the context of criticism of existing practices. The critical assessment of the real situation by the yardstick of the ideal expressed through tradition is used here again to reveal the hollowness of the ideal. The aim of the criticism is to bring the practice in line with the ideal. In the case of the ideal of the democracy of the Czech nation, it is usually Czech egalitarianism which is seen as hindering its realisation.

The pre-war custom of holding balls in the opera house was revived after the revolution of 1989, and the first charity ball was held in Smetana's Theatre in Prague in February 1992. The tickets were cheap in comparison with those for similar charity events elsewhere in the world but very expensive by Czech standards and out of reach of ordinary people. The proceeds from their sale went to the fund for the restoration of the theatre. Members of the Czechoslovak Anarchistic Association and the Left Initiative, who considered the ball an unacceptable provocation by the rich, shouted slogans about dirty money and the vampires' ball, pelted the participants with rotten tomatoes and oranges, and distributed 'vegetarian soup to the poor'. A few guests at the ball suffered slight injuries, and five demonstrators were detained by the police for breach of the peace. A comment printed a few days later in the daily *Lidové noviny* seized on the contradiction between the asserted democratic tradition of the Czech nation and Czech egalitarianism:

It is surely easier to throw a rotten tomato than to make a lot of money. It is easier to hit a successful person with a rotten orange than to be successful oneself. The demand of equality in poverty is deeply rooted in us, having been carefully watered for fifty years with a nutritive ideological solution.

However, the real cause of this peculiar state of mind probably lies deeper. For years the Czech nation has been suffering from constantly burnished superstition about some deep democratic traditions which, nobody knows exactly why, are supposed to have their root in the area between Aš and Znojmo.[3] These traditions have never been at home here, unless, of course, we confuse democratic traditions with plebeian traditions. The Communists were well aware of this, and they polished up the plebeian traditions to the sparkling lustre of socialist democracy. An obscure booklet by Zdeněk Nejedlý, 'Communists: Heirs of the Best Traditions of the Nation', is the basic text in this respect. Other building blocks of 'democratic traditions' are still with us: anyone else's success is immoral; we all have the same stomachs; education is parasitism.

We want to be democrats, or at least so most of us say. In no way will it be easy. Each of us will have trouble overcoming the plebeian habit of equality in poverty. I admit that it is difficult for us to tolerate wealth of almost Babylonian proportions, accustomed as we are to an undemanding life secured, as it were, through being homebodies and through our provincialism. We have to tolerate the success and wealth of others. We have to return a proper value to education, for education is one of the necessary, albeit not always sufficient, conditions of success . . .

We are not heirs to the democratic traditions which include listening to the opinions of others, tolerance, and the wish for success. We are heirs to the 'best traditions of the nation'. If we were not, we would be interested in one thing only about the ball in Smetana's Theatre: how many crowns, Deutschmarks, or dollars it raised for the restoration of the building . . . The demonstrators helped the theatre with rotten tomatoes. It is not difficult to recognise which is more helpful.

(Lidové noviny, 11 February 1992)

This is just one example of a more general negative evaluation of individual Czechs resulting from the comparison of their conduct with the ideals embodied in national traditions. What this negative evaluation expresses is the recognition of their failure to live up to these ideals. It is an explicit or often only tacit recognition of the fact that the traditions are indeed only ideals, expressing what Czechs would like to be, but are not or are not yet. The recognition of the fact that individual members of the nation constantly fail to live up to national ideals creates the ever-present tendency to see them in a negative light.

Envious and intolerant Czechs

Because traditions are invoked to mobilise people for the achievement of highly desirable goals, the self-image of the nation which is embodied in them has to be, and indeed is, highly positive. This positive image is not at all adversely affected by the fact that individual Czechs tend to see themselves in a distinctly negative light. I would suggest that the coexistence of these two contradictory images is the result of the way in which the nation is constructed in the nationalist discourse – not as a collectivity of heterogeneous individuals but as a supraindividual entity which exists in its own right. If the nation were seen as a collectivity of individuals, these individuals too would have to be ascribed positive characteristics, for their characteristics would affect the nation as a whole. However, although this construction makes it possible to ascribe negative characteristics to individual Czechs, it does not make it necessary; the positive image of the nation would not be challenged if its individual members too were ascribed positive traits.

The two most often mentioned negative characteristics of Czechs are envy and intolerance. The selection of these two particular characteristics – like the selection of the assumed traditions of the nation – is not arbitrary and is ultimately determined by the logic of the cultural construction of the individual as part of the nation. This construction inevitably engenders egalitarianism. When national identity is seen as the primary identity of every individual, the identities of individuals are derived from their membership of a collectivity united in purpose irrespective of any differences in class or rank, occupation, level of education, lifestyle, or regional characteristics. The culturally constructed primary identity is derived from the membership of a collectivity which surpasses and ultimately negates any vertical or horizontal stratification. As parts of a whole which recognises no internal differences, individuals are identical and equivalent units.

In practice, the appearance of ideologically asserted equality is disrupted by social stratification and particularly by the existence of individuals whose achievements are seen as beyond the capabilities of the majority. Given the cultural premise of equality of all members of the nation, the role model cannot be an overachiever or an exceptionally successful or gifted individual. It can only be an individual whose achievements are accessible to all: an underachiever or at best an average performer. This is recognised in the saying 'Our strength is in the average', sarcastically commented upon by Voskovec and Werich in one of their plays: 'The author of the saying was most probably himself below average so that he would profit even on that average.' As it is practically impossible for the majority to emulate the successful minority in achievements, conduct, and lifestyle, the successful and exceptional individual has to be brought down to the average level of the majority if any semblance of inherent equality among the members of the nation is to be maintained in behavioural practice. This is widely recognised as a typical characteristic of Czechs and incessantly commented upon. Smetana, for example, sees Czech art criticism as belonging to

> that kind of noisy and opinionated journalism which ostensibly subscribes to heightened criticism, even to national pride, but which gains its spurs and its pay by making everything dirty: the more outstanding the personality whom the reviewer noisily attacks and rubbishes, the more God-like he feels. 'It is grist to the mill of one negative Czech characteristic', complained the singer Karel Kyncl . . . 'When something is pure, let us rubbish it as much as we can – not to rise with someone but to pull him down to our level.'   *(1991: 93)*

It may appear incongruous that, in a nation which prides itself on being exceptionally cultured and well educated, 'You intellectual' is a common term of abuse. It is, however, just one of the manifestations of the effort to maintain an assumed and expected equality. The various stratagems employed to maintain this semblance of equality among people who see themselves as ideally equal parts of the transcendent whole which is the nation have been perceived as manifestations of envy and intolerance. The pejorative use of 'You intellectual' does not mean that intellectuality is universally negatively valued in Czech culture. Its negative aspects derive from contravening the expected equality of all Czechs generated by the nationalist discourse's construction of individuals as part of the nation and as emanations of collective Czech nationhood. The nationalist discourse is of course not the only one which creates and re-creates Czech cultural values and premises. It is in competition with the discourse which espouses the ideology of individualism and values intellectuality as a sign of individuality. In their discourse on individualism, Czechs construe intellectuality as a positive characteristic. As I shall suggest in chapter 5, most Czechs are distinctly proud of the intellectuality of their past and present leading personalities, whose individuality is used to evidence the ideal embodied in the national traditions. Seen as part of a specific discourse, intellectuality – like individuality – is a constant value which competes with egalitarianism and the denial of the individuality of the members of the nation for its moment of legitimate expression. In situations perceived as national crises, the values espoused in the nationalist discourse come to prominence whilst those espoused in the competing discourse on individualism may be temporarily submerged, but in fact both sets of values feed into the premises of Czech culture.

The creation of tradition
The fact that a specific attitude or mode of expected and approved social conduct has become established as the characteristic response of a collectivity in a certain historical period is not in itself sufficient for perceiving it as that collectivity's tradition. A tradition can be, and indeed is, substantiated by pointing to a few selected historical events which, because they function as standardised proofs of the existence of the tradition, are made to stand out from the regular flow of ordinary historical events and constituted as significant. Their significance does not derive from any possible impact they may have had on the course of history; on the contrary, it is the assumed present traditions which provide the prism through which events are selected and constituted as significant. This means that for this process of proving the tradition to work, the tradition has to exist, as it were, independently of the way in which its existence is proved. In other words, it has to be perpetually re-created in the present.

Awareness of a nation's tradition, as of any other aspect of national identity, crystallises only in relation to another nation perceived as different. During the national revival, Czechs defined themselves as a nation in conscious opposition to the Germans, who were culturally, politically, and economically the dominant element in Bohemia. The conscious aim of the revival was the development of the Czech language, which, as a language of literature, science, and philosophy, became the main instrument for creating a Czech culture equivalent to German culture in every respect. The *kulturnost* of Germans has never been denied by Czechs (at least Czech intellectuals). The first generation of revivalists wrote in German and began writing in Czech as an outward sign of their Czech identity only gradually and, at first, with great difficulty (Macura 1983: 144–5). Even after the Czech language had become established as the language in which they communicated among themselves and as their literary language, they remained bilingual or at least fluent in German. German literature, science, and philosophy were their main sources of stimulation. Their success in creating Czech literature and science in a short time became proof of the *kulturnost* of the Czech nation: Czechs had proved that they were as cultured as Germans.

The notion of Czech *kulturnost* based on the perception of Czech cultural achievements as fully equivalent to those of the Germans is perpetuated by the authors of these achievements. For ordinary Czechs, the image of the German is not that of a scholar or philosopher but that of an aggressor and oppressor or a warrior. Many ordinary Czechs today view with distaste the penetration of German capital into Czech industry, the proliferation of German firms, the growing quantity of German goods on the Czech market, and in particular the appearance of advertising slogans and inscriptions in German. They express their fear that, having failed to subjugate the Czech nation militarily, the Germans will succeed in subjugating it economically.

Although intellectuals and ordinary people differ in their perception of Germans, they share the idea of a cultured and well-educated Czech nation. For ordinary people the source of this image is not so much the perceived similarity between Czechs and Germans as the perceived difference between Czechs and Slovaks. To appreciate fully how this difference is perceived and expressed it is necessary to examine Czech–Slovak relations as they have unfolded throughout the modern history of the Czech nation. This discussion serves two purposes. First, it illustrates the specific ways in which the Czechs perpetually re-create the image of themselves as a cultured and well-educated nation with a deep-rooted tradition of democracy. Secondly, it provides the necessary background for understanding the significance of the Czech nationalist sentiments which have accompanied the demise of communism in Czechoslovakia and the creation of independent Czech and Slovak states which was its most important political outcome.

Czechs and Slovaks

The Great Moravian empire, considered by both Czech and Slovak historians to be the first historically documented state in Central Europe, collapsed at the beginning of the tenth century. Slovak historians tend toward the opinion that Slovaks were its dominant element and see it as the first Slovak state. Czech historians tend toward the view that it was the first common state of Czechs and Slovaks. Whatever its ethnic composition, during its existence a new political centre emerged in Levý Hradec[4] and later in Prague, which became the centre of the Bohemian kingdom. After the collapse of the Moravian empire, Slovakia became part of the Hungarian state, in which it remained without any autonomy as an integral part of St Stephen's crown until the collapse of the Austro-Hungarian Empire in 1918.

The population of Slovakia spoke several dialects which were closely related not only to each other but also to the various dialects of Bohemia and Moravia. By the end of the sixteenth century the language of the first printed Czech Bible (1579–94) became established as a literary language not only in Bohemia but also in Slovakia. Some of the leading personalities of the national revival in the first half of the last century, for example, J. Kollár, P. J. Šafařík, and F. Palacký, were active in both Bohemia and Slovakia or at least familiar with the culture, history, and contemporary political situations of both of these countries. One of the questions which was hotly debated during the national revival was whether Czechs and Slovaks were one nation or two closely related but separate ones. The view that Bohemia, Moravia, Silesia, and Upper Hungary (i.e., Slovakia) were all part of one Czech region, expressed, for example, by Dobrovský in 1792 (Pražák 1929: 27), began to be articulated during the nineteenth century in terms of the common ethnic identity of this region. Its inhabitants began to be referred to first as Czechoslavs (Pražák 1929: 28) and later as Czechoslovaks – a nation speaking a single Czechoslovak language and bound together by common history, tradition, and culture (Pražák 1929: 56–70). However, efforts to create a common Czechoslovak national identity binding together the inhabitants of Bohemia, Moravia, Silesia, and Slovakia were paralleled by efforts to assert a separate Slovak identity.

These efforts were motivated by two considerations. The first was uneasiness about the Czech linguistic and cultural dominance expressed in the image of the common nation drawn, for example, by Kollár, for whom the Czechs were the trunk and roots of the common Czechoslav tree of which the Moravians, Silesians, and Slovaks were branches and twigs (Pražák 1929: 57). The second was the strong Czech Protestant tradition, viewed as alien to the deep-rooted Catholic faith of most ordinary Slovaks. The decisive act in establishing a separate Slovak identity in relation to the Czechs was the creation of a Slovak literary language. The

Catholic priest Antonín Bernolák published a Latin treatise about the Slovak language in 1787 and a Slovak grammar based on the dialect spoken in western Slovakia in 1790. He thus laid the foundation of the Slovak literary language used since then by Slovak Catholics. Slovak Protestants continued to write in Czech until 1844, when, under the leadership of Ľudevít Štúr, they adopted the central Slovakian dialect as their literary language. Their argument against the Slovak language of Bernolák was that it was based on a dialect too close to Czech ones. Štúr's Slovak language then gradually became the literary language even for Slovak Catholics (Agnew 1992).

The creation of a Slovak literary language became the subject of a discussion among both Czech and Slovak intellectuals which lasted for almost a hundred years. The nationalistically oriented Czech intellectuals called it the 'language schism' and considered it a hindrance to the common struggle of Czechs and Slovaks for cultural and political autonomy. Some of them explained it as a move triggered by the increasing threat of Magyarisation of the Slovaks. Attempts to resolve the language schism were made by both Czechs and Slovaks. On the Slovak side the most important among them was Hurban's unsuccessful effort to return to the use of literary Czech in the 1870s; on the Czech side there were numerous appeals to the Slovaks in the 1890s and at the beginning of this century to return to the literary Czech language and thus to strengthen the awareness of a common national identity and increase the numerical strength of the common nation.

After the creation of the Slovak literary language, the idea of a single Czechoslovak nation speaking one language, embraced by most nationalistically minded Czech intellectuals in the first half of the nineteenth century, began to be replaced by the idea of a single nation speaking two languages or having two branches. These ideas and images acquired political significance shortly before World War I and particularly during the war itself, when Czech and Slovak politicians began to consider seriously the possibility of creating their own independent state following the defeat and the expected disintegration of the Austro-Hungarian Empire.

During the war, the Czech and Slovak political émigrés in the United States who were campaigning under the leadership of T. G. Masaryk for the creation of an independent Czechoslovakia referred in their various documents, memorandums, and speeches not so much to Czechs and Slovaks but to either the Czech or the Czechoslovak nation. For example, Masaryk's memorandum 'Independent Bohemia', written for the British foreign secretary in 1915, envisioned the Czech state as a monarchy in which the 'Slovak regions in northern Hungary' would be linked to the Czech lands. The memorandum mentions explicitly that 'Slovaks are Czechs in spite of using their dialect as a literary language.' The 1915 memorandum of the Czech Committee Abroad, which later became the Czechoslovak National Council, spoke of the struggle for sovereignty of the *Czech* nation and demanded the creation of an 'independent Czechoslovak state'. The so-called Washington declaration of 18 October 1918 talked on the one hand about the 'Czechoslovak nation' and on the other hand about the right of Czechs to be united with their 'Slovak brothers in Slovakia'. In Bohemia, a declaration of Czech members of parliament in 1917 demanded 'the unification of all branches of the Czechoslovak nation in a democratic Czech state also containing the Slovak branch of the nation'. In June 1917 the representatives of the Czech Social Democrats in Stockholm similarly demanded the unification 'of all members of the Czech nation who inhabit a continuous territory, that is, also the Slovaks' (Z. Urban 1988: 23–4). Other documents could be mentioned which in their rhetoric clearly expressed the idea of a Czechoslovak nation insisting on exercising its right to national self-determination by creating its own state. On the one hand, this rhetoric was motivated by the image of the Czech and Slovak branches of a single nation, which crystallised during the period of national revival and was shared by most Czech intellectuals in spite of the efforts of some Slovak intellectuals to establish a separate Slovak identity. On the other hand, it was determined by pragmatic political considerations, aimed at creating the image of a future Czechoslovak state which, though containing German, Hungarian, and other ethnic minorities, could nevertheless be seen as a proper nation-state in that the majority of its inhabitants were of a single ethnic stock.

Talk about the Czech or Czechoslovak nation was sometimes the conscious strategy of Czech and Slovak diplomats in their effort not to confuse the politicians of the Alliance, who were expected to be unfamiliar with the history and ethnic composition of Central Europe. Describing how the name of the Czechoslovak National Council (Conseil National des Pays Tcheques) was chosen, Beneš says, 'The Slovak Štefánik defended the expression "des Pays Tcheques" – of the Czech lands – because, given the Allies' complete lack of knowledge of Slovak matters, he did not want to complicate our political struggle by accentuating the Slovak question. He was afraid that it would not be understood and that our adversaries might even use it against us' (Beneš 1935: 117). The rhetoric was thus aimed at alleviating the Allies' fears of balkanisation of Europe and defusing their possible objections to the Czechs' and Slovaks' creating a new state in Central Europe which in its ethnic heterogeneity would, on a smaller scale, resemble the Austro-Hungarian Empire which they were determined to dismantle.

Among themselves, Czechs and Slovaks had to determine the form of their coexistence in a future common state. During the war Czech and Slovak politicians signed various agreements which the Slovaks later invoked as justification for their demands of greater autonomy within Czechoslovakia or outright political separation from the Czechs. The most important of these were the Cleveland agreement of October 1915 and the Pittsburgh agreement of May 1918. The Cleveland agreement, signed between the Czech National Assembly in America and the Slovak League, mentioned the future coexistence of 'the Czech and Slovak nation in a federative union' and proposed the 'full autonomy of Slovakia, with its own assembly, own administration, and Slovak official language'. The Pittsburgh agreement similarly mentioned separate Slovak administration, assembly, and courts and Slovak as the official language in the Slovak part of the independent state of the Czechs and Slovaks (Z. Urban 1988: 22).

At first, the diplomatic campaign of the Czech and Slovak politicians for the dismantling of the Austro-Hungarian Empire and the creation of a Czechoslovak state met with an ambiguous response from the Allies, who were much more concerned with the Polish and Yugoslav questions. But from the beginning of 1916, when Czech and Slovak diplomatic efforts were being centrally coordinated by the Czechoslovak National Council, the Czechoslovak rhetoric began to have its effect. Toward the end of the war, when the Polish and Yugoslav political organisations were facing difficulties in gaining recognition by the Allies, the Czechoslovak National Council and later the provisional government were recognised without any serious objections, and the Czechoslovak question became part of the official diplomatic negotiations even before the creation of an independent Czechoslovak state. This gave a strong voice to the Czechoslovak political representatives at the Versailles peace conference.

Czechoslovakia, as Czechs never failed to remind themselves, became 'the darling of the Allies' – an exemplary state emerging from the ruins of the Austro-Hungarian Empire. Although the officially embraced principle for the creation of new nation-states in Central and Southern Europe was the self-determination embodied in Wilson's declaration, Czech demands for the constitution of their new state within the historical borders of the Bohemian kingdom were accepted by the Allies. The result was that the new Czechoslovak Republic contained some three million ethnic

Germans. The Allies also recognised as legitimate the demand that the borders of the new state be defensible in the event of any future armed conflict. As a result, the southern border of Slovakia did not follow the Slovak–Hungarian ethnic divide but was drawn farther south along the Danube River, leaving a three-quarters-of-a-million-strong Hungarian minority in southern Slovakia. Apart from the Germans and Hungarians, there were half a million Ukrainians and about a hundred thousand Poles living in the new state.

Czechoslovakia was thus clearly a multiethnic state. Numerically, the strongest ethnic group was the Czechs, of whom there were about seven million. The second largest was the Germans, who with their three million considerably outnumbered the Slovaks, with only two and a quarter million. The Germans, as a defeated nation, were expected by the Czechs to be hostile to their state-building efforts. Immediately after independence, the Hungarians were politically even more of a problem for the new Czechoslovak government. Mihály Karolyi's Hungarian government tried to save the integrity of pre-war Hungary at the cost of granting autonomy to Slovakia. Through incessant propaganda it tried to awaken Slovak nationalism and to persuade the Slovaks that they would lose their national identity in a single state with the Czechs (Chaloupecký 1930: 72). The Czech political elites felt that treating the Slovaks as an ethnic minority and granting them cultural and political autonomy might play directly into the Hungarians' hands. By constructing the Czechoslovak nation as a *státotvorný národ* ('state-forming nation') (Felak 1992: 143) of which the Slovaks were an integral part, the Prague government tried to defuse any possible separatist tendencies in Slovakia. The notion of a single Czechoslovak nation also played a significant political role in relation to the ethnic minorities in the country. It ensured the numerical majority of the Czechs and Slovaks against all other nationalities in the state, particularly the Germans (Leff 1988: 35). Internationally, it made it possible to preserve the image of Czechoslovakia as a nation-state in spite of its ethnic heterogeneity.

Thus, although building on a strong sense of cultural and linguistic proximity, the construction of a single Czechoslovak nation or of the Czechs and the Slovaks as two branches of one nation was primarily determined by pragmatic considerations of the Czech, and also some Slovak, political elites both before and after the creation of Czechoslovakia. The idea that the Slovaks did not constitute a separate nation from the Czechs – that they spoke a language which was only a dialect of Czech or, bluntly expressed, were Czechs speaking Slovak – forms the basis of the ideology of Czechoslovakism (Leff 1988: 133–40) which became the official state doctrine of the new republic. The construction of the Czechs and Slovaks as one 'Czechoslovak nation' was enshrined in the Czechoslovak constitution of 1920. As a branch of one Czechoslovak nation, the Slovaks were part of the state-forming nation and not an ethnic minority like the Germans, Hungarians, Ukrainians, or Poles. Unlike them, the Slovaks did not need either cultural or political autonomy.

In the light of Herder's notion that language is the defining phenomenon of the nation, which was fully adopted by the nineteenth-century Czech nationalist movement against Bolzano's territorial conception of the nation (see Stern 1992: 29–43; Pynsent 1994: 185) and has been entertained ever since, the language schism between the Czechs and Slovaks was regrettable. It would have helped the construction of a single Czechoslovak nation if this schism could have been overcome, and until the late 1920s the view was still being expressed by Czech scholars and leading politicians that Czech and Slovak were in fact a single language. For example, Pražák wrote in 1929 that 'literary Slovak is not a definitive value in spite of its eighty-five years of history . . . Its definitive existence is still a question' (1929: 130). At about the same time, Masaryk wrote that the 'Czechs and Slovaks are one nation and have one language. The Czechs, who were more free, developed their language more intensively than the Slovaks. So it happened that the Slovaks preserved their older dialect' (1928: 13).

One of the important functions of the ideology of Czechoslovakism was to hide the fact that the Czechs considered Czechoslovakia their state and to mask their dominant role in it by creating the illusion that it was both Czech and Slovak. The dominant role of the Czechs manifested itself both on the symbolic level and on the level of social action, and the Slovaks eventually began to object to both these forms of domination (Felak 1992).

The dominant role of the Czechs in public administration, education, health service, and the administration of justice in the new state was at first a necessity resulting from the different levels of development reached in Slovakia and in the Czech lands before World War I. Especially after the federalisation of the Austro-Hungarian Empire in 1867, when the Slovaks began to be directly administered from Budapest, they were exposed to a Magyarisation much stronger than the Germanisation of the Czech lands of the Austrian part of the empire. The Magyarisation of the Slovaks culminated before the outbreak of World War I. Seton-Watson, attempting to raise European consciousness on behalf of an unknown and endangered nation, estimated that there were only about a thousand Slovak-speaking intellectuals left (1931: 30). According to some estimates, by 1918 there were only ten Slovak doctors and twelve high school-teachers.

As the Slovaks were unable to provide even a skeleton administration, they did not demand the fulfilment of the Pittsburgh agreement, and even future Slovak autonomists such as Juriga and Hlinka supported the Martin declaration of 30 October 1918, which pronounced the Slovak nation to be 'part of a linguistically and cultural-historically united Czechoslovak nation' and demanded for the latter 'an unlimited right to self-determination on the basis of complete independence' (Grečo 1947: 111–12). The Czechs undertook the tasks of building the new state, which were seen to be beyond the ability of the Slovaks, and Czech educators, doctors, judges, policemen, railway and postal workers, and so on, moved to Slovakia as state employees. Whilst according to the Hungarian population census of 1910 there were only 7,556 Czechs in Slovakia, by 1921 their number had increased to 71,733 (compared with only 15,630 Slovaks in the Czech lands) and by 1930 to 120,926 (Rychlík 1988: 19, 33). The image of Czechoslovakia as the Czech state and the legitimation of this image by the ideology of Czechoslovakism were also reflected in the ethnic composition of the central government institutions and of Czechoslovak political representation itself. Of the 1,300 employees of the Ministry of Defence in the 1920s, only 6 were Slovaks, and of the 131 generals in the Czechoslovak army only one was a Slovak. There were only 4 Slovaks among the 417 employees of the Ministry of Education in Prague. There were 94 Czechs and only 68 Slovaks in the Slovak branch of this ministry in Bratislava (Beránek 1988: 73). Only 2 of the 17 ministers in the cabinet formed in 1919 were Slovaks, and there were only 40 Slovaks among 254 members of parliament (Faltan 1986: 57).

This situation gradually began to be resented by many Slovaks. Already in the 1920s, for example, Slovak railwaymen demanded that only Slovaks be employed on Slovak railway lines, and when rumours spread that the state administration was planning a reduction of clerks and state employees, voices were raised in Slovakia that no Slovak should be dismissed while a single Czech retained employment in Slovakia (Nosková 1988: 9).

However much Czech administration of Slovakia was considered necessary in the 1920s owing to the lack of qualified Slovak personnel, it was difficult to justify it in the 1930s. By 1937 the number of Slovak university graduates had increased threefold since 1920 (Beránek 1988: 73). Although more Slovaks found jobs as state employees in Slovakia and in the central state institutions, the overall ratio of Czechs to Slovaks decreased only marginally. Given the higher rate of unemployment in

Slovakia than in the Czech lands during the recession years of the 1930s, it is understandable that Slovak aversion to the Czech presence in Slovakia increased. Also resented was the fact that many Czechs in Slovakia used Czech as the official language of administration. This was made possible by a 1920 law stipulating that the official language in the Czech lands would usually be Czech and that in Slovakia usually Slovak. The word 'usually' made it possible for Czechs in Slovakia to use Czech in administration and Slovaks in the Czech lands to use Slovak. However, as there were many more Czechs in Slovakia than Slovaks in the Czech lands, in the 1920s administration in Slovak in the latter was rather exceptional whereas administration in Czech was quite common in Slovakia. In the 1930s, even though Czechs remained in many administrative posts in Slovakia, their use of Slovak as the official language increased dramatically not only because of their linguistic assimilation but also because of official pressure to use Slovak as a means of defusing Slovak resentment (Rychlík 1988: 19–20, 33).

However, as Kertzer has argued, people make sense of the political process mainly through its symbols (1988: 6). That the Czechs were the politically dominant element in the new Czechoslovak Republic and that they saw the new state as the revival of the historical Czech state was for ordinary people symbolised not only by the fact that the capital of the republic was Prague, the capital city of the former Bohemian kingdom, but also by the fact that all the symbols of the new state had clearly Protestant overtones. Some 90 per cent of Slovaks were Catholics, and, especially among ordinary Slovak villagers, the Catholic faith played a more significant role than among the religiously lukewarm Czechs. From the outset Catholic believers in Slovakia, led by their bishops and village priests, objected to the celebration of 6 July – the day of the death of Jan Hus – as a national holiday on the ground that Hus had meaning only for Czechs. In the words of one village priest, 'he corrected their orthography and taught at their university; for the Slovaks he has no meaning whatever and remains a heretic'. The Slovak Catholics often disturbed the celebrations of Hus's anniversary by Czechs living in Slovakia, demonstrated against them, or celebrated the anniversary of Cyril and Method[5] in protest (Nosková 1988: 10–11).

All these various strands of resentment were politically articulated by the Slovak People's Party under the leadership of Andrej Hlinka, which campaigned for Slovak autonomy and regularly attracted the electoral support of almost a third of Slovak voters (Felak 1992). After the Munich agreement of 1938, when Czechoslovakia had to surrender to Germany the third of its territory in which Germans constituted the majority of the population, Hlinka's party, supported by other Slovak political parties, formed an autonomous Slovak government, which was recognised by the Czechoslovak parliament. Slovakia began to function as an autonomous part of the state, now officially designated Czecho-Slovakia. In 1939 the Slovak leader Jozef Tiso yielded to Hitler's pressure and declared Slovakia an independent state under the official protection of Nazi Germany. The Slovak government soon became a puppet regime and pursued Nazi-inspired policies including the forced transfer of Slovak Jews to Nazi concentration camps. Slovak opposition to Nazi rule culminated in 1944 in a national uprising which aimed to free Slovaks from Nazi control and to reunite them with Czechs in a single Czechoslovak Republic. The uprising was eventually crushed by German military forces, but it laid the basis for the autonomous role of Slovakia in post-war Czechoslovakia. An agreement reached in 1945 by the Czechoslovak government in exile in London and the rival communist faction in exile in Moscow confirmed Czechoslovakia as a state of two equal nations and accepted that the Slovak National Council, which had inspired and led the uprising, would be the supreme legislative Slovak organ in independent Czechoslovakia and the Slovak government its administrative branch.

The Czech National Council established during the 1945 uprising in Prague was dissolved by the Czechoslovak government which assumed power after the war. The result of this decision was the creation of an asymmetrical model, with a central Czechoslovak parliament and government ruling the whole country and a Slovak National Council and government in Bratislava. There was no corresponding Czech council and government in Bohemia and Moravia. This model, which existed until 1968, was thus the result not of Slovak demands for equity but of the power ambitions of the Czech-controlled Czechoslovak government. To most Slovaks it indicated once more that Slovakia might well belong to the Slovaks but Czechoslovakia belonged to the Czechs (Pithart 1990b: 109).

Once in power after 1948, the Communist Party increasingly subjected Slovakia to centralised rule. The legislative power of the Slovak National Council was in practice limited to certain aspects of cultural and educational policy, and the Slovak government was fully subordinated to the central government, with the Slovak ministers acting only as deputies to the ministers in Prague. The 'socialist constitution' of 1960 abolished the Slovak government and even further reduced the role of the Slovak National Council. All this, as well as the earlier fate of Slovak Communist politicians such as Vladimír Clementis, the former foreign minister, who was executed in 1952, and Gustáv Husák, who was imprisoned in 1951 on charges of 'bourgeois nationalism', contributed to increasing dissatisfaction among Slovak intellectuals.

During the 1960s, opposition to the centralising tendencies of the existing political system grew stronger even within the Communist Party in Slovakia. It was not accidental that when the process of liberalisation gained momentum in 1968 a Slovak – Alexandr Dubček – was chosen to lead the Czechoslovak Communist Party. Alongside economists and writers, the Slovak Communists represented the most important opposition to the bureaucratic centralism of the communist system. But while the main aim of the Czech intellectuals was the democratisation of the whole system of government and economic reform, the Slovak opposition aimed first of all at achieving recognition of the equality of Czechs and Slovaks and the institution of a federal system of government. Eventually, the constitutional law creating a Czechoslovak Socialist Federal Republic consisting of Czech and Slovak republics was the only result of the reform movement of 1968. Each republic had its own government and legislative body (national council) empowered to pass legislation which did not contravene the constitution of the federation. The legislative organ of the federation became the Federal Assembly, consisting of the Chamber of the People and the Chamber of Nations, in which the Czechs and Slovaks had the same number of deputies. The voting system in the Chamber of Nations, which had to approve legislation passed by the Federal Assembly, ruled out the possibility of an automatic majority of one nation over the other (Henderson 1993: 25). Whilst the federal state retained central control over foreign policy, defence, internal security, and economic planning, considerable powers were granted to the governments of both republics, particularly in the spheres of social, educational, and cultural policy (Skilling 1976: 49–56; Kusin 1971: 69–75; Leff 1988: 121–8; Rupnik 1981: 117–21; Wolchik 1991: 30).

During the period of 'normalisation' which followed the crushing of the Prague Spring, power was once again concentrated at the centre through various subsidiary legislative acts as well as in practice, leaving Slovak autonomy preserved only in its formal aspects. The result of two decades of this 'normalisation' was bitter disillusionment among many Slovaks (Leff 1988: 245–52).

Czech images of Slovaks

According to an opinion poll conducted in 1946, 65 per cent of Czechs maintained that Czechs and Slovaks were two branches of the same nation and only 21 per cent that they were separate nations. This view did not change much during the forty years of communist rule, in spite of the fact that the 'bourgeois' ideology of Czechoslovakism was vehemently denounced and vigorously replaced by the construction of two brotherly nations harmoniously coexisting in a common state. More than half of Czechs supported the idea of one Czechoslovak nation in an opinion poll conducted in October 1990. Nevertheless, 66 per cent of the Czechs in 1946 were, and according to my estimate many more today are, of the opinion that Slovaks differ considerably from Czechs in many respects (Timoracký 1992: 70–1).

This difference is expressed from numerous perspectives and in terms of various images. 'Slovak' frequently evokes the image of a well-built lad in folk costume – wide white trousers, a wide leather belt with strong brass buckles, and a short linen shirt which leaves his bare stomach exposed – brandishing an ornamental long-handled axe and singing a mournful folk-song. This image is the creation of a whole range of artists, film-makers, and journalists, many of them Slovaks, aimed at demonstrating their appreciation of ordinary Slovak folk. However, among many Czechs it perpetuates the belief that if it were not for their own civilising efforts, the Slovaks would still be walking around with their bellybuttons exposed. In this imagery, the Slovak is an exotic Other living in a traditional and pic-turesque mountain village, and Slovakia is an exotic and unspoiled wild country epitomised by the rocky mountains of the High Tatra, slivovitz, and ethnic dishes made of sheep cheese.

Toward the end of the nineteenth century, the writers and journalists who created this image were joined by professional ethnologists and folk-lorists, whose emphasis on the antiquity of Slovak culture was part of an attempt to reconstruct the image of an original society and culture for each particular nation. The traditional folk culture – even in its isolated remnants, whether vernacular architecture, folk costumes, or folk-songs – was for them the main building material for such reconstructions. Their description of the traditional way of life and culture of the Slovak peasant penetrated into the consciousness of the general public through their pub-lications, which were widely read, and through articles in encyclopaedias.

In their purely visual form, the images of the Czech lands and Slovakia are collapsed into straightforward images of culture and nature: the Czech lands are symbolised by the image of Prague, and the silhouette of the Hradčany Castle is the most common visual image of Bohemia; Slovakia is symbolised by the Tatra Mountains. These images were drawn upon in a newspaper article pleading for the preservation of the common state of

Czechs and Slovaks: 'what unites us is certainly more than a large slice of bread. The pride of Slovaks in mother Prague of the hundred spires is equal to the pride of Czechs in the clear peaks of the Tatra Mountains' (Marie Mandelíková in *Lidové noviny*, 23 November 1990).

The image of the healthy Slovak lad in his folk costume correlates not only with an image of an exotic Other but also with an image of youth and connotes a more general image of the young Slovak as against the old Czech nation. In spite of their perceived differences, when asked which nation is most similar to them, most Czechs without hesitation mention the Slovaks. Not only have most Czechs been to Slovakia but almost a quarter of them have relatives of Slovak origin, almost half count Slovaks among their personal friends, and a third have met Slovaks regularly in the course of their work. These personal contacts are even stronger among the Slovaks: 31 per cent have relatives who come from Bohemia or Moravia, 57 per cent have personal friends among Czechs, and 30 per cent have been in regular contact with Czech colleagues in the course of their work (Timoracký 1992: 83). Czechs see Slovaks as their 'brothers'. However, this kinship metaphor does not express feelings of equality. Not only is the expression 'brother Slovaks' very often intended ironically – as is made clear by quoting from the text of the Slovak national anthem and rendering the word 'brother' in Slovak – but the basic notion of inequality in spite of close kinship is expressed through the image of the Slovak as the Czech's younger brother. Like most other images, this image dates back at least to the period of the political aspirations of nineteenth-century Czechs and Slovaks to create their own common state. The implications of the image of a younger brother were explicitly stated, for example by Karel Kálal who wrote several articles and books about Slovakia at the turn of the century:

The Czech is the elder and the Slovak the younger brother. The younger brother is usually inclined to believe that the elder aims in his advice only at his own advantage. He rejects your helping hand, he kicks you . . . And what about you, elder brother? Your duty is to look after the younger brother even more carefully, to make sure that when alone he will not lose his way or drown.   *(1905: 143)*

These notions of the wisdom and mature rationality of the elder brother and the consequent paternal responsibility and of the youthful irresponsibility, immaturity, lack of experience, and recourse to emotions rather than to rational calculation of the younger have been variously implied whenever the image of elder and younger brothers has been invoked (see, e.g., Vaculík in *Literární noviny*, 3 May 1990).

Most ordinary Czechs have hardly any factual knowledge of the history of Slovakia. Nevertheless, they are aware that Czechs have a rich history during which they have often played a decisive role in European politics, whereas Slovakia has always been just a mountainous region of Hungary which has been bypassed by history. Even more than the image of a rural community in which the traditional culture and way of life remain preserved, the image of Slovakia as a land without history is the creation of historians, often themselves Slovaks. Motivated by their nationalist aspirations, they have refused to treat Slovak history as part of Hungarian history. The result is a simple periodisation of Slovak history, the first example of which is perhaps the work of the Slovak revivalist Čerwenák published in 1844. He emphasises the period of the Great Moravian empire of which the Slovaks were allegedly the main component, and then hesitantly describes the period between the eleventh and the eighteenth centuries in which he pays attention only to Matuš Čák Trenčanský (see Pynsent 1994: 166), for him the model of the power and glory of the true Slovak leader. He then describes in detail the activities of the protagonists of the Slovak national revival in the nineteenth century. This periodisation of Slovak history, more or less embraced by the whole of Slovak historiography (see Pynsent 1994: 62), led the Slovak writer V. Mináč to express the view that 'we have no history, and what we have is not our own' (1970).

The image of Slovakia as a land without history is also created through the usage whereby Bohemia and Moravia are described as a single entity as an alternative to the expression 'the Czech Republic'. These are lands which were part of the Bohemian kingdom and are referred to as 'the lands of the Czech crown'. In relation to Slovakia, they are habitually referred to as 'the historical lands'. The contraposition of 'the historical lands' and Slovakia denies Slovakia any historicity. Czechs are quick to point out that, because the Slovaks have no history, they have never produced any important historical personalities and that the only state they have ever had was the Czechoslovak Republic. Only 21 per cent of Czechs are of the opinion that the Slovaks had no alternative but to create their own state after the Munich agreement; most believe that in doing so they betrayed the Czechs and the common Czechoslovak cause (Timoracký 1992: 81). The Czechs consider laughable the claim of some Slovak politicians that Slovaks are the oldest European nation because they were the main element of the Great Moravian empire, which was the first historically documented state in Central Europe. A consequence of the perception that the Slovaks have no history is the prevailing Czech view that they have no significant national culture. Allusions to Slovak writers, composers, playwrights, and scholars are easily dismissed by pointing out that none of them has ever become internationally famous.

In comparison with Slovaks, Czechs see themselves as part of a cultured and civilised Europe from which they were only temporarily excluded while under communist rule, and quite a number of them are willing to blame the Slovaks even for that. Shortly after the November 1989 revolution, an overwhelming majority of the Czechoslovak population supported radical economic reforms and there appeared to be no significant differences in attitude between Czechs and Slovaks. However, according to an opinion poll conducted in March 1990, 63 per cent of Slovaks but only 48 per cent of Czechs advocated a slower rate of economic transformation. During 1990 two different attitudes toward economic reform became apparent. The first, predominant among Czechs, supported reform in the form in which it was being carried out, while the second, predominant among Slovaks, critically pointed to its negative social consequences, the most important of which was the increase in unemployment and the loss of basic social security. Whereas in the Czech lands economic reform was considered the most important aspect of the post-communist transformation of the society, in Slovakia the most important task was seen as the solution of its social aspects. This was interpreted by the Czech media as a Slovak preference for an economy with socialist elements (Timoracký 1992: 85–7). This view was strongly reinforced by the 1992 election results in Slovakia and eventually led to the view that it was predominantly the Slovaks who were responsible for the excesses of communist rule in Czechoslovakia. According to an opinion poll conducted in October 1990, 70 per cent of Czechs considered the pre-war Czechoslovak Republic an exemplary democratic state, and 62 per cent were of the opinion that the Slovaks had managed to survive as a nation only because of the republic's existence. Fifty-eight per cent thought that most Slovaks had adapted well to the communist regime after 1968 and presented no effective opposition to it. The view that the Czechs had suffered more from 'normalisation' than the Slovaks was shared by 60 per cent of Czechs (Timoracký 1992: 81–2).

As most Czechs now tend to see socialism as an alien system imposed on them by the uncultured Asiatic East, they also tend to see the boundary between the 'historical lands' and Slovakia as the boundary between Western rationalism and Eastern emotionality (Timoracký 1992: 72) or, even more explicitly, as the boundary between the cultured West and the uncultured East. This is not a new view; in the 1950s I heard Czechs jokingly express the view that Asia began immediately east of Luhačovice (a

Table 2. *Czech images of Czechs and Slovaks*

Czechs	Slovaks
Modern society	Traditional community
History	Lack of history
Statehood	Lack of statehood
Progress	Underdevelopment
Adult	Young
Culture	Nature
Rationality	Emotions
West	East

town in eastern Moravia). Nowadays, however, it is not so masked but made respectable by the tone of numerous articles in the press and the discussion on Czech television. For example, an article which argued for the necessity of dividing Czechoslovakia into separate Czech and Slovak states was published in 1992 in *Respekt*, the recipient of a 1991 award from the World Press Review for the 'deepening of world understanding, defence of human rights, and journalistic professionalism'. The article was entitled 'On Our Own into Europe, Together into the Balkans'. *Lidové noviny* printed the opinion that Slovakia 'has never belonged economically and politically to Western Europe' and that 'the contemporary reality of the Slovak political scene echoes the Balkan-oriented trends' (9 April 1991). The right-wing *Metropolitní telegraf* expressed the view that

the acceptance . . . of the constitution of the Slovak Republic moved Slovakia back into its traditional space. It meant that the eastern part of Czechoslovakia lost its connecting link with the Central European region and it is gradually becoming a part of Panonnia. *(5 September 1992)*

Český deník commented that

Slovakia differs from the Czech lands in its historical development, which is directed more toward the East than the history of the more Western-oriented Bohemia . . . We should not be indifferent as to whether the Commonwealth of Independent States or the Balkans or both would begin across our [i.e., the Czech state's] new border. *(1 September 1992)*

By holding certain images of the Slovaks which contrast with images they have of themselves, the Czechs ascribe certain attributes to themselves as a nation. These contrasting images can be set out in a classical table of binary oppositions (table 2). Every term in the set associated with Czechs carries positive connotations in relation to the corresponding term associated with Slovaks. This explicit comparison, carried out through a number of fixed images of the Slovaks, perpetually re-creates the tradition of the Czechs as a cultured nation.

The self-perception of the Czechs as an inherently democratic nation is also continually re-created through the comparison and juxtaposition of the political processes in Slovakia and in the Czech lands. In post-1989 Czech political rhetoric, 'democracy' is one of the most often used terms. In particular contexts it stands for a multiplicity of specific political and social arrangements, practices, and attitudes, of which the ones most often invoked are the recognition of civil rights, freedom of opinion, freedom of the press, and the rule of law which guarantees these various rights and freedoms. When employed rhetorically, the meaning of 'democracy' is not circumscribed by any one of these political and social arrangements, practices, and attitudes. Neither is democracy defined as a specific form of government, political process, or political culture. The term is employed rhetorically as a symbol which gains its meaning in relation to what is perceived as its opposite or its negation: totalitarianism (*totalita*). Although 'totalitarianism' itself is, in certain contexts, defined as state control over ideology and economy or over most aspects of citizens' lives, in most political rhetoric it is also employed as an overarching symbol whose meaning derives from its opposition to 'democracy'. Both democracy and totalitarianism are thus symbols which allow the possibility of a discourse without any necessary agreement on the meaning of the symbols which it employs and at the same time creates. The existence of this discourse is made possible by its underpinning by a shared notion of communism and fascism as tokens of totalitarianism.

A Czech publicist aptly characterised the popular conceptualisation of democracy as an understanding that 'the Communists should not govern and certainly not alone and forever' (František Schildberger in *Lidové noviny*, 22 June 1992). Democracy is construed as the opposite of totalitarianism or of any of its concrete tokens not only in popular opinion but also in the rhetoric of professional politicians: 'Democracy must be understood not only in its moral dimension but as a set of measures in the functioning of society which make any return of totalitarianism impossible' (Ladislav Dvořák, chairman of the Czech Socialist Party, *Svobodné slovo*, 20 February 1992). The statements of various Czech and Slovak political leaders during the negotiations about the future form of Czech–Slovak political relations have been widely reported on television and in the Czech press, and have of course significantly contributed to the image of Czech and Slovak political cultures as radically different.

However, the perception of this difference is even more significantly nourished by what the Czechs see as clear symbols of totalitarianism in Slovak political culture.

One of these symbols is the independent Slovak state declared on 14 March 1939. According to an opinion poll conducted in October 1990, of the 69 per cent of Slovaks who had an opinion about the character of the independent Slovak state, half saw it in a positive light and half negatively. However, 47 per cent were convinced that the existence of the Slovak state fulfilled Slovak desires for independence. In contrast to Slovak ambivalence, 66 per cent of Czechs are convinced that the independent Slovak state was unambiguously fascist in character (Timoracký 1992: 81–2).

For many Slovaks, the period of Slovak independence in 1939 represents a time when they were for the first and last time masters of their own destiny. In post-communist Czechoslovakia the independent Slovak state became a powerful symbol invoked in demonstrations expressing a Slovak desire for sovereignty. This desire was first articulated by the Slovak National Party and gradually embraced by both the Christian Democratic Movement and the Movement for Democratic Slovakia, the strongest political party to emerge from the Public Against Violence. The most important of these demonstrations were the 14 March celebrations. During the demonstration held in 1990 in Bratislava, the crowd shouted slogans such as 'Independent Slovakia!', 'We've had enough of Prague!', and 'We've had enough of Havel!' The demonstration was reported on Czech television and in the Czech press and widely commented upon. With their attitude to the Slovak state, Czechs saw the demonstration as a clear sign not only that the Slovaks were proudly celebrating their fascist past, of which they should be ashamed, but also that the political scene in Slovakia was again acquiring a distinctly fascist character. This view was reinforced by the fact that the slogans shouted at the demonstration included 'Hungarians across the Danube!' and 'Jews to Palestine!' For many Czechs it was evidence that the Slovaks were unable to distance themselves from their fascist past that Jan Čarnogurský, then prime minister of the Slovak Republic, objected to the preamble of the new Czechoslovak–German treaty affirming the legal continuity of Czechoslovakia after the Munich agreement on the ground that this continuity had been interrupted by international recognition of the independent Slovak state between 1939 and 1945.

The straightforward conclusion of many Czechs that the Slovaks were fascists was reinforced by many other events in Slovakia. One of them was the next celebration of the anniversary of the declaration of the Slovak state in Bratislava in March 1991, when President Havel was verbally abused and physically assaulted by the demonstrators. On 28 October 1991, during the celebration in Bratislava of the anniversary of the founding of the Czechoslovak Republic in 1918, demonstrators threw eggs at him, whereupon he left the platform and the celebration ended. Other events which reinforced the Czech view of Slovaks as fascists were the commemorative celebrations of the birthdays of Hlinka, the founder of the Slovak People's Party, who died before Slovakia gained its independence in 1939 but whose party was the ruling party in the Slovak state, and particularly of Tiso, the president of the Slovak state, tried and sentenced as a war criminal. Strong disapproval on the Czech side was also expressed when Čarnogurský attended the burial of Gustáv Husák, the Communist boss of post-1968 Czechoslovakia. The prevailing Czech feelings were summed up in a reader's letter to the daily *Český deník*:

I admire the Czech representation – Mr Klaus and others. They have to deal with people who one day go to pay their respects to the memory of and to give homage to the fascist criminal Tiso and a few weeks later go to pay their respects to the memory of the Communist criminal Husák. Even the Slovak citizen can surely imagine the fate of an active politician in Germany who celebrated Hitler or some other Nazi criminal.   *(8 September 1992)*

Not only what are perceived as fascist tendencies in Slovakia, but also all the signs of Slovak political culture reminiscent of the political culture of the communist regime, are seen by Czechs as indications of Slovak totalitarianism. Prominent among these are acts and statements which Czechs see as attempts to curb the freedom of the press in Slovakia, first manifested when the Slovak weekly magazine *Kulturný život* published an allegedly blasphemous story and the minister of culture of the Slovak Republic, a member of the Christian Democratic Movement, refused the magazine any further government subsidy. The founding of For the True Image of Slovakia, an organisation of Slovak journalists – in fact a response to Slovak prime minister Vladimír Mečiar's exclusion from his news conferences of journalists whose reporting he saw as 'hostile' to his government and damaging to Slovak 'legitimate interests' – was interpreted by the Czech media as an attempt to curb the freedom of the press in Slovakia. Disapproving comments were also made on Mečiar's criticism of Slovak television, which in his view was unwilling to grant him the right to inform the public regularly about his and his government's views. His appeal in September 1992 to Slovak journalists to print only 'objective news' and to respect, in the interest of Slovakia, 'the rules of ethical self-regulation' was the subject of debate on Czech television; comments on it unanimously denounced it as a call for self-censorship. Under the title 'Is Jakeš the Example?', a Czech newspaper expressed the view that

> attempts to introduce censorship manifest themselves clearly in Slovakia today. It makes no difference under what mantle censorship hides itself, whether the former [communist] Office for Press and Information or today's association For the True Image of Slovakia . . . pressure from a political party official on the publisher or editor and efforts to differentiate between journalists who may attend press conferences and those for whom there is 'no more room' in the conference hall or at important events are nothing other than political censorship.
>
> *(Lubomir Kohout in* Metropolitní telegraf, *5 September 1992)*

Such views were echoed by a great number of Czech intellectuals. Ordinary people were more sensitive to rhetoric reminiscent of that of representatives of the communist regime. Thus Mečiar's talk about opposition parties, journalists, and newspapers critical of the Slovak government as 'enemies' of the government or 'hostile' to the Slovak nation was not only commented upon in Czech media but also the subject of people's comments in their discussion of contemporary political events. In the course of this discussion, political process in Slovakia came to be perceived as a 'totalitarianism [*totalita*] of one person, one opinion, and one way of thinking', as Štefan Hřib expressed it in *Lidové noviny* (2 September 1992). A similar reaction on the Czech side followed the public vote of the deputies of the Slovak National Council on the Slovak constitution in September 1992, when the deputies stood up, announced their names, and declared whether they were for acceptance or rejection of the proposed constitution. This was viewed by the Czech press and public as undemocratic, being against council rules requiring a secret ballot and an intimidating tactic of the Slovak ruling party (the Movement for Democratic Slovakia), which was seen as assuming a 'leading role' reminiscent of that of the Communist Party.

Any signs of Slovak political culture reminiscent of the political culture of the communist regime are noted and critically commented upon by Czechs. Even more than the similarity in rhetoric, the televised images of Slovak political culture remind people of communist practices. After the television transmission of the ceremonial session of the Slovak National Council at which the Slovak constitution was signed by the prime minister and the chairman, many Czechs with whom I spoke commented with disapproval on the applause which followed. The tone of these spontaneous comments was summed up in the following description of the incident:

The chairmanship of the Slovak National Council stood up as one prime minister and collectively started applauding themselves in a rhythm conspicuously reminiscent of 'Long Live the Communist Party'. It was moving to see those eyes turned with a dog's affection to the prime minister to see whether he had stood up (and when he stood up, all did so as if on command), whether he was still applauding . . . or had he already stopped? And if he had not stopped, they would still be applauding there now.   *(Vladimír Just in* Respekt, *1992, no. 36: 14)*

All these various signs which the Czechs observe with disapproval in Slovak politics reinforce their view that 'the virus of nationalism accompanied by the signs of totalitarianism is the Slovak reality' (Štefan Hřib in *Lidové noviny*, 2 September 1992) and that 'in Slovakia, [communist] totalitarianism driven out through the door returns through the window dressed up in "national costume"' (F. Gál 1992: 27). During the last months of the existence of the Czechoslovak federation, the Slovak political scene was habitually characterised as a 'totalitarian regime pursued by the national-socialist government' (*Metropolitní telegraf*, 5 September 1992); many Czechs saw Slovakia as 'an explosive mixture of nationalism, communism, and authoritarianism' (Jirák and Šoltys 1992: 56). Such attitudes were to a great extent refractions of comments appearing in the Czech press. The comments published in *Český deník*, a daily with ties to the Civic Democratic Party, can serve as an example of the reporting typical of much of the press at the time:

Slovakia is governed by a dangerous neo-Bolshevik faction which is capable of anything and for which the supposedly democratic institutions [the Slovak National Council] serve merely as a screen from domestic and foreign public opinion.

. . . a thousand-year old dream of the Slovak nation is fulfilled in the post-communist neo-Bolshevik national regime whose godfathers are Lenin, Mussolini . . .

. . . the problem of the Czechs is that they inhabit, at least formally, a single state with this red–brown clan.   *(Josef Mlejnek Jr in* Český deník, *27 August 1992)*

This perception of the Slovak political scene leads to the construction of the 'velvet revolution' as primarily a Czech endeavour which the Slovaks at best joined but certainly did not initiate. The view that it was Czechs and not Slovaks who instigated the end of the communist regime derives from the belief that the former had more reason to be dissatisfied with it. This is reflected in the perceived difference in the opposition to the communist regime between the Czech lands and Slovakia. Václav Benda, chairman of the Christian Democratic Party represented in the post-1992 ruling coalition, articulated this Czech view in the following way:

whilst [the opposition] in Bohemia was a civic opposition in which various Christian associations also of course played a significant role, civic opposition in

Slovakia was quite marginal. Opposition trends manifested themselves primarily within the Catholic church, and their political articulation was only individual and insufficient. *(Lidové noviny, 1 September 1992)*

In the Czech view, these deep-rooted differences manifested themselves in the result of the 1992 elections:

In the Czech Republic, the democratic forces won a victory over the non-democratic crypto-communist left . . . But in the Slovak Republic, 85 per cent of mandates were won by nationalistically or even separatistically oriented, predominantly left-wing, and strongly anti-reformist parties.

The election results confronted us basically with the decision of whether we want another relapse of socialism in a common state or a democratic development in an independent Czech Republic.

(Václav Benda in Lidové noviny, 1 September 1992)

Like Czech *kulturnost*, the deep-seated democratic tendencies which give credence to the asserted democratic tradition of the Czech nation are continually re-created through the comparison and juxtaposition of the political processes in Slovakia and in the Czech lands. The Czech democratic tradition is confirmed and thus perpetually re-created by rejection of the totalitarianism which most Czechs see as dominating the Slovak political scene. This rejection manifested itself most vividly in the change of attitude of the Czech government to its Slovak counterpart which emerged from the 1992 elections and in its efforts to terminate the existing federation and create a separate Czech state. Rhetorically, this effort was presented as an effort to safeguard the Western-style democracy of the Czech lands threatened by political development in Slovakia. Most Czechs understood it as an effort consistent with the democratic tradition of the Czech nation.

4

National traditions and the imagining of the nation

Whether people behave in accordance with their traditions may be questionable, but in the Czech view the existence of the traditions themselves is beyond doubt. Individual Czechs or even most Czechs may be autocratic and intolerant of the opinions of others, but Czechs as a nation are inherently democratic; many Czechs may have no more than the compulsory education and not even a modicum of manners, but the Czech nation is well educated and highly cultured. National traditions make it possible to find the behaviour of most members of the nation wanting at specific times without such behaviour's adversely affecting the positive image of the nation as a whole. Thus, for example, the collaboration of a considerable number of Czechs with the German occupation during World War II and the compliance of most Czechs with the communist system have not shattered the democratic tradition of the Czech nation.

All this seems to suggest that a nation can be a nation only when it has traditions. This is something that has probably always been intuitively felt. The contemporary Czech philosopher Jaroslava Pešková expressed this feeling when she said that 'a nation without a tradition loses the meaning of its existence' (1988: 118).

Anderson argues that a nation 'is an imagined political community – and imagined as both inherently limited and sovereign' (1983: 6) and that it was the emergence of press capitalism that made this imagination possible. A nation is, however, imagined also as a transcendental whole endowed with agency and with its own history, and it is belief in the existence of the nation's traditions which makes such imagination possible. The view of a nation as a transcendental whole is the result of seeing not individuals but the nation as the carrier of the traditions. Thus the nation can also be seen as acting on its own – being oppressed, resisting foreign domination, rising in a struggle, and so on. Although the state is also endowed with agency in that it can be spoken of, for example, as going to war, spending money, or pursuing a certain kind of foreign policy, the nation still acts independently of the state at least in the sense that it creates, follows, and perpetuates its traditions. It is thus through the persistence of traditions that the nation's acting becomes imaginable.

Although traditions are always determined by present practical interests, people themselves do not see them as such. They see traditions – as a Czech saying goes – as the result of their historical experience. The notion of 'historical experience' implies the movement of an experiencing subject through time, and the experiencing subject is obviously not a particular warm-blooded human being but the nation. Its historical experience gives rise to what it sees as its traditions, and the same historical experience is invoked to explain the characteristic traits which its members attribute to themselves as individuals. For example, Arnošt Lustig explains Czech hypocrisy in the following way:

The motives were born of reality. Who knows where it began? I can return to White Mountain, to what and how one had to pretend during the Austro-Hungarian Empire, then during Hitler's time. During communism many people pretended a loyalty which they did not feel. *(*Nedělní Lidové noviny*, 11 January 1992)*

What this explanation suggests is that hypocrisy has become a trait of the Czech character because Czechs' historical experience has taught them that it is the best way of surviving under foreign domination. What it leaves unexplained is why it persists when it can no longer be seen as adaptively advantageous. I would suggest that this is to be expected. The invocation of historical experience does not aim primarily at explaining why Czechs possess certain characteristics and not others. Rather than an explanation (at best *ad hoc*), it is a rhetorical device or discursive strategy through which the Czech nation is construed as a nation. It is a device through which the nation is imagined as a community of people sharing not only a language but a set of traits and traditions (which we would call culture), and, moreover, as a community of considerable historical antiquity which legitimates its present position among other such communities. By referring to specific historical events and periods, an explanation in terms of historical experience establishes their significance. In this respect, it is a device through which the nation's history is constructed in the sense that from the multiplicity of past historical events only some are selected as significant.

'Nation', 'tradition', and 'historical experience' form the core of nationalist ideology. The way in which the relation between these notions is conceptualised is another specific characteristic of the nation. It is a supra-individual whole not only endowed with agency (and capable of acting independently of its constituent parts – individuals), but also created not as the object but as the subject of history. It is through its history that the nation acquires its historical experience, and it is this historical experience which equips it with the characteristics conceptualised as its traditions. This is how we commonsensically talk about the nation. But in talking unproblematically and unreflectively about it in this way we are doing much more than merely describing something that exists independently of the way we talk about it and that would not change in its essence if we talked about it differently. On the contrary, it is precisely by speaking of the nation as having historical experience that we construe it as such and imagine it as an entity which moves through time and in the process gathers that experience. It is this image of a supraindividual entity moving through time that creates that 'imaginary collective subject – a transhistorical national identity going by the name of "we"' (Wright 1985: 163). And it is this image that makes it possible to think of a Czech nation which does not change its basic characteristics – the result of its historical experience – in spite of the fact that the particular warm-blooded human beings who now constitute the Czech nation are quite different, and have quite different personal experiences, from the concrete individuals who constituted it fifty, one hundred, or one thousand years ago.

The notion of an entity moving through time gives rise to the notion of history as always a history of something, this something being in this particular case the Czech nation. Although the concept of the Czech nation as a community of people speaking the same language and sharing a culture is a concept which crystallised only during the national revival of the nineteenth century, Czechs conceptualise this community as a natural entity which has existed virtually from the dawn of historical time. Czech historiography, as we have seen, places its beginning in the first half of the tenth century, when Wenceslas consolidated his rule over the Slavonic tribes in Bohemia. Folk legend places its beginning in the mythological time when Čech, the ancestor of the Czechs, stopped on his migration on Říp Mountain in central Bohemia, found the land around him to 'abound in milk and honey', and decided to settle there.

On the one hand, the notion of history – which is the source of accumulated experience – makes possible the construction of a nation, and, on the other, the unproblematic acceptance of the nation as a significant collectivity necessitates thinking in historical terms. Nationalism thus both makes history a necessity and generates thinking in historical terms. However, history is not simply everything that happened in the past or the record of it. From the multiplicity of past events only those which are seen as significant are recorded (and hence remembered), and this significance is determined by their being perceived as having some consequence for the present. History thus needs to be constructed through selecting events from the chaotic past which are deemed to have historical significance in the sense of their contribution to the present: we are what (or where) we are because this or that happened in our past.

The possibility of such a construction of history requires the construction of an object which can be seen as both enduring and changing over time. If it did not change it would not have history: we cannot imagine a history of God; we can only imagine a history of the imagination of God. The very notion of history thus implies both the endurance and change of the object of history. When the object of history is the nation, it is its imagined existence over time which makes possible the construction of the enduring 'we' who imagine 'our history' and unproblematically utter, as Czechs do, the phrase 'We have suffered for three hundred years.'

The change of an object over time also has other consequences. In order for the history of a nation to be constructed, it has to be agreed. Awareness that some things happened in the past and should therefore be part of the historical narrative is determined by the meaning which they have for the present. What was the present of the nation at a certain point in time is now its past. The construction of the nation's history thus has its own history. The consequence is that this construction, which is appropriated by ordinary people and presents itself to them as valid through their schooling, through references to the nation's past in the media, and through what is inscribed in the historical monuments around them, itself changes over time. What is presented as the 'true' historical narrative at any given time is the construction of the ruling elites and, in particular, of professional historians.

Under totalitarian regimes, ruling elites subscribe to one official ideology and present one official image of the past. That there is only one official historical narrative does not mean, however, that it is necessarily accepted as valid by everyone to whom it is addressed. Many people may cling to the image which they considered true before. This was the case not only during the German occupation but also during the communist regime, when the construction of the past by communist historiography was seen by many people as a myth, a distortion, or an outright lie. Alongside the currently constructed images of the nation's past, old ones

constructed under different political circumstances coexist. The acceptance or rejection of any particular image is mainly determined by generational and political differences and differences in level of education. Calls
to historians to 'fill in the blanks in our history' and 'tell the truth about
our history' accompany every change in the political system. The history
of the Czech nation, and indeed to some extent of every nation, is a
history of rewriting its history. In this respect, nationalism can be seen as a
discursive agreement that history matters without necessarily agreeing on
what that history was and what it means.

In the Czech lands today, several lines of cleavage permeate the ongoing
discussion about the 'true image of the nation's past' and about the meanings of the particular events which become part of the historical narrative.
One of these distinguishes those who construct Czechoslovak history from
either the Czech or the Slovak point of view (whether they are Czechs or
Slovaks) from those who construct Czech history from either the Czech or
the German point of view and those who construct it from either the
Catholic or the Protestant point of view. Needless to say, particular dis-
putes are justified in terms of 'telling the truth about the past'. However,
all these specific forms of the appropriation of the construction of the
national past produce a widely shared idea of the thousand years of existence of the Czech nation. It is based on an often vaguely drawn image of
a community of people speaking Czech and their identification with the
Bohemian kingdom and on the image of humanity divided from time
immemorial into national wholes. Underlying this widely shared image of
the nation's history are, nevertheless, two distinct images of the past.

Contrasting images of the past

One of the two images which underlie the multivocality of the discourse
about Czech history is that of the glorious history of a nation which has
pursued democracy and humanism from time immemorial. It is an image
first explicitly formulated by František Palacký and its obvious function is
to rally the nation in what at any given time is seen as its historical struggle
– to define its purpose and to inspire hope that it can be accomplished.
This image of history is an important part of Czech nationalism, which
like all nationalisms, constructs an image of a great nation which has
always been an active subject of history. Its most extreme expression is the
formulation of 'the Czech question' as a 'world question'. The question
was first posed in the period of the national revival and the succeeding
struggle for the existence of the Czech nation in its own state by such
thinkers as Palacký, Havlíček,[1] and Masaryk. In their view, Czechs as a

nation would either contribute to the solution of universal human problems such as democracy and humanism or lose any right to an independent existence, which depended not on their numerical or military but on
their spiritual and intellectual strength. Although originally formulated to
provide moral justification for the Czechs' struggle for independent existence as a nation, the question is far from dead today and is raised again
and again during various national crises. It was raised, for example, in
1968 by the Czech philosopher Karel Kosík (Pithart 1990b: 129–31) and
again by Václav Havel at the height of Czech–Slovak tensions in 1992,
when the formation of a separate Czech state began to be discussed as a
solution to the crisis:

In Czech spiritual history, in Czech statehood, there are some motives on which it
is possible and, in my opinion, necessary to build. One of them is the idea that
'Czechness' itself is not enough and that it is not something hovering somewhere at
the summit of all values but gains its meaning and fulfilment only by the way in
which it accepts, so to speak, pan-human tasks and responsibility for a general
human destiny. We are here not only for ourselves, and if we followed only our own
interest we would not get very far. I think that a revived Czech statehood must have
its spiritual and moral dimension – that it should be founded in a new way on our
humanistic tradition, which can be found in the sphere of thought as well as in the
sphere of statehood. It is the tradition of faith, spirituality, tolerance, education. It
is expressed, for example, by St Wenceslas, Karel IV, Hus, Chelčický,[2] Komenský,
Jiří z Poděbrad,[3] the Hussites, and also T. G. Masaryk. Of course, we also have
other traditions, possibly equally strong ones, such as, for example, Czech collabo-
rationism or Czech quarrelsomeness.   *(Respekt, 1992, no. 29: 4)*

The particular problem of the construction of the Czech nation as an
active subject of history is explaining past periods in which Czech efforts
to achieve democracy and humanism obviously failed. These failures are
seen as the result of foreign betrayal and oppression, and the course of
Czech history is construed as discontinuous, full of breaks, interruptions,
and schisms (three hundred years of 'darkness' following the Battle of
White Mountain in 1620, German occupation during World War II, the
communist period of 1948–89). According to this image of the past, Czech
history is the history of a nation which often made European history
through its actions but was frequently blocked by its powerful neighbours
because its ideas were ahead of their time. In the Hussite wars, for
example, which ended in the battle of Lipany in 1434, Czechs made
European history as enthusiastic proponents of the Reformation; the first
Czechoslovak Republic, which was effectively ended by the Munich agreement of 1938, shone as a beacon of democracy in a Central Europe dominated by autocratic fascist regimes; and in the Prague Spring, which was

ended by the invasion of Warsaw Pact armies in August 1968, in the words of the Czech writer Milan Kundera, the Czech nation tried to

> create at last (and for the first time in its own history as well as in the history of the world) a socialism without the all-powerful secret police, with freedom of the written and spoken word, public opinion which was heeded and served as the basis for politics, a freely developing modern culture, and people without fear; it was an effort in which Czechs and Slovaks stood again for the first time since the end of the Middle Ages in the centre of world history and addressed their challenge to the world.   *(quoted in Pithart 1990b: 16)*

Being thwarted in its efforts to make European history constitutes a break in the course of Czech history. After each of these breaks or discontinuities Czech history picks up again, and the Czech nation starts building again where it left off.

The notion of breaks and discontinuities presupposes that of a continuous development against the background of which one can perceive them. In this construction, the 'meaning' of Czech history is distilled not from what actually happened in the past but from the imagination of what would have happened if, as it were, Czechs had been left to their own devices. If that were the case, Czech history would indeed have been an uninterrupted striving toward democracy and humanism. To construe its meaning as such, certain periods must be declared as anomalous discontinuities. For Czech history to return to its proper course again, the consequences of the historical event which marked the beginning of the discontinuity, have to be 'undone' (*odčiněny*). History can then start again where it was interrupted by foreign interference, and through redressing historical wrongs it can be corrected.

The most important of the events marking the beginning of a discontinuity in Czech history was the Battle of White Mountain, which Czech historiography (including the Catholic historiography of Josef Pekař) and popular Czech historical consciousness consider a 'national tragedy'. It ended the uprising of the Protestant Bohemian nobility against the absolutist rule of the Catholic Habsburgs established on the Czech throne since 1526. The estates of the rebellious nobility were confiscated by the crown and given to Catholic noble families loyal to the monarchy – all of whom were Germans in popular perception. The defeat of the uprising effectively meant the end of the sovereignty of the Czech state. The period of re-Catholicisation and gradual Germanisation of Bohemian towns which followed is seen as three hundred years of 'darkness' and suffering under foreign domination from which the Czech nation was liberated only in 1918, with the establishment of the Czechoslovak Republic.

One of the first legislative acts of the parliament of the new republic was the land reform bill, hastily introduced before the first parliamentary elections not only to prevent a socialist revolution, but also to ensure its smooth passage before the German members of the parliament had been duly elected. In accordance with this bill, the estates of members of the imperial family were confiscated in full and without compensation. Other noble families were allowed to hold 150 hectares of agricultural land or 250 hectares total (in exceptional cases up to 500 hectares). The rest of their land was sold to more than half a million Czech smallholders, and some 2,000 'remnant estates' of about 100 hectares each were created to be sold for considerably less than the land allocated to individual farmers. These were meant to create an agricultural base for the new state which would efficiently employ the agricultural technology then available. They were also destined to become an important base for the Czech element in the German-speaking areas along the borders of Bohemia and in Slovakia and Ruthenia.

The land reform was carried out under the slogan of 'undoing' White Mountain. A simple monument erected in 1921 in a small village in southern Bohemia, probably by grateful new landowners, states explicitly that 'the land reform redressed the wrong of White Mountain' (*Pozemková reforma odčinila křivdu bělohorskou*). This purpose of the reform was undoubtedly supported by the overwhelming majority of Czechs, including the Catholic and conservative historian Josef Pekař, despite his articles in *Národní listy* criticising its implementation and some of its legal aspects (see Pithart 1990a: 71–103). The reform was generally perceived as accomplishing historical justice after three hundred years. Its purpose was to deprive the foreign (primarily German) nobility of the property which it had wrongfully acquired at the expense of the rebellious Czech nobility after the Battle of White Mountain. In the perception of most people, the land stolen from the Czech nation through confiscation three hundred years ago was now simply to be returned. It is unnecessary to dwell here on the party-political aspect of the reform[4] and on its accompanying scandals. In the context of the discussion of Czech nationalism what is important is that 'for millions of citizens of the new state, it was a clear lesson in how to understand history easily, how to correct it retrospectively, and how to achieve ostentatious national satisfaction for a lost battle' (Pithart 1990a: 81).

The next land reform was carried out on the basis of the 'Decree of the President of the Republic concerning confiscation and speedy redistribution of the agricultural property of the Germans and Hungarians as well as traitors and enemies of the Czech and Slovak nation', issued on 21 June 1945. The reform was again legitimated as finally 'undoing' the wrongs of White Mountain. The decree was followed by a popular demonstration symbolically held on the plain of White Mountain on the outskirts of Prague. The minister of agriculture of the first post-war coalition government gave the following speech:

Czech farmers, workers, friends: three and a quarter centuries have elapsed since the Habsburgs, aided by adventurous foreign nobles, defeated Czech nobility on this plain of White Mountain and subjugated the Czech lands and the Czech people for three hundred years. The foreign conquerors were victorious then because the Czech nobility included traitors and because it was split into Catholic and Protestant but, most important, because it separated itself from the people – because instead of going with them it went against them . . . The weak Czech bourgeoisie preserved the remnants of feudalism throughout the old democratic republic as we can see today when confiscating the 70,000-hectare estates of the Lichtensteins, the Dittrichsteins, and the Hungarian grofs. However, we feel the consequences of White Mountain and of the survival in the old republic of the Austro-Hungarian feudalism of 1848 in other ways as well . . . After three and a quarter centuries, the Czech land stolen is finally being returned to Czech hands. Not only are the Lichtensteins and Dittrichsteins liquidated but also the traitors from the years 1621 and 1938–45 . . . And now, once and for all, this long, sad history of our nations ends. White Mountain is undone [*odčiněna*].

(quoted in Pithart 1990a: 99)

The political rhetoric which justified both reforms clearly indicated their dual purpose: to eliminate the political power of the aristocracy by depriving it of the property on which its power was based and, especially during the reform after World War I, to strengthen the Czech element in the multinational but Czech-dominated state by allocating the land confiscated from the Germans to Czech farmers. In the case of the land reform after World War II, the breaking of the economic power of the Germans and other 'traitors and enemies of the Czech and Slovak nation' was aided by the forcible removal of some three million Germans to Germany, thus making the population of Bohemia and Moravia – with the exception of the gypsies – ethnically homogeneous for the first time.[5] The perception of the land reform as returning to the Czechs as a whole what had traditionally always been theirs is evidence once again of Czech collectivism. The land which was redistributed in the land reform after World War I was land belonging to individual noble families. The noble families of Bohemia who rebelled against the Habsburg monarchy and whose estates were confiscated can hardly be classified as Czechs when the notion of what it means to be a Czech became established only during the past century. Any attribution of ethnicity to a particular noble family is necessarily retrospective and depends on how that family was classified in the nineteenth century, after the modern Czech nation came into being.

Even if the problematic nature of the attribution of ethnicity to the noble families of the seventeenth century is disregarded, the fact remains that many of the confiscated estates later changed hands through purchase and at least some of them were acquired by noble families considered to be Czech. But such historical arguments seem to have been of interest only to a legalistically minded historian like Pekař. For politicians and ordinary people alike the only thing that mattered about the reform was returning Czech land, unjustifiably misappropriated by the Germans, to Czech hands. That this land did not belong to the Czechs as a whole but originally had individual owners and was again acquired as private, heritable property by individual farmers did not seem to matter. It was treated as if it had been the collective property of the Czech nation and was being returned to it; its private owners were seen as trustees of some collective Czech good. The land was not 'mine' or 'yours'; it was 'ours', that of the Czech nation as a whole. One can entertain the notion that the land reform 'undid' or redressed the Battle of White Mountain only by interpreting the events of the seventeenth century in a particular way. This interpretation is that the victorious foreigners – perceived as Germans – punished the rebellious noblemen not as individuals but as members of the Czech nation. During the land reform, individual farmers received land not because they needed it, but because as members of the Czech nation, they had the right to have restored to them what had historically belonged to them as Czechs. That the land, at one time privately owned, was now being sold to different private owners was not the issue; the issue was returning Czech land to its rightful Czech owners. It was not a wrong done to particular individuals which the land reform redressed but one done to a collectivity, then, as now, perceived as the Czech nation.

Another event which interrupted the continuity of Czech history was the loss of the Sudetenland to the German Reich after the Munich agreement of 1938. This historical wrong was 'undone' by the forcible repatriation of the German population from Czechoslovakia to Germany in 1945, which at that time met with the explicit approval of virtually all Czechs. The issue was reopened by Václav Havel after he became president of the Czechoslovak Republic. He questioned particularly the principle of collective guilt which motivated the expulsion of an ethnic group as a whole as punishment for actions carried out before and during the war by particular members of it. He apologised for the atrocities committed by Czechs during the transfer of the German population. Most Czechs saw this as his biggest political blunder, and in the eyes of many it affected the tremendous popularity which he had up to then enjoyed. In 1993, 76 per cent of Czechs approved of the 1945 transfer of the Sudeten Germans and considered the issue closed (*Lidové noviny*, 10 August 1993).

What happened in history cannot, of course, always be 'undone' in such a straightforward way, but it helps to maintain the veracity of the reading of certain historical periods as anomalous interruptions of the natural course of history if these periods can officially be attributed to the illegitimate interference of foreign powers. In 1989 Czechoslovak diplomacy saw as its great success its extraction from the Soviet government of a statement declaring the Soviet invasion of Czechoslovakia in 1968 to have been a violation of international law. And it was seen as a failure of Czech diplomacy that the German government could not be persuaded to declare the Munich agreement null and void and to include a statement to this effect in the Czechoslovak–German treaty signed in 1991. It was seen as a diplomatic success when the British prime minister John Major agreed to the annulment of the Munich treaty in a joint statement signed by him and Havel during his visit to Czechoslovakia in 1992.

The second image of the past construes Czech history without any notion of discontinuities. It sees it not as the history of a nation which through its actions often made European history, but as a history which has always been part of European history. It envisions a nation not so much the subject of its history as the object of historical forces beyond its control. Whereas the first image of the past was articulated by the 'father of the nation', Palacký, who characteristically ended his monumental history of the Czech nation with the accession of the Habsburg dynasty to the Czech throne, the second image was most explicitly formulated by what may be seen as a consciously non-nationalistic historiography whose main proponent was Josef Pekař (see Pynsent 1994: 182). This historiography saw Czech history not as the unique achievement of the Czech nation but as the unfolding of events in the wider context of European history to which the Czechs were responsive. Among contemporary Czech intellectuals, this view is most explicitly articulated by Petr Pithart. In view of the fact that the first image of the past is an important ideological construction of Czech nationalism, it is not without significance that Palacký was a Protestant and Pekař a Catholic. The two images differ most significantly in their respective evaluations of the period of re-Catholicisation after the Battle of White Mountain.

According to the first image, this was a period of 'darkness'; according to the second it was a period of unprecedented cultural and spiritual flowering of the Czech nation during which the cultural development of Bohemia was once more in tune with cultural development elsewhere in Europe after the disruption of the Reformation (see Pynsent 1994: 176): the country not only accepted cultural impulses from elsewhere but creatively transformed them into its own style, known as Czech Baroque. Considering that the Baroque period has contributed more to the contemporary image of Prague than any other period in its history (Pynsent 1994: 184) and that the Baroque style affected virtually every Czech town and village and the whole Czech countryside (in architecture, music, folk costumes, etc.), the first image of the past could easily be seen as idealistic and the second as realistic. In adopting such a view, however, one would inevitably be taking sides in the Czech discourse about the past. It is more appropriate to see them as two views of the past, one emphasising the political and the other the cultural aspect. Czech intellectuals themselves hotly debate which of these two views more accurately reflects the objective historical facts.

Historical facts are, however, not objective in themselves but construed as such through the interpretation of the past, part of which is the selection of the events which are to be mentioned or disregarded. The two images of history are thus part of an ongoing discourse whose authors and participants are not only the intellectuals who write about Czech history and the politicians who argue among themselves about the validity of their particular interpretations but ordinary people as well. It is through this discourse that a historical memory is perpetually constructed. A historical memory is not something a nation has because it has a history; it is something created through a nation's reminding itself that it has a history. To ordinary people this history is accessible not through the study of historical documents but through what they have learned about it at school and through its inscription in the historical monuments around them and, eventually, in the very countryside. Most important, they are made aware of it through what they read about it in newspapers and hear on television and on the radio. References to specific events in history permeate the discussion of contemporary political problems in daily press coverage and in the televised debates of politicians and journalists. For example, in 1992, when politicians began speaking openly about the inevitable demise of Czechoslovakia, the chairman of the Czech Socialist Party wrote in a daily newspaper:

In the present stormy time, we often ask what should be the meaning and purpose of Czech politics. If we want to answer this question seriously, we have to think about the conception of Czech politics in our modern history. It has always had to spring from the context in which the Czech nation found itself both historically and as the consequence of its geographical position. It has always had to formulate its task as that of defending the existence and identity of a Czech nation surrounded by the powerful German nation. At the same time, it has had to take into consideration that the Czech state was incorporated into the multinational conglomerate of the Habsburg empire, which had little consideration for the aspirations and interests of the nations within it. Efforts to assimilate the Czech element in the Central European region have repeatedly emerged with powerful force from White Mountain until World War II, and it was because of the nation's vitality that these efforts eventually failed.   (*Svobodné slovo, 20 February 1992*)

Here specific historical periods and events (the Battle of White Mountain, Habsburg rule, World War II) are mentioned to illustrate the dangers which the Czech nation has faced during its history. They are invoked as symbols of the nation's character, traditions, aspirations, fears, and aims or as symbols of its uniqueness among other nations. But in much of the popular discourse about Czech history, specific historical events or persons are mentioned without being given any explicit meaning. References to history in popular discourse often take the form of a simple listing of the names of particular persons from the nation's past: 'our national history is unambiguously dominated by the line Hus–Chelčický–the Czech Brethren[6]–Komenský–Havlíček–Palacký–Patočka'[7] (M. C. Putna in *Literární noviny* 3 (1992), no. 34: 5; see also the quote from Havel on p. 119). There is no need to explain what these persons did; mentioning their names is enough. Reciting the 'genealogy' of the nation's spiritual ancestors makes the reader or listener aware both of the long and glorious history of the Czech nation and of the existence of the national traditions which are its product. The actual knowledge of history of course varies tremendously depending on the person's education, interests, and other factors, but all Czechs, even those with only a basic education, are able to mention a number of events and persons from the nation's past. These events and names are the means through which their knowledge of the nation's history is constructed, even if that knowledge is little more than the notion that the Czech nation has a long and glorious history. The discourse about the nation's past is thus a discourse in which the knowledge, awareness, and perception of its participants are unevenly distributed. It is also a discourse which oscillates between tacit and explicit articulation, the latter coming into prominence when particular political issues have to be decided, particular political causes have to be formulated and fought for, or particular political actions are being taken. The two images of the past can be summarised in a standard table of binary oppositions (table 3).

The image of the past in which the Czech nation is the subject of its

Table 3. *Contrasting Czech images of the past*

Nationalist ideology	Non-nationalist ideology
The nation as the subject of history	The nation as the object of history
Discontinuous history	Historical continuity
'Undoing' history	Acceptance of the whole past as national history
Failures attributed to our being too progressive and misunderstood	Failures attributed to our not appreciating the world in which we live

history is part of the nationalist ideology. An important part of it is the construction of the image of the well-educated and highly cultured nation with strong traditions of democracy. The image of the past in which the Czech nation is the object of European history is part of a consciously non-nationalist ideology which posits different national traditions: 'With us reigns the tradition of giving up: the years 1938, 1939, 1948, 1968 – we have always given up everything without a fight; Schweik became the role model for the people' (*Mladý svět*, 1990, no. 4: 20). In their extreme formulation, the two images of the past emphasise different traditions and different attitudes as characteristic of the Czech nation in times of national crisis: heroism versus cowardice, resistance versus collaboration. During the first Czechoslovak Republic, the first image of the past was articulated in its extreme form by the Czech politicians and intellectuals who published their views in the weekly *Fronta*. It came into prominence in the interpretation of the events which led to the creation of independent Czechoslovakia. In his wartime memoirs and interpretation of World War I *The World Revolution* (*Světová revoluce*, 1925), Masaryk argued that the Czechoslovak Republic was created through his and his collaborators' diplomatic efforts in the United States because they managed to present the Czech cause in the context of contemporary world events and contemporary political thinking.

In this interpretation, the creation of an independent Czechoslovakia was part of world history; rather than the creator of its own destiny, the Czech nation was once again an object of history, albeit in this case history favourable to the Czech cause. *Fronta* called this interpretation a 'liberation legend' and emphasised instead the heroic struggle of the Czech legions alongside the Allied armies in Russia, France, and Italy, their fight against the Bolsheviks (which, in its view, effectively prevented the collapse of the eastern front after the October Revolution and thus facilitated the final victory of the Allies), the fight against the Austrian police at home, and the importance of the 'revolution' in Prague on 28–30 October 1918 (see Pithart 1990a: 144–56).

The interpretation of events which led to the creation of the Czechoslovak Republic in 1918 is determined by the two differing images of the past or their combination. Petr Vopěnka, minister of education in the government formed after the 1990 elections, speaking at a conference on the idea of Czech statehood in Prague in October 1992, said,

Let us not forget that the Czechoslovak Republic after 1918 was not founded through the favour of the victorious powers. The gravity of this state was also founded on the blood of Masaryk's legions shed on all the battlefields of the World War I.   *(Lidové noviny, 20 November 1992)*

Just as the two images of the past are invoked in imposing meaning on the events of 1918, they are invoked in the interpretation of the events of 1989. On the one hand, the 'velvet revolution' is seen as the work of students, dissidents, and actors. According to this view, the Czech nation liberated itself from the communist regime and can thus be seen again as the subject of history. On the other hand, liberation from the communist regime is seen as the consequence of the changed international situation, and the nation can thus be seen again as the object of history:

The totalitarian system was not defeated by students, dissidents, and actors. Its end had for a long time been predetermined by the changed international situation and by its gradually increasing internal impotence, and at the moment of mass protest meetings it simply collapsed.   *(Martin Schmarcz in* Český deník, *17 November 1992)*

Although the two images of the past can be formulated as ideally distinct, they rarely enter into everyday discourse in their pure ideal-typical form. In this discourse, which is always about Czech identity and its meaning, various elements of the two images are often embraced and variously combined by the same individual. Czechs who are distinctly proud of Baroque architecture, music, or literature as part of their 'national heritage' can view the period of re-Catholicisation during which this heritage was produced as a period of darkness and suffering under foreign oppressors. For example, Masaryk subscribed to Palacký's view of the discontinuity of Czech history and explicitly formulated the view of the Czech nation as an active subject of history. His 'liberation legend' nevertheless clearly sprang from the view of the Czech nation as the object of history. Present-day official political thinking, in contrast, reflects the view of the Czech nation as object rather than subject of history. In his insistence on accepting the office of president only on condition that a suitable political role be found for Dubček (who subsequently became chairman of the Federal Assembly), however, Havel was attempting symbolically to 'undo' the invasion which in 1968 had crushed the Prague Spring, of which Dubček remained the living symbol. This effort can be seen as motivated by the image of the Czech nation as an active subject of history and of Czech history as discontinuous. Such mixing of elements of the two images is characteristic not only of the discourse of professional historians, intellectuals, and politicians but also of much of the popular discourse.

On the one hand, there is an official tendency to 'draw a thick line under history' (*udělat tlustou čáru za historii*) which follows from Havel's view that the communist system in Czechoslovakia was the creation not just of the then-ruling communist elite but of everyone, because everyone in one way or another complied with its demands, however formally. In practical political action this attitude, which tacitly adopts the view of the Czech nation as an object of history beyond its control, manifests itself in a reluctance to investigate the sources of the wealth of emerging entrepreneurs, in an absence of reprisals against judges and civil servants who, whatever their formal political affiliations and sympathies, did not contravene valid communist law, and in strictly controlled action against former agents and collaborators of the communist secret police. On the other hand, there was a call for the recognition of the resistance to communist rule as a third official resistance movement (the first two having opposed the Austro-Hungarian Empire and the German occupation), for discrimination in the emerging market economy against those who had enriched themselves under communist rule by controlling the distribution of scarce goods (not necessarily only material ones), and for publication in full of the list of agents and collaborators of the communist secret police. These are the demands of those who once more would like to see history 'undone' and its wrongs redressed.

The easy mixing of the elements of the two images of the past in political discourse is made possible not only by the fact that political and cultural history need not be seen as congruent but also by the fact that in both images the Czechs are construed as a numerically small nation in Central Europe, itself seen as a traditional crossroads of the political, religious, and cultural movements of the Continent. In one view, the Czechs themselves were sometimes instigators of these movements and would have been so all the time if their enemies had been as receptive as the Czechs to the progressive ideas or had not predominated over them numerically. History is seen as the history of Czech defeats which can, however, be seen as moral victories. As František Palacký expressed it, 'Whenever we were victorious, it was always through the supremacy of the spirit rather than through physical power.' Part of this image of the past is attributing responsibility for failure to others (alternatively Catholics, Germans, Communists, Russians, or Slovaks), and achieving moral victory by 'undoing', often after centuries, particular defeats of the 'Czech cause'. In the other view of the past, the Czechs have always been objects of the political, cultural, and religious movements of Europe. Because they have never been numerically strong, they could not have prevented what others did to them. Part of this image of the past is attributing responsibility for failure not to others but to Czechs themselves, particularly for their lack of appreciation of the world of which they are an integral part. The strength of the nation is not in its moral victories, as the first image of the past would have it, but in its ability to survive three hundred years of Habsburg oppression, six years of German occupation, and forty-three years of communism through pretended loyalty and tacit or explicit collaboration. This accounts for the popularity of Good Soldier Schweik, a survivor *par excellence*.

The two images of history are formulated on the basis of a shared view of Czech history as a succession of defeats and failures to which there seem to be only two exceptions: the founding of the Czechoslovak Republic in 1918 (which was positively evaluated by all Czechs) and the demise of communism in 1989 (which is positively evaluated by most but certainly not all). The two images differ only in their interpretation of the reasons for the course of Czech history. In Bohemia there are few monuments of victorious battles, no monuments of great military leaders (with the exception of Žižka, whom I shall discuss later) and no triumphal arches (Pithart 1990b: 13). In neither image of the past are there any heroes in the sense of individuals who fought in arms victoriously for their cause – or, more exactly, efforts to construct images of such heroes (e.g., legionnaires of World War I or the partisans of World War II) have never been successful. Heroic images have either not lasted long or not been unambiguously accepted by the whole nation. The Czechs celebrate their suffering rather than their victories (Pynsent 1994: 190–6), and the heroes of the Czech nation are its martyrs (Macura 1993: 76).

I have already mentioned the two most important Czech martyrs – St Wenceslas and Jan Hus. One need only take a stroll through Prague to appreciate the importance which Czechs ascribe to these two figures: the two largest monuments erected in the two largest squares in the city centre belong to them. The significance of these martyrs derives from their having become powerful symbols. The case of the modern Czech martyr Jan Palach illustrates a point of general significance: when symbols function in a political context – that is, when they are used to express identification with particular political causes and forces – they are contested by the opponents of these causes and forces in two ways.

First, because symbols serve as vehicles for meaning through their linkage to other symbols, their meanings can be altered by explicitly linking them to different symbols. As we have seen, the government, in an effort to reduce his perceived symbolic significance, tried to construe Palach's death as emulation of Buddhist monks rather than of Jan Hus. Another important Czech martyr – Jan Nepomucký – was the object of similar manipulation as a symbol. Nepomucký, the capital vicar of the archbishop of Prague, was drowned by order of the king in 1393 because he opposed the king's plan to create a new bishopric in western Bohemia. He was canonised as a saint in 1729 on the basis of a widely circulated popular legend, according to which he had met his death because he refused to reveal to the king the contents of the queen's confession (Piťha 1992: 119–40). Toward the end of the last century, when Hus had become the most important symbol of Czech nationalism, Czech Protestant journalists and writers began to express the view that Jan Nepomucký had not really been so worthy as he was made out to be by the Catholic church and had been canonised simply because the church (and implicitly, the Habsburg monarchy) had needed a new Czech saint to reduce the significance of Hus (Vlnas 1993). In this view, Hus was so significant for Czechs even during the period of re-Catholicisation that the church felt able to suppress this politically dangerous consciousness only by vigorously promulgating the cult of a new Czech saint and martyr. Opponents of Nepomucký's cult linked him to Hus not only to reduce his importance but also to bolster Hus's. The battle over the relative significance of Hus and Nepomucký in keeping Czech national consciousness alive was still being waged in the pages of Czech newspapers in the 1920s (see Pekař 1990: 275–313). The meaning which the Czech Protestant nationalists imposed on Nepomucký was not confined to the intellectual circles in which it originated. During the Jan Nepomucký holiday in 1893 Prague youths demonstrated not for this Jan but for Jan Hus (O. Urban 1982: 417), and after the establishment of the Czechoslovak Republic in 1918 a number of Nepomucký monuments were pulled down as symbols of Habsburg oppression (Pekař 1990: 311).

A second way of contesting the symbolic significance of martyrs derives from the fact that martyrs are not fictitious mythological figures but historical persons and are venerated for what are perceived as their actual deeds and views. The symbolic potency of martyrs' actions derives precisely from the perception of them as something that really happened in the past. This perception can thus effectively be undermined or altered by showing that the martyrs did not in fact do what they are believed to have done or were not in fact what they are believed to have been. This form of contesting their significance consists of showing that what is being venerated is not a historical truth but a myth (in the sense of something fabricated) created because of some specific contemporary political interest.

This effort to demolish the myth and reveal the historical truth is of course as much motivated by present political interests as is the perpetuation of the myth. Part of contesting the symbolic significance of Jan Nepomucký was the discovery by some historians (disputed, of course, by others) that the fourteenth-century Prague vicar had in fact been much less concerned with spiritual matters than with using his high church office for his material benefit and, worse, that he was in fact not a Czech at all but a German (see Pekař 1990: 284–5, 302). From this perspective his canonisation was seen at best as an error and at worst as a fraud. When the celebrations of Jan Hus during the first years of the Czechoslovak Republic led to concentrated attacks on the Catholic church, the Catholic historian Pekař argued that Hus himself had never meant to break away from the church and instead had intended to reform it from within. He urged all those who invoked Hus for their anti-Catholic crusade to study his actual teachings rather than be inspired by the politically motivated image of a Hus who never was (Pekař 1990: 115–27). Again, during the German occupation, German propaganda emphasised the fact that St Wenceslas had put his country under German protection and paid an annual tribute of 300 pieces of silver and 120 oxen to the Saxon king, the predecessor of the Roman emperors – rulers of what the ideologists of the Third Reich saw as the first German Reich. German propaganda was in this way able to claim that the Czech nation, which had put itself under the protection of the German Reich, was fulfilling at last the true historical legacy of St Wenceslas.

The role of martyrs in Czech culture and politics is by no means exhausted at this point – martyrs have always been used as the main symbols of specific political ideas and doctrines. Even the Communists relied on a martyr rather than on the heroes of the class struggle to build up the myth of the Communists as the leaders of the Czech resistance against the fascists during the German occupation and to present themselves as appropriate leaders of a nation that had always seen itself as well educated and highly cultured. This martyr was Julius Fučík, a journalist who became a member of the underground Central Committee of the Communist Party during the war. He was arrested by the Gestapo in 1942 and executed in Berlin in 1943. He is best known for his *Report Written on the Noose*, written in prison with the assistance of a Czech warden who smuggled his writing out. In the book he describes his arrest and interrogation. The book was first published after the war and in later editions underwent a gradual metamorphosis whereby various passages were left out which did not fully fit his image of a martyr tortured and executed by the Gestapo for his patriotism. The communist regime declared him a national hero, the anniversary of his death was celebrated as the 'Day of the Press', and members of the Czechoslovak Union of Youth competed for the Fučík medal, awarded for knowledge of his writings and knowledge of novels by selected Czech and Soviet authors (Pynsent 1994: 207–8).

Like other political symbols, this one too was contested. This happened for the first time during the Prague Spring and then again after the overthrow of the communist regime in 1989. It was suggested that Fučík's *Report* was a fabrication, for he could not possibly have written it under the strict regime of a Gestapo prison. These allegations eventually proved unfounded, but the view persisted that far from being a Czech patriot he was in fact an informer of the Gestapo. This allegation is based on the assumption that otherwise he could not have written his *Report* and would not have been treated by his interrogator in the way he describes. The places named after him reverted to their old names after the revolution of 1989, and his statue in Prague, erected in 1979, was removed.

After the student demonstration on 17 November 1989, one of the representatives of Charter 77 reported to the world press that a student had been killed by the police during the demonstration. Although it soon transpired that no one had actually been killed, the report of a student's death had some factual basis. During the parliamentary inquiry into the events of 17 November it was established that the students had been actively encouraged by provocateurs within the ranks of the police to march on the city centre and that during police assault on the students one of the policemen, who was marching in civilian clothes at the head of the procession, pretended to have been killed and his 'body' was whisked away in an ambulance. A representative of Charter 77, which was normally very careful to check the accuracy of its information, reported to the world press that a student had been killed by the police; the logic of the situation made the rumour perfectly plausible to any Czech.

This incident gave rise to a rather convoluted conspiracy theory that the radical wing of the Communist Party had tried to stir up street protest in order to get rid of the conservative leadership and that this plan had misfired when Havel had hijacked the Communists' own plot. I think that a simpler explanation is more likely. The Communists wanted a 'dead' student, knowing that the opposition would immediately see him as a martyr to the cause. By being able to demonstrate that there was in fact no dead student, they would effectively discredit the opposition, which would be seen as resorting to lies to foster its aims. The strategy could only have worked, of course, in a society in which martyrs as political symbols evoke strong emotions. It seems to me that Czech society is precisely such a society. The military commander of the Czechoslovak troops fighting the German and Austrian armies in Russia during World War I whose name is best remembered is Colonel Švec. He is remembered not because he led his troops to heroic victories but because he shot himself to raise the sinking morale of his troops (Pynsent 1994: 205–6).

Heroes and martyrs can equally be used as political symbols. The Czechs have a long list of martyrs but are distinctly short of heroes. They have no Bismarck, Napoleon, Wellington, Nelson, or even Kossuth. The only Czech hero of any significance is Jan Žižka, the leader of the Hussite armies, who, interestingly, appears to be more remembered in folk legends than invoked as a political symbol. Plans for erecting a monument to him in Prague emerged only after Czechoslovak independence in 1924, and the monument was eventually erected only in 1950. It is quite possible that the long time it took to build reflects the ambivalence toward him.

The names of historical persons of whom the Czechs are proud have not changed over the past twenty years. According to an opinion survey conducted in October 1968 in the atmosphere of strong opposition to the recent invasion of Czechoslovakia by the Warsaw Pact armies, respondents mentioned in order of frequency T. G. Masaryk, Jan Hus, Karel IV, and Jan Amos Komenský (Comenius) (*Lidové noviny*, 17 July 1992). In October 1992 a similar survey among the population of the Czech Republic yielded the list of table 4.

Some of the persons are leading politicians of the pre-war Czechoslovak Republic, particularly its two founders and subsequent presidents T. G. Masaryk and Edvard Beneš, as well as its other 'founding father', Milan Rastislav Štefánik, and post-war politicians who equally symbolise the nation's striving for political independence: Ludvík Svoboda, who was the Czechoslovak president during the Prague Spring and is popularly perceived (albeit incorrectly) as its most determined

Table 4. *Historical persons Czechs
mention with pride (percentages)*

T. G. Masaryk	46.2
Karel IV	13.2
E. Beneš	11.9
J. Hus	10.0
J. A. Komenský	8.6
L. Svoboda	8.5
J. Masaryk	8.0
J. Žižka	4.2
M. R. Štefánik	4.0
A. Dubček	3.1

Note:
Percentages add up to more than 100
because respondents could mention as
many names as they wished.
*Source: Aktuálne problémy Česko-
Slovenska*, November 1990: 16.

defender against Soviet pressure; Jan Masaryk, the Czechoslovak foreign minister who is seen as the victim of the communist coup d'état in 1948; and Alexandr Dubček, the leading figure of the Prague Spring. When the list is extended to include the living as well as the dead, as it was in my own independent survey, the name of Václav Havel comes out at the top. To some extent both Jan Masaryk and Dubček are seen as martyrs in that they have obviously suffered for their beliefs as, of course, has Havel.

A second group includes persons from earlier Czech history. One of these is the Czech king and Roman emperor Karel IV, and two others are Jan Hus and Jan Amos Komenský. The popular image of Komenský is not only that of the 'teacher of nations' but also that of a martyr who, as a Protestant, had to leave his country during the Counter-Reformation following the Battle of White Mountain and spend the rest of his life in exile. The last mentioned in this group is Jan Žižka. Some of the informants whom I asked for the names of persons who, in their view, 'did most for and meant most to the Czech nation' thought about Hus but did not include him. Although they valued Hus himself positively, they did not value the Hussite movement which followed his death, of which Žižka was the main protagonist. The reasons which I received from respondents for not mentioning Žižka included his burning of churches and monasteries and his general destruction of what we now see as cultural monuments. Those who did not mention Hus at all were mainly motivated by their negative view of the Hussite period. For some, this was to some extent a reaction to the Communists' interpretation of the Hussite movement as the first social revolution in the history of the Czech nation and as part of the Czech revolutionary tradition; others were Catholic believers who did not approve of Hus's criticism of the Catholic church and particularly of his open rejection of papal authority.

The list of historical figures of whom the Czechs feel particularly proud includes a significant number of martyrs or at least of persons who are perceived as having suffered a fate close to martyrdom (Hus, Komenský, Jan Masaryk, Dubček). Obviously, the important thing about martyrs is their high morality, manifested beyond any doubt in their willingness to die or suffer in some other way for their beliefs, but all the martyrs I have mentioned (with the exception of Colonel Švec) share yet another characteristic. They were all educated men and intellectuals – even the St Wenceslas legends emphasise his learning rather than his military prowess. Karel IV, Hus, and Komenský are remembered first of all for their intellectual and moral qualities. These figures are therefore fitting symbols of a nation whose self-image is that it is cultured and well educated. Žižka clearly does not fit this image: he was not an intellectual but a military leader. Apart from the tradition of *kulturnost* and education, another tradition which the Czechs invoke is the tradition of non-violence. They are distinctly proud of the non-violent character of their November revolution, which has confirmed to them the strength of this tradition as well as demonstrating yet again their *kulturnost*. As a military leader and hence a man of violence, Žižka again does not fit easily into the overall picture.

It is not only professional historians who distil a tradition from the course of history and then retell this history in the light of the tradition which gives it its meaning. This is also done by ordinary people, for whom the perception of history is reduced to the names of a few historical persons who are seen as embodiments of national traditions or a few selected events deemed to be of special importance because of the assumed traditions. In this popular perception of history, it is reduced to tradition, and it is through this tradition that the nation is both endowed with history and constituted as a historical entity. In this sense it can be said that the nation lives in and through its traditions.

The two images of the past with their different constructions of national traditions constitute two different ideologies: one overtly nationalist, the other consciously non-nationalist. Much as the two ideologies are simultaneously available to and can be differently accentuated by the same individual in everyday discourse, they are differently accentuated in discourses which become dominant in different historical periods. The result is that Czech nationalism remains tacit at certain times, giving rise to the feeling that there is no strong sense of Czech national identity, and explicitly artic-ulated at other times. The nationalist ideology gains ascendancy in situa-tions which are perceived as national crises or in situations in which what is tacitly understood as the Czech way of life is threatened by those per-ceived as the Other. As the opposition to the communist regime took the form of the nation's resisting what had been perceived as yet another form of foreign oppression, the image of the democratic and well-educated Czech nation, fostered by the nationalist reading of Czech history, became an effective rallying cry for the political mobilisation of the masses in opposition to the communist system and subsequently in support of a market economy, a democratic political structure, and an independent Czech state. In the remaining two chapters I concentrate on the role played by these images of the Czech nation and other premises of Czech culture in giving meaning to various political events in recent Czech history.

5

National traditions and the political process

A tradition is an asserted belief. This does not mean, however, that it is arbitrary. We can begin to appreciate this when we move beyond the description of its form and structure to consider how it is reproduced in social praxis and in whose particular interest it is formulated and invoked. Although a tradition is ostensibly invoked to make sense of the past, it is always invoked either from the standpoint of the present objective or from the standpoint of some future objective. It is the present or the future which determines certain presumed attitudes and characteristics to be 'our traditions'. A tradition is thus, on the one hand, invoked to legitimate or to alter the present state of affairs and, on the other, to mobilise people to pursue some envisaged ideal state of affairs in the future. The present is thus made sense of, or the envisaged future is seen as desirable, in terms of the past. Conceptualised as evidence of the past, the tradition is at the same time seen as a historical force continuing in the present or 'logically' pointing the way to the society's historically predetermined future. One of its important functions is to link past, present, and future.

Neither a democratic tradition nor the tradition of a cultured and well-educated nation was invoked under the communist regime in Czechoslovakia, when the traditions of revolutionary struggle, sympathy with the movements of national liberation from colonial oppression, and the long history of friendship with other peoples building socialism were part of the official political rhetoric. This is the reason the socialist period is seen as yet another anomaly and discontinuity in Czech history and the reason the assumed traditions of democracy and culture which form an important part of Czech nationalism became a powerful motivating force during the November 1989 revolution which toppled the communist regime. This is also the reason that numerous Czech politicians and journalists talk about the end of the communist system as 'the return to history' and the whole post-communist transformation of society is seen as 'undoing' the wrongs of the socialist period.

The 'velvet revolution'

As all revolutionaries worth their salt know, the precondition of a successful revolution is the widespread dissatisfaction of the masses, who can then be politicised and encouraged to act in the name of the envisaged change for the better. By this textbook formula, Poland in the 1980s and the Soviet Union in the late 1980s and early 1990s were probably in a more revolutionary situation than Czechoslovakia ever was before November 1989. However one interprets Šimečka's 1988 diary, from which I have quoted earlier (see p. 27), one can hardly read it as a description of politicised masses ready for revolutionary action. The leading dissidents themselves remained sceptical, until the very last moment, about the chances of overthrowing the communist system. The essay Petr Pithart wrote in August 1989 (Pithart 1990a: 345–61) depicts the communist regime in Czechoslovakia as extremely stable and Czechoslovak society as distinctly passive. A few days before the events of November 1989, Václav Havel said that he expected political changes in Czechoslovakia in the spring of 1990 and that the changes would not be connected with public demonstrations.

Yet, a few days later a revolution took place. When the students who demonstrated in Prague on 17 November were brutally beaten by the police, they declared an indefinite strike, in which they were immediately joined by actors and musicians. The day after the demonstration not a single theatre was open in Prague, and very soon thereafter theatrical and concert performances came to a halt throughout the country. The declaration of the students' and actors' strikes was followed by a week of daily mass demonstrations in Prague in which an estimated 750,000 people participated (in a city with a population of 1,200,000). The demonstrations soon spread to other cities and towns. Ten days after the students and actors in Prague went on strike, there was a general strike in protest against the rule of the Communist Party. According to a published survey, about half of the population actually stopped work for two hours on 27 November, and another quarter of the population joined the demonstrations which took place in cities and major towns throughout the country. Ten per cent refrained from participating in the strike in order to maintain essential services, and only 20 per cent did so either because they did not want to take part or because they were afraid of dismissal or other reprisals threatened by their superiors and by local party secretaries.

Two days after the strike the Federal Assembly abolished the article of the Czechoslovak constitution which enshrined the leading role of the Communist Party, and the Communist chairman of the Federal Assembly resigned. The new cabinet formed on 3 December consisted of fifteen Communists and five non-Communists. New mass demonstrations followed, and under the threat of another general strike the new government survived for only seven days. On 10 December the Communist president swore in a new government of national understanding which consisted of nine Communists and eleven non-Communists and then resigned. In January the prime minister and one of the deputy prime ministers resigned their party membership, reducing the number of Communists in the cabinet to seven out of twenty. On 28 December Alexandr Dubček was elected chairman of the Federal Assembly, and on 29 December the Federal Assembly elected Havel president of the republic (Wheaton and Kavan 1992). Allegiance to socialism was omitted from his constitutionally prescribed oath by agreement of all concerned. In contrast with Poland and Hungary, where reform-minded Communist leaders negotiated the end of communist rule in discussions with the opposition which stretched over several months, the communist system in Czechoslovakia fell within a few days.

A number of Western political commentators viewed this revolution led by actors and a playwright as a kind of absurd theatre in itself. Yet the change which it brought about was not only faster than the change anywhere else in Eastern Europe but also, with the possible exception of that in East Germany and Hungary, much more radical. Early in 1990 the People's Militia, the armed wing of the Communist Party, was dissolved, and the activities of the Communist Party in workplaces, the army, and the police were banned by law; most party property was put to new uses. Elections held in June 1990 involved twenty-three political parties and movements which covered the whole spectrum from ultra-right to radical left and resulted in the formation of a coalition government of the Civic Forum and Christian Democrats which began to pursue vigorously a policy of privatisation and transition to a free market economy.

How then do we explain the paradox that the most successful revolution in Eastern Europe was one which defied all textbook formulae – one which was started by students and led by intellectuals who had no support of the masses when they embarked on their political gamble? I want to argue that this paradox disappears once we begin to see 'politics' as an aspect of the cultural system. To sketch the role of Czech national traditions in giving shape to the course of political events known as the 'velvet revolution', I want to consider two questions: why the revolution was started by students, actors, and other intellectuals and why their public opposition to the communist regime was so swiftly followed by the masses.

An important instrument of communist propaganda was the unceasing comparison of the achievements of socialist Czechoslovakia with those of the pre-war capitalist Czechoslovak Republic. In this comparison socialist Czechoslovakia was far ahead: it had full employment, and basic education, medical care, and old-age pensions were available to everyone. It was also (naturally) winning hands down on the number of cars, bathrooms, radio sets, and other gadgets per family, not to mention television sets, of which there had been none at all in pre-war Czechoslovakia. Figures which were not to the advantage of the socialist system, such as the number of hospital beds in relation to the population or the average speed of passenger trains, were simply not mentioned, and pictures of Prague from the 1930s, portraying a lively and cosmopolitan city hardly resembling the drab and dilapidated Prague of the 1960s and 1970s, were nowhere to be seen.

This elementary trick of comparing the past with the present and presenting it as a comparison of one contemporary social system with another worked mainly because there were still enough older people around who could enliven the statistics with narratives of their personal experiences during the depression years of the 1930s. (Similar personal experiences of hardship in the 1930s were used to sustain the morale of the British miners striking against pit closures in the 1980s.) These narratives re-emerged in letters from old party members to the party newspaper *Rudé právo* in the early months of 1990 as arguments against privatisation and the introduction of an economic model based on market principles. The point is that it is 'lived' experience of this kind which gives credence to the statistics employed by official propaganda: statistical figures are experience-distant, and reality as it is understood by the people themselves can be apprehended only through concepts which are experience-near.

The proverbial denial of the values of the previous generation by the members of the subsequent one undoubtedly played some role, but the main reason for the politicisation of young people in Czechoslovakia was mainly that their experience was quite different from the experience of their parents and certainly of their grandparents. Most of those involved in the demonstration on 17 November and in the subsequent student strike had not even been born in 1968, and those who had been were too young to remember it. Their 'lived' experience was only with post-1968 Czechoslovakia, which they were comparing not with the Czechoslovakia of the past but with its contemporary neighbours to the West. In comparison with their counterparts there, they felt deprived in every respect: prevented from travelling, from playing and listening to music they liked, from reading books and looking at pictures they liked, from hearing more than one view on anything in the course of their education, and even from freely choosing whether to believe in God.

Another reason it was the young people who rebelled most openly against the state was that in their case one important tactic of the regime for forcing the population to toe the line was completely ineffective. Although the leading dissidents were given prison sentences after 1968, the main ways of controlling dissent were economic. Dissidents were prevented from getting employment appropriate to their qualifications and could at best earn their living in menial jobs. Examples of writers, journalists, actors, and priests employed as stokers, unskilled labourers, lumbermen, and – with luck – taxi drivers are legion. One of the most effective means of forcing potential dissidents to give up their subversive activity was discrimination against their children; irrespective of their academic achievements, they were denied access to higher education. It was one thing to engage in political opposition to the regime and suffer in consequence; it was another to engage in such opposition in the knowledge that one's children would suffer as well.

There is no doubt that using children as hostages was the most effective means of breaking down the widespread popular opposition which followed the invasion by Warsaw Pact armies in 1968 (Šimečka 1984). In 1989 young people were free from this particular kind of pressure. Of course, not only they themselves but their parents too could have suffered for their actions. But while it is difficult to justify the punishment of innocent children for the actions of their parents, it is not so difficult to justify the possible punishment of the parents for the actions of their children. After all, it was precisely the inactivity of the parents' generation which had created the mess in which the country found itself. The pride which people took in the students in November and December 1989 was remarkable. It was obvious that the students were managing to do what they themselves had always wanted, but never dared, to do.

The small circle of dissidents who stood in active opposition to the regime objected particularly to the systematic persecution of scholars, journalists, writers, poets, musicians, pop singers, and other artists who had declared their open support for the reforms of 1968 and who were unwilling to seek the regime's favour by publicly renouncing their 'ideological mistakes'. These active dissidents formed only a tiny minority of the country's intelligentsia, but their small circle included virtually all leading Czech and Slovak intellectuals, among them many of those who had contributed to the high international profile of Czechoslovak cinema, drama, and literature in the 1960s. Those who had not emigrated had been banned, forced to survive in menial occupations, and from time to time imprisoned; their creativity had been driven underground. The result was that hardly a novel, film, or drama of any significance had been published or performed in Czechoslovakia since 1968 (on Czech literature after 1968, see Pynsent 1994: 152). In the words of Heinrich Böll, Czechoslovakia had become 'a cultural Biafra'.

As the systematic creation of a cultural desert in post-1968 Czechoslovakia was seen as the gift of the state to people whose self-image was that of a highly cultured and well-educated nation, it is understandable that the persistence of rigid censorship and systematic and ruthless persecution of anyone expressing a thought which deviated from the official line was seen by the intellectuals as the state's betrayal of the very nation whose state it nominally was. The state's cultural policy turned the intellectuals against the state in the name of the nation of which they formed a part and in whose name they saw themselves as speaking. The actors joined the students in the strike not because they had any greater grudge against the state than other intellectuals but simply because they and the musicians who joined them were, because of their visibility, the only intellectuals who could strike effectively.

The idea that a strike in the theatres of London's West End could topple the British government when even miners and ambulance drivers had not come anywhere close to it is clearly laughable. Pursuing further this unimaginable parallel, we may amuse ourselves by contemplating how long a strike in the West End would have to last before workers in the Midlands and farmers in Northumberland or Cumbria would even notice it. The strike of actors in Prague theatres, however, not only spread like wildfire to all the other theatres and concert halls in the country and was emulated by other entertainers (such as the footballers who refused to play the scheduled league matches) but was followed in ten days by a country-wide general strike which made it clear to the ruling party that its time was up. Western commentators, who probably had in mind my hypothetical image of a strike in the West End, clearly thought that they were witnessing something approaching a miracle.

With hindsight it is clear that the general strike could have come much earlier; the intellectuals who led the revolution were themselves cautious in estimating the impact of their own action on the masses and thought that at least ten days were needed to rouse them from their apathy. Their caution derived from their awareness that Czechs and Slovaks did not suffer any significant economic deprivation. In spite of its technological backwardness, the Czechoslovak economy was in better shape than any other in Eastern Europe (with the possible exception of East Germany), and therefore one obvious source of widespread popular opposition to communist rule was missing. They were also very well aware that the specific grievances of the intellectuals did not motivate the population at large. Most people did not even know who the leading intellectuals were. When Havel first addressed the mass rallies, most people perceived him as one of 'those mysterious dissidents', and when he later emerged as the only serious candidate for the presidency, Czech newspapers hurriedly printed articles explaining who he was. There were cooperative farmers and factory workers who genuinely believed that if he really were a world-renowned playwright, his plays would surely have been staged in Czechoslovakia and they would have heard of him.

Whatever may objectively be the cultural and educational standard of those who expressed such views, they too were Czechs and saw themselves as part of a nation whose main characteristic was being cultured and well educated. What they resented as members of this nation was not the persecution of a few intellectuals but the affront of having to obey the orders of those who not only knew less than they should have in their positions but often knew less than those whom they were supposed to lead. The image of those in authority as blithering idiots was all-pervasive and an unceasing source of popular jokes. The Civic Forum skilfully exploited these feelings when it broadcast to the public in the street the secret recording of the general secretary's impromptu speech to the district party secretaries. The grammatically incorrect and syntactically incoherent speech of the once most powerful man in the country drove the point home without any need for further comment. The crowds of ordinary people who listened to this broadcast rolled with contemptuous laughter and in this act itself were displaying their own *kulturnost*; the message was 'Less cultured nations would shoot you; we laugh at you.'

What gave the 'velvet revolution' its impetus was the general feeling in the country that on 17 November, state repression had become unbearable. People's perception of themselves as a cultured and well-educated nation again played a significant role in fostering this general feeling. The 'uncultured' use of brute force by the state against the 'cultured' and peaceful demonstrators made it clear that the Czechs had a state that did not befit them as a cultured nation and that they deserved a better one. In an open confrontation of intellectuals and future intellectuals (students) with uncultured and uneducated power, the people's place could only be at the side of the cultured and educated. The myth of a nation whose leading personalities had always been intellectuals provided the charter for action and in the confrontation of intellectuals with the power of the state, perceived as uncultured and uneducated, the myth swayed the nation to the side of the intellectuals.

The rallying of the masses was of course considerably facilitated by the fact that the revolution took place in the television age. It was significant that the students were first joined in the strike by actors and that the actors were seen as the main representatives of the intellectuals, for actors have visibility which writers, poets, playwrights, and philosophers never do. Those in open rebellion against the state were not unknown dissidents but men and women whose names and faces were known from the television screen. This gave them an authority which the leading dissidents (including Havel) whose faces and often names were mostly unknown, could never have had. All this contributed to the perception of the 'velvet revolution' as a revolution of the cultured against the uncultured.

That the actors' strike had such a tremendous political impact derives to a great extent from the fact that the notion of the Czechs as a cultured nation and the notion of Czech history as giving meaning to contemporary events are encapsulated in the symbol of the National Theatre. Even those with only a smattering of knowledge of Czech history know two things about it. The first (which is not, in fact, historically accurate) is that the National Theatre, by keeping the Czech language alive, was instrumental to the survival of the Czech nation at a time when it was struggling by direct political means for its rights within the Austrian monarchy. The other (historically correct only to a certain extent) is that its construction was made possible only by the financial contributions of ordinary people (for many of whom it meant a considerable financial sacrifice) and that when it burnt down in 1881 before its construction was complete it was rebuilt in record time solely from such contributions. The words 'Nation to itself' above the proscenium arch call attention to this remarkable dedication to the national cause. The story of the building of the National Theatre is one of the most important national myths, and, in consequence, the theatre itself is one of the most important symbols of the Czech nation and, after Hradčany Castle, probably the most frequently visited: there are probably few Czechs who have never been to the National Theatre. It is known as 'the golden chapel' – a name which suggests that it is more important as a national shrine than as a venue for theatrical performances. Although the actors' strike did not start at the National Theatre, the fact that the actors of the National Theatre immediately joined it was of the utmost importance. The fact that the National Theatre was closed was an unmistakable sign that the nation was in crisis.

Both the tradition of the cultured and well-educated nation and the democratic tradition were instrumental in shaping the revolution of November 1989. Czechs manage unproblematically to preserve their belief in a democratic tradition as characteristic of their nation because all the past collapses of the democratic form of government can be seen as catastrophes imposed on it by others: by the Nazis in 1939, in a coup d'état inspired by Moscow in 1948, and by the Soviets in 1968. It was precisely the invocation of the Czech democratic tradition which enabled communist rule to be perceived as an imposition of an alien form of government upon the Czech nation. Although the Soviet Union did not govern Czechoslovakia in the same way as Nazi Germany governed its Protectorate of Bohemia and Moravia and although the Soviet troops were in no way instrumental in maintaining the post-1968 communist system, the Soviet army could still be perceived as an army of occupation and the Soviet Union as maintaining the Czech communist government in power. The tradition of democracy was invoked to inspire and mobilise the nation to rise against the undemocratic communist rule imposed from outside.

The invocation of the democratic tradition during the 'velvet revolution' and its aftermath helped to create hope that the Czechs could again achieve what they had – when left to their own devices – achieved in the past: a democratic society that befitted their tradition. One of the major aims of the 'velvet revolution' and the political and economic changes that followed it was to 'return Czechoslovakia to Europe'. The national traditions were invoked to foster the confidence that the Czechs, as a democratic, cultured, and well-educated nation, rightfully belonged to the West.

There were, of course, various other aspects of Czech culture which in many subtle ways played their role in the events of November 1989. Their significance is apparent from the fact that it was not only the actors' strike which led to the almost immediate politicisation of the whole population of the country, but also the brutal suppression of the students' demonstration by the police on 17 November. Like all the previous demonstrations, that of 17 November took place on a symbolically significant day: the fiftieth anniversary of the closing of all Czech universities in 1939 as a reprisal for student demonstrations against the Nazi occupation of Czechoslovakia. The demonstration of 17 November differed from the previous ones in two respects: it was allowed to take place after the city authorities had agreed with the students on the route of the march, and the police and what later appeared to have been specially trained anti-terrorist units brutally assaulted the students. Since the police blocked all possible escape routes after they had requested the students to disperse, the purpose of the attack was obviously not to break up the demonstration but to teach any potential demonstrator a lesson once and for all. The massacre, as it came to be called, occurred on one of Prague's major streets and, as a subsequent parliamentary inquiry indicated, had been planned by the police from the start (Wheaton and Kavan 1992: 41–8). On 17 November the state thus manifested its alienation from the nation in a doubly meaningful way: its repression became unbearable and, even more significantly, in its own way it repeated what the German fascists had done fifty years before.

Repression is the opposite of care, and the communist state spent a considerable amount of propaganda on presenting a caring image, mainly by stressing its role as the guarantor of the social security available to all citizens. In the Czech cultural conceptualisation, care is a typically feminine trait. The defining features of femininity are motherhood and the socialisation of children. Maternal sentiments are culturally assumed to be grounded in female nature and as such not susceptible to manipulation by culture and society. The result is a strong cultural affirmation of a naturally given association of women with the domestic domain (to the extent that the woman holds the purse strings and is responsible for running the domestic economy) and a naturally determined gravitation of women toward caring professions in the public domain. In 1990, 73 per cent of teachers were women, and the percentage of women employed in social services, retail trade, and health care was even greater (*Respekt*, 1993, no. 37: 1), and women outnumbered men not only as nurses but also as doctors. To give birth, to bring up children, and to be caring are the culturally assumed main characteristics of womanhood condensed in the image of the woman as mother.

The whole programme of the Czechoslovak Union of Women was built on this conceptualisation. (It may be worth mentioning in passing that one of the acts of the new government was to abolish the celebrations of International Women's Day and to reinstitute Mother's Day. This change met with no opposition, as if people were saying, 'Correct – what right does a woman have to be venerated unless she is a mother?') If motherhood, as a symbol with all its connotations, enters into the construction of the nation as a life-engendering entity, the state – construed as the guardian of the nation's interests – cannot but behave in a caring, that is, motherly way. It certainly cannot repress the members of the nation, the metaphorical children of the mother country. When it does, it alienates itself from the nation; it betrays it. And this is how it was perceived on 17 November, for then it was assaulting not just citizens – the metaphorical children of the nation – but actual children, 'the future of our nation'.

As is the case with many other cultural premises, those which motivated the perception of the events of 17 November were taken for granted rather than explicitly stated and their existence can only be inferred from discourses for which they served as unspoken assumptions. One such discourse was that concerning the action of the leadership of the Czechoslovak Union of Women after 17 November. The leadership expressed regret over the severity of the police action but instead of condemning it merely described it as 'disproportionate' to the task of maintaining public order. This formulation outraged the rank and file of the union, who saw in it a betrayal of the maternal feelings of the women whose interests the union was supposed to represent. The leadership was forced to resign, and at a congress called to discuss the future of the women's movement in Czechoslovakia the union dissolved itself, to be replaced by a number of independent women's organisations.

The revolution in Czechoslovakia was triggered by the state's assault on students (young people, our children) participating in an event for which it had itself given permission – an obvious sign of its betrayal of the nation. The nation's outrage against the state was given shape by intellectuals (mainly actors) and students, who were in the forefront of the popular revolt. The concepts brought into opposition during this revolt were not socialism and democracy – as most Western commentators were inclined to see it – but totalitarianism and freedom.

Demands for sweeping political change were articulated by representatives of Charter 77, other independent groups, and a few intellectuals and students who had so far stood outside these dissident circles in a meeting in a Prague theatre on 19 November. The opposition of the independent groups to communist power had always been formulated in terms of respect for citizens' legal rights, and the organisation which its representatives founded after the first street protests was appropriately called the Civic Forum. Its spokesman – Václav Havel – addressed the demonstrators on 21 November and subsequently presented the Forum's demands to the communist government and led the ensuing political negotiations. It was because of the Civic Forum that the conflict between the nation and its state was eventually redefined as a conflict between the citizens and the state.

Economic transformation

In present-day political rhetoric, Czech national traditions are invoked to buttress national identity and compensate for a lack of national confidence and solidarity. They are invoked to foster the identification of people with political goals construed as the goals of all Czechs. The national traditions are appropriate images for this purpose because the common national identity and goals which they invoke ignore the inequalities and conflicts within Czech society.

As elsewhere in the former socialist countries, the overthrow of the communist regime in Czechoslovakia was swiftly followed by the implementation of plans for a wide-ranging economic reform aimed at creating a market economy. Alongside the creation of a democratic political structure and a new system of central and local government and administration of justice, the reform of the systems of education and health care, etc., this was part of the revolutionary process of the creation of a post-communist social order. In many respects, it was the most important part of this process, for the introduction of a free market would inevitably effect changes in all spheres of social and political life. In contrast with the situation in many other countries of the former socialist bloc, the introduction of a market economy and the restitution of private property in Czechoslovakia were swift, successful, and welcomed by the majority of the population, although strong objections to particular aspects of the reform were also expressed.

In January 1990, when the government started to prepare the necessary legislation for the economic transformation and economic reform was being widely discussed by the public at large, 85 per cent of the people supported the programme of radical economic and social transformation and 68 per cent supported the introduction of a market economy with a substantial private sector which might lead to the bankruptcy of unprofitable firms. Fifty-six per cent of Czechs and 46 per cent of Slovaks expressed confidence in the eventual success of the reform and a belief that it would eventually lead to a general increase in the standard of living.[1] Only 9 per cent were opposed to the introduction of a market economy (*Forum*, 1990, no. 3; *Lidové noviny*, 14 December 1990, 24 February 1990). According to an opinion poll conducted before the official start of the economic reform on 1 January 1991, only 23 per cent of the people in the Czech lands (but

48 per cent in Slovakia) considered it a mistake; 75 per cent in the Czech lands (but only 57 per cent in Slovakia) were of the opinion that only economic reform would prevent the total collapse of the Czechoslovak economy (*Lidové noviny*, 28 December 1990).

The need to introduce a market economy was justified in both pragmatic and ideological terms. The view that the economy had to be restructured to avoid its eventual collapse predated the political change. Considered in terms of the economists' standard criteria of economic performance, the Czechoslovak economy had been in poor shape for a considerable time and had increasingly come to resemble that of a Third World country: productivity and the quality of manufactured goods were low, the rate of growth was declining steadily, the internal and external debt of the country and inflation (mostly hidden because of widespread subsidies) were increasing, and international trade was heavily biased toward the export of raw materials and the import of technology. All this had been recognised a long time before the political change at the end of 1989, and an important part of the old regime's political programme was the 'restructuring of the economic mechanism' – a phrase which replaced 'economic reform', ideologically tainted by its association with the reform attempts of Dubček's regime. 'Restructuring of the economic mechanism' envisioned some kind of strengthening of market relations but did not aim at abolishing central planning and the public ownership of property: its main aspects were better planning, tighter central control and more effective sanctions (mainly in the form of the distribution of state subsidies), and increased productivity through better work discipline.

In 1990, by contrast, the government programme of economic reform took the form of a complete abandonment of any central planning and its replacement by a liberal market economy in which the state would interfere only through its fiscal policies (taxation, control of the money supply, etc.). The possibility of a 'third road' which would combine some elements of a planned economy and some of a market economy was ruled out, and the only question remaining was the speed of the transition. Eventually the 'radicals' around the finance minister won the day over the 'gradualists', and a swift transition to a free market economy became the government's policy. The three main elements of the economic reform were the liberalisation of prices, to be determined solely by the market, the internal convertibility of the Czechoslovak currency, and privatisation of state and cooperative enterprises. The small ones, such as retail outlets, workshops, and restaurants, were sold at auctions and the large ones were converted into limited companies through the sale for a nominal price of 'investment vouchers' which could be redeemed for shares in the privatised companies or sold. Any citizen over the age of eighteen was entitled to purchase them and some eight and one-half million Czechoslovak citizens availed themselves of the opportunity.

However, the economic transformation was motivated by more than the need to boost the ailing economy. The market also had strong ideological connotations, and the transition to a free market was presented as the realisation of the goal of the 'velvet revolution'. The image which the Czechs have of themselves as a highly cultured and well-educated nation motivates what they call their 'return to Europe' and view as the ultimate goal of their revolution. Czechs have always detested being classified as Eastern Europeans and are quick to point out that Prague is west of Vienna and west of the line between Vienna and Berlin. For Czechs, Eastern Europe is Russia, Romania, Bulgaria, and possibly Poland, but their country is part of Central Europe and it is commonly described as lying in 'the heart of Europe' or even as being 'the heart of Europe'. Czechs use the concept of *kulturnost* to construct a boundary between themselves and the uncultured East into which they were lumped after the communist coup d'état in 1948, and they see their proper place as alongside the civilised, cultured, and educated nations of Western Europe. The idea of the 'return to Europe' dominated the election campaign in June 1990, and the transition to a market economy was construed as a necessary part of this re-entry. This notion was clearly articulated by Václav Klaus, the Czechoslovak minister of finance and chief architect of the economic reform:

As a slogan of our 'gentle revolution' we chose 'the return to Europe', including the adoption of an economic system which is characteristic of the civilised world and which shows that, in spite of all its shortcomings, no better arrangement of economic relations exists. *(Lidové noviny, 10 March 1990)*

The rhetoric in which the necessity of the transition to a market economy was couched constructed the market as a symbol of the civilisation to which Czech society now again aspired. As this symbol, the market was an integral part of the package of ideological notions, the other important elements of which were democracy and pluralism of ideas, all 'civilising mechanisms' which were destroyed under socialism. As Radim Valenčík expressed it in his analysis of 'real existing socialism',

the society which wanted 'to command the wind and the rain' grossly distorted the forms of the organisation of production based on market relations which had gradually been created in the process of historical genesis. The suppression of the market by centralist administrative-bureaucratic management resulted in the emergence of pre-capitalist relations – feudal ones, characteristic of the Asiatic mode of

production and even of lineage society. This social atavism led not only to stagnation (as it was euphemistically called) but also to an ever-accelerating rot.

(Tvorba, 1990, no. 42)

Shared cultural values were marshalled, however, not only in support of
the market but in support of objections to particular aspects of the economic reform. One of these values was national pride, distinctly heightened by the sweeping political change that took place in Czechoslovakia at
the end of 1989 and, particularly, by the style of this change. Czechs take a
distinct pride in the 'gentleness' of their revolution, which for them is a
sign of their *kulturnost*. They compare themselves favourably not only
with the Romanians, whose revolution was distinctly bloody and messy
and showed that they lacked the Czechs' *kulturnost*, but also with the Poles
and East Germans, who took much longer than the Czechs to achieve the
change. That the Poles and East Germans paved the way for the Czechs is
conveniently disregarded.

At the start of the economic reform, the self-image of Czechs as a cultured and civilised nation was often invoked in the moral condemnation of
money-changers and the emerging private entrepreneurs. As they offered
their services mostly to foreigners who did not know their way around,
they were perceived as destroying the Czechs' reputation as a cultured
nation and creating the undesirable image of Czechs as cheats, swindlers,
and profiteers. In so doing, they were seen as hampering the Czechs' return
to Europe: 'Would Europe really want us if we are not able to behave in a
civilised manner?'

National pride and the notion that Czech is best (expressed in the rhyme
Co je české, to je hezké, 'Czech is beautiful') also led to opposition to the
participation of foreign capital in Czech enterprises. This was spoken of as
the sell-off of national wealth, and three reasons were given for opposing
it. It was argued that the sale of shares in Czech enterprises to foreigners
would lead to the exploitation of Czech labour by foreign capital, to the
cheap export of labour and national wealth, and to the subjugation of the
Czech economy to foreign rather than to national interests. While, according to an opinion poll conducted in June 1990, 46 per cent of the people
approved of the sale of large unprofitable companies, only 23 per cent
approved of their sale without its being restricted to Czechoslovak citizens
and firms. Large firms in particular were the object of national pride, and
the objection to foreigners' participating in their ownership was particularly strong: while 44 per cent approved of the sale of small enterprises to
foreigners, only 18 per cent approved of the sale of large ones (*Lidové
noviny*, 18 June 1990). In January 1992, 43 per cent of Czechs were afraid

that the negative aspect of economic reform would be the sell-off of national wealth to foreign capital (*Aktuálne problémy Česko-Slovenska*, January 1992: 59).

Beyond being a symbol of 'civilisation' and 'modern society', the market was also a symbol of the rational organisation of society or even of rationality itself, and economic reform was often talked about as 'the return of rationality to our society' (*Forum*, 1990, no. 10) or as 'an experiment in the return to reason' (*Lidové noviny*, 11 July 1990). The introduction of a market economy was a return to 'the normal order' of things (Václav Klaus in *Literární noviny*, 2 August 1990).

The rationality of a market economy was seen as deriving from the fact that unlike a centrally planned economy, it was the result not of an ideological construction imposed artificially on society but of society's normal historical development. It was seen as 'a great historical invention of humankind' (*Forum*, 1990, no. 11) and in this respect, it was 'natural', whereas a planned economy was 'artificial':

[In a centrally planned economy] the price of labour and goods was determined *artificially*[2] and, moreover, even nonsensically according to ideological directives. However, modern society is organisationally directly dependent on the free exchange of services and goods, i.e., on a monetary principle.

(Vladimír Ulrich in Tvorba, *1990, no. 42)*

The planned economy is an *ideological construct* . . . in essence it is violence imposed on economics by politics. Nobody *constructed* the market economy – it developed *naturally*; what was useful survived, what was not useful died out.

(Otakar Turek in Literární noviny, *14 June 1990)*

The market economy and democracy are *natural* conditions of mankind, and it should be possible to return to such a *natural* state . . . At the beginning there may be only a few [entrepreneurs], but they will be heroes, the new pioneers who will breach the dam separating us from the *natural* state of affairs and take others along with them. *(Dušan Tříska in* Mladá fronta dnes, *12 September 1990)*

The market economy not only operated as a process of natural selection but was itself the result of the process of natural selection, and it was precisely this aspect of it which accounted for its effectiveness:

The market mechanism is the most perfect means to the satisfaction of the needs of all people created in the process of the historical development of society.

(Lidové noviny, *26 May 1990)*

The market economy achieved this perfection because it was not guided by political or ideological considerations but left to develop according to its own principles.

Table 5. *Images of the planned and the market economy*

Planned economy	Market economy
Atavistic survivals of pre-capitalist societal forms	Civilisation, modern society
Stagnation	Development
Irrationality	Rationality
Artificial	Normal, natural
Ideological construct	Result of pragmatic considerations
Subject to politics	Independent of politics

In this package of notions in terms of which economic reform was legit-imated, the various characteristics of a planned and a market economy were seen as in opposition (table 5). Each term in which the market economy was constructed in opposition to the centrally planned economy invoked a different kind of agency from the one invoked in socialist ideol-ogy. Part of that ideology was the construction of man as the master of nature, which he could shape to his own will. In terms of this ideological construction, man was the sole agent of social and economic processes: he was constructing socialism, the first just society, and he was constructing an economy in which people were rewarded according to their merits, not in virtue of inherited privileges, and in which they would ultimately be rewarded according to their needs. Human agency also positively affected natural processes, for the new man whom socialism brought into being could 'command the wind and the rain' as the slogan, now the object of ridicule and routinely invoked as the ultimate proof of communist folly (see the quotation from Valenčík, pp. 151–2 above), proclaimed.

It now became part of the ideological packaging of democratic plural-ism and the market economy to point out that man's tampering with society had led not to the freeing of human potential but to the suppres-sion of all human rights, not to the creation of a just society but to the cre-ation of a totalitarian system, not to the gradual withering of the state but to its increased interference in all aspects of its citizens' lives, not to the creation of a higher form of morality but to the destruction of all moral principles and a disregard for even the most rudimentary principles of 'civilised' behaviour. The rudeness of those employed to serve the public too was directly attributed to the absence of the market:

Anyone who has been in the West can testify that willingness, regard for others, and respect for their needs are quite common there. This is not in spite of but because of the fact that the market has reigned there for more than two hundred years and its 'invisible hand' has educated citizens in this way. 'The baker bakes good, cheap rolls not because he is an altruist but because he is an egoist' is one of the basic maxims of classical economics. Readiness to serve, a friendly attitude, and interest in the needs of the customer are basic conditions of survival in the competition of the market, and these qualities are then reflected in other interpersonal relations.   *(Anna Červenková in* Lidové noviny, *3 September 1990)*

Television commentators especially explain [the market mechanism] as a kind of self-salvation which will automatically deliver smiling shop assistants, waiters ready to serve us, correct measures of beer, and anything else we may ever wish for.
(Jan Hýsek in Forum, *1990, no. 44)*

It was stressed that man's attempt to 'command the wind and the rain' had resulted in unprecedented levels of pollution and ecological devastation which only the market could correct. In the words of the minister of finance,

The only solution to our ecological problems lies in the introduction of a *normal* market economy. We know very well that the environment is the most devastated in countries which lack a market economy. A *normally* functioning market economy is the crux of everything because it is an economy which lends to all goods, including water, air, and everything else, their correct price.
*(*Lidové noviny, *20 December 1990)*

As far as the economy itself was concerned, it was argued that man's tinkering with it had resulted in the transformation of Czechoslovakia from a country which before World War II enjoyed the tenth highest standard of living in the world into a country which at the end of the 1980s occupied forty-second place, well below many Third World countries. The message was easy to grasp: the prosperous countries were prosperous because, unlike us, they had never tinkered with their economies; they had let the market do the job rather than trying to do it themselves. Speaking of the aims of economic reform, Václav Klaus clearly expressed where the agency should lie: 'The aim is to let the invisible hand of the market act and replace the hand of the central planner' *(Forum, 1990, no. 18)*.

However, the necessity of introducing a market economy was justified not only in terms of the agency of the market, which, as a self-regulating mechanism, was capable of avoiding all the errors and deficiencies of an economy whose agents were planners, bureaucrats, and ideologists, but also in terms of the agency of those who participated in the market. In particular, the notion of the natural character of the market was predicated on both types of agency. On the one hand, the market was 'natural' as a self-regulating mechanism which itself determined prices and values in opposition to a centrally planned economy, in which prices and values were 'artificially' determined by human agents. The return to a market economy was, then, a return to the 'natural' state of society. But the market was also 'natural' because it was an arrangement of economic relations that corresponded to human nature. In consequence, when human nature was not interfered with, it always gave rise to the market:

[The market] is a great historical invention of humankind and it is never possible to destroy it completely. The striving of its participants for a bigger share has so far been the only basis of innovative movement and economic growth that corresponds to human *nature*.
(Forum, *1990, no. 11*)

This 'human nature' is the people's propensity toward private property, which is the main factor that motivates them to work:

In the case of small firms combined with the owner's direct work participation, private property is the most effective motivational factor.
(*Jaroslav Smrčka in* Forum, *1990, no. 10*)

It is a fact established through years of experience that in most branches of human activity private ownership is socially the most effective way of the management of material goods.
(Forum, *1990, no. 2*)

Repression of private property leads to diminished work motivation.
(Lidové noviny, *21 July 1990*)

During the November events, freedom was defined not positively (freedom for what) but negatively (freedom from what). The calls for freedom implied freedom from the oppression of the totalitarian state: freedom from constant surveillance by the secret police, from restrictions on travel abroad, from censorship (which concerned not only writers but also various pop groups and aficionados of contemporary Western pop music), from restrictions on access to higher education, from political qualifications for most non-manual jobs, and from many other forms of state intervention in personal lives. The positive content was given to freedom not by the demonstrators themselves but by the politicians who came to power during and after the revolution. While equating freedom with democracy in political terms, in economic terms they equated it with private ownership, the restitution of which became the main element of the economic transformation.

Although no demands were expressed for the restitution of private ownership during the mass demonstrations of November 1989 and although the initiation of the economic transformation met not only with approval in some quarters but also with scepticism and apprehension in others,[3] privatisation and the restitution of private property were soon accepted by most people. This is because the institution of a market economy basically legalised the effective private ownership which had prevailed in the official socialist economic system. In that system, enterprises in 'socialist ownership' were officially declared to be in the common ownership of all people and in the popular perception they were seen as belonging to no one. In fact, from the economic point of view they were the effective property of their socialist managers. It was impossible to buy a lucrative petrol station, a workshop, a shop, or a restaurant, but for those whose right it was to make decisions about the management of such enterprises and outlets, it was possible to place a relative or – for a price – an acquaintance there as manager. For the manager the enterprise was a source of financial gain through overpricing, pilfering, and in other ways cheating the legal owner – the state. It also offered the possibility of providing goods in short supply to those who were, in this 'market system', able to supply desirable counterservices, including other goods in short supply, labour in servicing one's car or building or extending one's house, medical treatment in a state hospital, or even admission of one's child to a high school or university (Možný 1991: 19). Anyone who had scarce goods, skills, or favours to 'sell' was in one way or another involved in this hidden 'market economy', in which all goods and services were obtainable for their realistic 'market price'.

The most tangible expression of any private ownership that was left in communist Czechoslovakia became the ownership of weekend homes ranging from little wooden cabins to substantial cottages and farmhouses. The intellectuals who justified private ownership ideologically as the basis of freedom argued that the 'possibility of caring about [even a small] part of the world is something so basic that even the communist states eventually had to allow it' and had to tolerate the private ownership of holiday cabins and cottages.[4] 'That was that bit of the world where even our "working man" was free for two days of the week', for he could, in his own way, without any interference from the state, care about a small part of the world:

A *natural* expression and a tangible form of this care about a piece of the world is private property: a house, a garden, a workshop, a shop. Ownership and property are, in this form, a condition of normal human *freedom*.

(Jan Sokol in Přítomnost, *1990, no. 1: 8–9)*

Because the opposing notions in November 1989 were not socialism versus democracy but totalitarianism versus freedom, the debate surrounding the economic reform in Czechoslovakia did not suggest an ideological link of the free market to democracy through the notion of individual freedom, as most Western analysts are inclined to argue. In their conceptualisation, just as only democratic pluralism guarantees individual freedom of political choice, only the market guarantees individual freedom of economic choice. Individual freedom of economic choice is ultimately freedom of choice among competing products, that is, consumer choice. In this conceptualisation, the notion of a free market is part of an ideological package including pluralism, competition, and freedom of choice as opposed to the centralism, cooperation in the realisation of a common societal goal, and equity of needs which formed the package of notions characteristic of socialist ideology.

In the Czech conceptualisation, the link between the market and freedom is construed differently. It is not so much freedom in the sense of the exercise of choice as freedom in the sense of an unconstrained expression of human nature that is linked to the concept of the market. If private property is construed as part of human nature, only a free market economy based on private ownership of the means of production offers people real freedom, for, in contrast to the planned economy, it does not constrain their natural propensity toward it:

> Private ownership is not only the basis of a market economy but one of the main guarantees of human *freedom* in general.
>
> *(Josef Mlejnek Jr in* Český deník, *12 September 1992)*

The tangible symbol of freedom is not consumer choice but private ownership, and this symbol was invoked to justify the economic reform: to achieve freedom we must have a free market, the precondition of which is private ownership. Privatisation then logically becomes the key element of the economic reform.

This construction of freedom as the freedom not of consumers but of producers (who are owners) was consistent with the emphasis on the production side of the economy. In the early days of post-communist Czechoslovakia, consumer choice appeared to be at best only a distant ideal. Demand considerably outweighed supply, and the emphasis on production reflected the reformers' goal of boosting the productivity and increasing supply. They openly admitted that achieving this goal would mean at least a temporary tightening of belts, for prices would rise when subsidies were eliminated. This emphasis on productivity is similar to the policies of the International Monetary Fund and the World Bank, which insist on the introduction of various austerity measures as the condition for credit. That the terms 'market' and 'world market' themselves entail an emphasis on production rather than consumption is suggested by the rhetoric of 'penetrating the market' or 'gaining new markets'. The market is understood as a place where commodities can be disposed of, and who or what is the source of the countervalue which is exchanged for the commodities in the market seems to be of little concern. The Czech conception of the market corresponds to this conceptualisation.

In line with this conceptualisation of the market is the fact that most people see themselves as the market's passive objects and not as active agents who through the exercise of choice influence the quantity, quality, and price of commodities. What they experience is not the working of incipient market forces but the practices of emerging entrepreneurs, which they evaluate by moral rather than economic criteria. The private entrepreneurs who have taken advantage of the government's policy of price liberalisation to set their prices above the level previously established by the state are seen as profiteers. The state, pursuing a policy of minimum administrative interference in the running of the economy, tends to see these activities as excesses that will automatically disappear once the free market is fully established. The pressure on the government to control overcharging (a criminal offence when all prices were centrally determined) is countered by elementary lessons about people's envisaged role as active agents in the market and the power they exercise as consumers. At the beginning of the economic reform, women's magazines and daily newspapers printed articles whose message was 'If you think it is expensive, do not buy it. If they cannot sell it for its asking price, they will have to lower the price.'

However, the practical policy of economic reform has not been able to ignore all the objections to market economy which stem from the perception of entrepreneurs as the active agents of the market and customers as its passive objects. When the privatisation of retail outlets, restaurants, and workshops (the so-called 'small privatisation') was being discussed, the concern was often expressed that the new owners would stop selling the goods which until then had been retailed in the shops and begin selling merchandise which would guarantee them more immediate profit. If the new private entrepreneurs were allowed unlimited freedom in choosing the goods they wanted to sell, it was argued, the customers would suffer. The government eventually yielded to these arguments, and legislation was passed which forced the new private owners of grocery shops to continue selling groceries for at least a year. In the early days of the economic reform, the main objects of moral indignation were the street money-changers (*veksláci*). As they operated without licences, their activities remained illegal as they had been under the previous regime, but after the collapse of the communist system they operated virtually with impunity. Like entrepreneurs who drove prices above what they should be, they drove up the exchange rate, and this was seen as immoral because it undermined the 'just' price.

However, the government did not yield to the public's outrage. The opening of the country's borders and the resulting influx of tourists had not yet been matched by the necessary expansion of banks and exchange bureaux. In this situation, street money-changers provided a service without which the tourist industry – an important source of badly needed foreign currency – would break down. With the subsequent devaluation of the Czechoslovak currency, the difference between the official and the black market exchange rates had narrowed considerably, and the government did not see the money-changers as a serious threat to the economy. Providing companies with the hard currency they needed, they offered services which were a welcome addition to those available through the underdeveloped banking system. Moreover, their activities were seen as those of entrepreneurs who operated effectively according to the principle of supply and demand and thus contributed positively to setting the only 'realistic' exchange rate. The government was, on the whole, inclined to see them as people who would either gradually be absorbed into the emerging banking system or eventually go out of business once the currency had become fully convertible and the necessary number of licensed exchange offices had been established as a result of a fully operational market. All that in fact quickly happened, and the once ubiquitous illegal money-changers have become a rare sight on Prague streets.

Irrespective of whether a collectivity is imagined as a collection of heterogeneous individuals or individuals are imagined as parts of a whole (giving rise to the opposed notions of individualism and collectivism), the relationship between the individuals themselves can be imagined as either hierarchical or egalitarian. Seen in terms of these two dichotomies, Czech society is characterised by egalitarian collectivism. Suppression of individual difference and personal autonomy engenders a strong egalitarian ethos ('We all have the same stomach'), which in socialist Czechoslovakia was realised in practice to a much greater degree than anywhere else in Eastern Europe. In 1979, for example, the highest income was only two and one-half times the lowest and according to a 1984 survey of attitudes and values there was widespread support for a further decrease in wage differentials (Wolchik 1991: 172–5). In an opinion survey conducted in 1990 before the start of the economic reform, four-fifths of the respondents said that their efforts and work products had no influence on their salaries (*Lidové noviny*, 21 December 1990). These facts and perceptions were seen by the economic reformers of the Prague Spring as dampening personal initiative and hindering economic development but they were never an issue of popular concern. If anything, Czechs found it distinctly comforting: so long as no one has much more than I do, things are as they should be. Although it would be foolish to deny that forty years of socialism in Czechoslovakia had played their part in strengthening the egalitarian ethos, it seems to me that the ideal of egalitarianism was the aspect of the socialist ideology to which Czechs objected least, precisely because it built upon Czech cultural values which, like individualism in England (McFarlane 1978), had deep historical roots. After the demise of the Czech nobility during the Counter-Reformation the major class and status division paralleled the basic ethnic division and this situation did not change during the eighteenth and nineteenth centuries when the rising capitalist class in Bohemia was German or at least spoke German. National legends have always taken cognisance of this egalitarian ethos, and this in fact may have helped make it possible to eliminate the private economic sector to a much greater extent than anywhere else in the socialist bloc.

The Masaryk legend put great emphasis on his ordinariness. Every schoolchild knew that he slept on a simple military iron bed and enjoyed simple food, and nothing symbolised his hatred of ostentation more than the simple military-style tunic and military-style hat with a ribbon in the national colours which appeared to be almost the only items in his wardrobe. Stories about the headaches of the personal bodyguards whose watchful eyes he constantly tried to escape communicated his dislike of privilege. President Havel has gradually been acquiring a similar image. Soon after his election, Czech newspapers and television reported that after his visit to the largest factory in Prague he stopped at the local pub for a beer. Although he has consistently enjoyed great popularity, the fact that he comes from a wealthy family and as an internationally successful playwright has always been rather well off, even under the communist regime, diminishes his standing in the eyes of many Czechs. When in 1993 he bought a large villa and moved into it from his flat, it was reported in virtually every Czech newspaper and the price which he allegedly paid was for a time the main topic of everyday conversation. In contrast, the popularity of Václav Klaus was greatly enhanced by the fact that he has continued to live in his flat in a prefabricated tenement house even after becoming prime minister. To discredit him before the elections, his political opponents spread the rumour that he was buying a villa in one of the most prestigious Prague suburbs.

A market in which entrepreneurs were perceived as active subjects and everyone else as a passive object offended the cultural ideal of equality and minimal material disparities and differences in lifestyles within society. The market economy was perceived as a system which increased differences in wealth, and only 40.3 per cent of those who expressed their intention to vote for non-Communist parties in the June 1990 elections and only 18.5 per cent of those who intended to vote for the Communist Party found the increased differentiation acceptable. By contrast, 70 per cent of the potential non-Communist voters and 42.9 per cent of the potential Communist voters supported the transition to a market economy (*Forum*, 1990, no. 6). According to an opinion poll conducted in December 1990, 57 per cent feared that economic reform would make it possible for some people to become extremely rich (*Lidové noviny*, 28 December 1990). Fear of increased inequality was also reflected in differing attitudes toward the different forms of privatisation. According to an opinion poll conducted in the first year of the privatisation programme, 81 per cent of Czechs had confidence in small-scale privatisation, but the restitution of property to its original private owners or their heirs was supported by only 49 per cent (*Aktuálne problémy Česko-Slovenska*, January 1992: 60).

The deep-rooted commitment to social equality was seen by the architects of the economic reform as perhaps the most serious potential danger to its success. This led to exhortations that 'to be responsible for oneself is the sign of human and civic maturity' (*Lidové noviny*, 27 July 1990), that 'a market economy gives the capable and hard-working a chance', and that 'each of us has to learn to look after himself', as the former prime minister Marian Čalfa expressed it (*Lidové noviny*, 11 July 1990). In its turn, this rhetoric led to the expression of feelings that 'the economic reform and all the changes which are connected with it address the citizens of the republic as if they all were only businessmen, managers, and entrepreneurs' (Václav Slavík in *Rudé právo*, 15 November 1990).

Acknowledging the strength of egalitarian feelings, the reformers argued that this ideal had never been achieved. It had existed even under communism, although then it was based on ideological and political privileges rather than on the degree to which one contributed to the creation of wealth which guaranteed a high standard of living for all. Given that inequality was a necessary condition of living in society, they argued, a market economy was just, or at least less unjust than the centrally planned economy, for 'only market relations will show who really deserves what' (V.

Klaus in *Literární noviny*, 2 August 1990). The market economy 'builds on the ability, skill, and wits of all, not only on the wits of the leading "elite" as was the case in the system of centrally planned economy' (Otakar Turek in *Literární noviny*, 14 June 1990). This view was, however, far from widespread. Those who had 'worked honestly' under socialism saw themselves as discriminated against because they had never been able to accumulate the capital which would have enabled them to become entrepreneurs. Some commentators argued that the ideologically motivated preference for private property was 'the betrayal of the programme of the November revolution, which expressed equality of all forms of ownership and not only a preference for one of them' (Jiří Vraný in *Tvorba*, 1990, no. 45). People expressed a similar view in complaining that the market was privileging those who had once controlled the distribution of housing, higher education, cars, and other scarce goods and commanded substantial bribes – that only those who had prospered under totalitarianism were destined to prosper under the market economy. These people were referred to as 'the mafia', and the prevailing collective image of them was as an octopus with society firmly in its tentacles. The question of the laundering of dirty money became a prominent element of the debate over economic reform. The government's attitude that attempting to regulate the sources of capital of the new private entrepreneurs would only delay the economic reform and thus worsen the already dismal economic situation strengthened fears of a new totalitarianism.

Democratic tradition and political culture
Czech national traditions are not generalisations of actual events of Czech history but formulations of ideals. For the ideals to remain credible, the gap between the ideal and the real has to be bridged; the ideal must be realised in practice at least from time to time. This realisation is most effective if accomplished by those in the public eye, whose practical conduct and attitudes are open to public scrutiny and with whom the public can empathise. If the chosen representatives of the nation can be seen to be living up to the ideals embodied in national traditions, the existence of the traditions, like the existence of the characteristic traits which Czechs attribute to themselves, can be proved by ostension ('Are we not a well-educated and cultured nation? Look at Havel'). I would suggest that it was once more the invocation of the ideals of a democratic, cultured, and well-educated nation which led to Havel's being unopposed for president after the November revolution. As a world-renowned playwright and intellectual and a man who persistently fought for democratic rights at the cost of

great personal suffering, he was the man who could be seen as best embodying Czech national traditions. The choice of Masaryk – a philosopher and social thinker – as the first president of Czechoslovakia in 1918 was largely motivated by the same considerations. After two years in office, Havel still enjoyed the support of 80 per cent of Czechs (his popularity was less in Slovakia), who, pointing at Havel, compared themselves favourably with the Poles, who in their view had in Wałensa, an electrician and trade unionist, the president they deserved.

To embody the ideals whose carriers are not particular individuals but the nation as a whole, the chosen representatives of the nation have to be able to transcend the characteristic traits which Czechs ascribe to themselves and which are embodied in the image of the little Czech. Because one of these traits is intolerance of individual difference, they must be individualists, by definition – people able to approach their own lives as conscious objects and to make a selection among the attitudes and customs existing in their social environment. They have to be able to distance themselves critically from the social and cultural environment in which they live and seek ways of putting the imprint of their own individuality on the world that has emerged from the given situation (Heller 1984: 22–3). In other words, they have to be capable of living up to the ideal embodied in the national traditions and subscribing in practice to different values from those to which most Czechs pragmatically subscribe. The ideology expressed in terms of national traditions is holistic in that it 'valorizes the social whole and neglects or subordinates the human individual' (Dumont 1986: 279). Yet, paradoxically, to remain credible it has to be enacted by people whose own personal philosophy is highly individualistic. Havel's individualist attitude is best described by himself:

When all power in the communist countries is in the hands of the bureaucratic apparatus of one political party, then it is of course understandably worse than when there are two parties which are under control of freely expressed public opinion and when the public can choose between them in elections. Nevertheless, I do not consider even that to be ideal. It would appear to me more meaningful for people to be elected rather than parties . . . for politicians to canvass for the favour of the voters in their own right as concrete human beings and not merely as members of the party machine or as its favourites . . . I am not against the solidarity and cohesion of different interest groups; I am merely against anything that dilutes personal responsibility or that rewards anyone for his obedience to a power-oriented group.
                                                                    (1990a: 19–20)

To venerate the collective ideal, the nation which imagines itself to have a strong democratic tradition, must, paradoxically, venerate an individual hero and thus create its specific political culture.

Pointing to the fact that Czechoslovakia was the only democratic country in Central Europe between the two world wars, a number of analysts have stressed the democratic tradition as an important part of Czechoslovak political life. However, the Czechoslovak political culture before the war was based on the notion of power concentrated in the centre and its infallibility. Numerous historians today point to authoritarian elements in pre-war Czechoslovak democracy, particularly in relation to the role of Masaryk in Czechoslovak politics. Although he was not a dictator, Masaryk was generally seen as the central political figure of the republic, in which political decision making effectively involved only a small group (Leff 1988: 48–50, 61). This quasi-presidential form of government is perhaps best captured in the phrase 'Masaryk's republic'. Although he never publicly challenged the constitutional constraints on the presidency, he managed to circumvent them in the actual running of the state, and for this reason, Campbell (1975) describes Czechoslovak democracy as 'directed democracy'.

During the pre-war republic, the list system of the Czechoslovak form of proportional representation 'led to highly oligarchic party organisations, with party bosses exercising near-dictatorial powers' (Barnard 1991: 138). Parliament did not, however, play a decisive role in political decision making. Political decisions were made in the 'Fiver' (*Pětka*) – a coordinating body consisting of the leaders of the most powerful parties which Masaryk created in 1920 and which lasted for six years as a kind of 'state council' in spite of the fact that the party leaders themselves often had no seat in the parliament. The decisions reached by the 'Fiver' were binding on all the deputies of the five parties. During the crisis of 1938, the parliament was replaced by the 'Twenty' deputies delegated by the ruling coalition parties. The ultimate responsibility was placed in the hands of the president, who never declined to play the decisive political role and who distinctly preferred to work with a small, knowledgeable elite than with elected politicians, most of whom were in his opinion 'still insufficiently educated politically to bear the responsibility for leading a state' (Barnard 1991: 138). The general acceptance of Masaryk as the charismatic leader of the new Czechoslovak state led to the general acceptance of his nominating Beneš as his successor, making the constitutionally prescribed election of the president by the parliament a formality. According to the constitution, anyone could become president, but in fact there always was only one serious candidate – the heir apparent. Serious politicians avoided this role, and anyone who tried to assume it was suspect.

In 1989 Václav Havel personified all the required characteristics of a president. He symbolised the opposition to the communist regime with which most people wholeheartedly agreed but very few were willing to demonstrate through their actions. He thus represented an almost messianic figure, metaphorically bearing the cross of the oppressed nation. Significant in the meteoric rise of his popularity after the 'velvet revolution' was not only that he was seen as its leader but also that he never reproached anyone for not having behaved as he had during the communist regime and publicly acknowledged that everyone, himself included, through compliance with the formal demands of the totalitarian regime, had contributed to its maintenance (Havel *et al.* 1985; Havel 1990b: 12).

In the presidential elections in 1992 he was again the only candidate but this time he was not elected because the Slovak deputies in the parliament – for whom he epitomised Czech domination over the Slovaks – did not vote for him. This was seen by most Czechs as a clear manifestation of Slovak separatism and betrayal of the ideals of the Czechoslovak state. The only candidate put forward in the second round was the leader of the ultra right-wing Republican Party. Other Czech political parties, concerned for their reputations, recognised that it would be political suicide for them to nominate a candidate for the presidency. The leader of the Republican Party was not elected. The fact that some deputies of other parties voted for him was generally seen as a scandal. That the leader of the Republican Party was perceived as an usurper of the throne rightfully belonging to Havel was vividly demonstrated by the fact that he was physically assaulted by an angry crowd when he was leaving the parliament building.

A relatively strong tendency to emphasise the authority of the leading political personality over the formal political structures manifests itself in the continuing debates whether, for example, Beneš could or should have acted differently during the Munich crisis in 1938 or whether Dubček could or should have acted differently in 1968. In February 1948 the Czech people were willing to show their confidence in Beneš and to accept his authority at the cost of fundamental constitutional changes and the curbing of traditional civil liberties. This tendency to accept the charismatic authority of political leaders, which during the pre-war republic facilitated the creation of political consensus and political decision making, manifested itself equally strongly in 1945. Skilling (1976) speaks in this respect about the 'domestic roots of Stalinism'. In his speech on the occasion of the second anniversary of 17 November, in an attempt to resolve the paralysis of the parliament, Havel questioned its authority in favour of the authority of the president. His appeal led to mass support during public street demonstrations.

A political culture determined by the notion of power concentrated in the centre and its infallibility (such as that of the Soviet Union (White 1979: 107)) produces a cult of the leader manifesting itself in the erection of monuments to the living person, the naming of streets, institutions, and encyclopaedias after him, and the official celebrations of his birthdays. In pre-war Czechoslovakia Masaryk was the object of such a cult (see Pynsent 1994: 193–4). It is paradoxical that people were taught democracy almost single-handedly by this philosopher-president. The role of Havel in present-day Czech politics is analogous to Masaryk's. Although certain of his advisers have often been the object of popular criticism and scorn, criticism of Havel is seen by most Czechs as in bad taste. The analogy with legends about good kings and their treacherous and unfaithful courtiers is striking.

But perhaps there is nothing paradoxical in this situation: by being chosen to represent the traditions of the nation, the hero relieves others from the necessity to live up to their ideals and makes it possible to maintain the credibility of an ideal which would otherwise be challenged by the historical experience of the masses. It is ultimately through venerating his heroes that the autocratic, intolerant, begrudging, and not exceptionally cultured or educated little Czech can still consider himself to belong to a democratic, cultured, and well-educated nation.

6

Nation and state in the context of Czech culture

The discourse surrounding the beginning of the economic transformation in post-communist Czechoslovakia explicitly contrasted the socialist planned economy with the market economy. The opposition between a natural process and human design which it articulated was explicitly posed by Prime Minister Václav Klaus in a television interview in October 1992 in which he objected to the interviewer's formulation 'instituting a market economy' and his question of when the process would be completed. In Klaus's view, a market economy was not something that could be instituted by human beings and certainly not something that could be declared as having been successfully instituted from a specific date. Rather it was a 'spontaneous process', and all people could do was to create the legislative conditions that would allow it to take place. The opposition between the naturally constituted or given and the artificially created through deliberate human design is an opposition that not only articulates and gives form to economic discourse but is regularly invoked and pervasive in many other discourses and in that sense can be seen as an important dichotomy of Czech culture.

Like any other culture, Czech culture is not isolated from others. Czechs constantly compare themselves with others, and Czech culture accepts new ideas and values from other cultures. This process is, however, highly selective, and it is again the opposition between the naturally constituted and the consciously created that provides the gauge for the acceptance or rejection of new trends. In the past several decades, the two most important trends that have emerged in the West have been the ecological and the feminist movements, and each has had a distinctly different impact on Czech culture.

The ecological discourse

Ecological awareness is now firmly a part of Czech culture, and the ecological movement was an important form of opposition to the communist regime, whose policy of extensive economic development was seen as the main cause of the increasing destruction of the natural environment evident in the dying forests of northern and western Bohemia, the polluted air and water of much of the country, and the deterioration in the quality of agricultural land. The supporters of the ecological movement considerably outnumbered the dissidents, and during the last years of communist rule in Czechoslovakia ecological protest became the most important form of expression of disagreement with the communist system. Whereas the regime tried to suppress the dissident movement, its main strategy vis-à-vis the ecological movement was to co-opt it (Wheaton and Kavan 1992: 24, 29).

In communist Czechoslovakia, private ownership acquired a different meaning from ownership in Western European countries with highly developed consumer societies. The ideal of most Czechs was to own a flat (or at least its contents), a car, and a holiday home and thus to create a space into which they could withdraw from the public sphere of employment and politics with which they were unable to identify. The visible deterioration of the environment was felt as an intrusion of the public domain into this private sphere and a violation of its sanctity. People who had their own cars but were forced to drive on congested roads and to breathe poisonous emissions, who could spend two days a week in their holiday homes but remained as exposed there as anywhere else to air polluted by numerous industrial plants, or who were able to buy enough food but were aware that it was highly contaminated came to see ecology as the main problem.

For the most part, the ecological movement in Czechoslovakia was not motivated by the perception of the environment as a whole of which humans are an integral part which has been gaining ground in ecological discourse in the West since the 1960s. According to this perception, nature has an intrinsic value that exists independently of human needs, experiences, and evaluations. In the centre of this perception is not man-in-the-environment but the interrelationship of all the elements of the biotic whole. The movement in Czechoslovakia instead embraced for the most part the traditional Western perception, rooted in Christianity, of people's relationship to the environment. The book of Genesis enjoins people to dominate over nature, which God gave them to use. With Protestantism

emerged the notion of individual responsibility for the rational understanding and harnessing of nature which modern theologians express in
the idea of stewardship: people have the right to use nature for their
benefit but also have duties toward it; they must respect it as God's creation and are responsible to God for it.

In this view, nature has an instrumental value in that it provides
resources which people use. It is the means for the creation of new value.
This conception of the environment forms the basis of many Czech environmental concerns. Differences in average life expectancy in areas polluted to different degrees, for example, are pointed out. The necessity of
protecting domestic animals against mistreatment is legitimated by bio-
chemical evidence that their suffering diminishes the quality of their meat
for human consumption. The main argument for the protection of environment is people's health and the health of their children and future generations; one of the most visible environmental groups is the 'Prague
mothers', who, with their children in protective masks, occasionally
demonstrate against the polluted atmosphere and who in 1991 threatened
to keep their children home from school on days when the concentration
of sulphur dioxide in the atmosphere exceeded the officially acceptable
level.

Against the background of this perception of people's place in the environment, the expressed concerns with environmental issues reflected, on
the one hand, an awareness of the deep crisis of the socialist system and,
on the other, a radical critique of it. Awareness of the crisis was most
forcefully driven home by the fact that Czechoslovakia had both a lower
standard of living and lower life expectancy than Western capitalist countries. In 1960 Czechoslovakia occupied eleventh place among the nations
of the world in average life expectancy, but by 1989 it had dropped to
approximately fortieth place. Whilst in Western industrial countries life
expectancy for women was 79.0 years and for men 72.5 years, life
expectancy for women in the Czech Republic was only 75.4 years and for
men 68.1 years, approximating that of countries such as Uruguay, Chile,
or Panama. In the highly polluted areas of northern Bohemia, life
expectancy was even lower. The figures for infant mortality were even
worse. Whilst in Western industrial countries the rate of infant mortality
(measured in the number of children deceased before the age of one year
in relation to the number of children born during the same time) was 122.5
in 1989, in the Czech Republic it was 188.6 (*Data a fakta*, no. 4, December
1991). This clearly indicated that the constant growth and progress
through extensive industrialisation on which the building of socialist

society was predicated had failed dismally. Socialism had delivered neither a higher standard of living nor a healthier and longer life.

The ecological movement in Czechoslovakia reflected anxieties resulting from living in a society which was perceived to be in crisis. It not only expressed dissatisfaction with the ways in which life in a socialist society was shaped but articulated concerns over important moral and existential realities. Issues of the physical environment, being tangible and therefore perceived as 'objective' in terms of the scientifically biased Western culture, were readily understandable symbols of these wider moral and existential issues (see Grove-White 1993). In the Czechoslovak case, an additional reason for concentration on the issues of the physical environment stemmed from the fact that under the communist system no discourse openly voicing moral and existential anxieties would have been tolerated. For these anxieties to be voiced at all they had to be expressed in terms of a discourse in which the party and the government were forced to take part. Not even they could have denied the deterioration of the environment during the previous twenty years. The party's leading role in society, enshrined in the constitution, gave it not only a monopoly of power but also a monopoly of responsibility. When reminded of this responsibility by people concerned with ecological problems, it could not simply label them as agents of Western imperialist agencies aiming at the destruction of the socialist system, as it did the dissidents campaigning against the violation of human rights.

The fact that in the ecological discourse the environment figured primarily as a tangible symbol of the wider ills of the socialist system is attested to by the development of the ecological movement since November 1989. Although the quality of the environment has not greatly improved, there has been a noticeable decline of ecological awareness. In opinion surveys, protection of the environment dropped from the first place which it still occupied in March 1991 among society's problems (*Data a fakta*, no. 9, March 1992) to seventh place in 1992 (*Respekt*, 1993, no. 1: 9). Whilst in June 1990, 44 per cent of the inhabitants of the Czech Republic were dissatisfied with the quality of the environment, their number had dropped to 28 per cent in July 1993, although in northern Bohemia, where the pollution and the general environmental degradation have reached record levels, 61 per cent of the people expressed dissatisfaction with the state of the environment even in 1993. The government ascribes this trend to the strengthening of environmental legislation and to people's belief that the overall transformation of society will bring about improvement in the environment as well. Ecological activists argue that people's interest in environmental issues has been overshadowed by the political and social concerns which the transformation of the society naturally brings in its train, and that their diminishing interest in the environment is the result of propaganda presenting the government as deeply concerned with ecological problems and systematically working toward their gradual alleviation (*Lidové noviny*, 11 August 1993).

The gender discourse

In contrast to the ecological movement, which began to have its impact long before the final overthrow of the communist regime, the feminist movement came to affect Czech discourse only gradually after the November events. The first public debate on feminism was broadcast on television in the autumn of 1992, and a book hailed as the first Czech feminist writing appeared only in that year (Biedermannová 1992), which also saw an issue of the main Czech philosophical journal devoted mostly to feminist philosophy (*Filozofický časopis*, 1992, no. 5). The public debate was triggered by a series of light-hearted articles on sexual harassment by Josef Škvorecký in the political and cultural weekly *Respekt* (1992, nos. 32 and 39). In these he dismissed the notion of sexual harassment as a misguided and ludicrous idea which, if taken to its logical conclusion, would make it impossible for men to communicate with women at all. It is symptomatic that most of the adverse reactions to Škvorecký's views, which can be seen as part of the male backlash against radical feminism, were written by Czech men and women living in the West rather than by those living in the Czech Republic.

Although a few middle-class, university-educated Czech women call themselves feminists, most women reject this label and distance themselves from the premises and aims of the feminist movement. The representatives of some of the women's organisations which emerged alongside and partly replaced the pre-revolutionary Union of Czechoslovak Women (now the Czech Union of Women) emphasise that they do not want to be feminists. Women's organisations, such as the Movement for the Equality of Rights of Women of Bohemia and Moravia, campaign for a greater role for men in the family and women in society, to be achieved by raising women's self-consciousness. The activists of the movement themselves admit that their efforts have not met with much interest among Czech women.

Basic socio-economic differences between capitalist and socialist systems account to a great extent for the differences in the impact of and attitudes to the feminist movement in the West and in the Czech lands. As did all of the socialist countries, Czechoslovakia legislated the right of women to work and education, equal pay for men and women, and six months' maternity leave at full pay. By placing women in public posts on the basis of quotas, the socialist system opened public institutions to women to a much greater extent than is usual in Western liberal democracies. One legacy of the socialist system is that 88 per cent of Czech women of productive age work full-time and that women constitute 45 per cent of the total labour force, with 12.5 per cent of women considering themselves sole and 48 per cent partial breadwinners for their families (*Data a fakta*, no. 13, September 1992; *Respekt*, 1993, no. 1).

Communist ideology emphasised the value of the working woman, and the communist government always argued that women in socialist countries did not need a women's movement of the Western type because under socialism they had already achieved full emancipation. The impact of this ideology on the consciousness of Czech women is reflected in the belief that the feminist movement's campaign for women's emancipation is justified in Western liberal democracies but unnecessary in the Czech situation. The socialist state made the full incorporation of women into the work process possible by providing not only generous maternity leave but also nurseries and kindergartens in local communities and workplaces. According to a sociological survey carried out in December 1991, most Czech women are of the opinion that neither men nor women enjoy any advantages or suffer any disadvantages in law, that the social security system treats men and women equally, and that the educational system does not discriminate against either sex. The family offers the same advantages to men as to women. Private entrepreneurial activity, employment, and particularly politics are the only areas in which women see men as having an advantage. The percentages of women who expressed opinions on the advantages of men and women in particular social spheres are summarised in table 6.

The argument of those campaigning for equality of rights for men and women is that, far from emancipating women, socialism exploited them to a degree to which they never had been exploited before. By making it impossible for the average family to live on a single income, it forced women into full employment without relieving them of their traditional household work and child care, which the system of nurseries and kindergartens helped only to a limited extent. As a result, women enjoyed three hours less leisure per day than men. Even their seemingly increased participation in the public sphere was far from the ideal of true emancipation. In spite of the legal guarantee of equal pay for men and women, the average woman's pay was 30 per cent less than that of a man because many more

Table 6. *Opinions of women (percentages) on advantages of men and women by social sphere*

	Men advantaged	Neither sex advantaged	Women advantaged
Law	9	82	9
Social security	7	68	25
Education	16	83	1
Family	28	49	23
Private entrepreneurial activity	50	49	1
Employment	52	46	2
Politics	89	10	1

Source: Data a fakta, no. 13, September 1992.

women than men were employed in low-paid unskilled and semiskilled jobs. In the 1991 survey mentioned above, 45 per cent of women reported that their pay was less than that of men in the same jobs in spite of equal performance, and 62 per cent of women mentioned various forms of discrimination of the work teams in which women predominate. Women are also more likely than men to be made redundant (*Data a fakta*, no. 13, September 1992).

The socialist system probably fostered the present attitude of most Czech women to feminism in that it militated against the development of antagonism between men and women, which many analysts see as a form of class antagonism. Socialist reality robbed men as well as women of their dignity. Men felt degraded by not being able to fulfil their traditional role of breadwinners solely responsible for the financial security and material well-being of their families; women felt degraded by not being able to fulfil properly their traditional role as homemakers. The division between 'them' and 'us' was drawn not along gender lines but between the state and the people who felt manipulated by it even in the most private aspects of their lives. The feeling of solidarity between men and women in the face of their common adversary was thus much stronger than in liberal-democratic political systems.

However, the specific aspects of communist ideology and socialist reality, although undoubtedly significant, are not in themselves sufficient to account for the differences in the intensity of the impact of ecological and feminist movements on Czech society before and during its post-communist transformation. The issues on which the women's movement in the Czech lands concentrates are also greatly affected by the unquestioned and taken-for-granted premises of Czech culture, which in feminist terms is distinctly patriarchal and sexist.

The Czechs see gender differences as embedded in nature and as resulting directly from the biological differences between men and women. Women, in particular, emphasise their unique experience of gestation and childbearing which men can never share, and deduce from this experience all the other differences which they attribute to men and women. Both men and women argue that women's desires are almost entirely directed to the bearing and upbringing of children and that because of their biological differences men and women have different natures and different psychological dispositions and think differently. Even people who are unable to specify how male and female mentalities differ assume that they must. Gender identity is seen as something that is not socially constructed but biologically given. A female university student argued that biological differences between men and women were undeniable and, given these differences, it was only to be expected that men and women would also differ in their psychological dispositions, mentalities, and interests. She did not think that women were inferior to men; they were just different, and in her view any effort to achieve equality with men was foolish: 'I have never heard of men's striving for equality with women; why should women strive for equality with men?'

The characteristics of men and women which my informants mentioned most often resemble the standard gender stereotypes of male-dominated Western culture. Thus, for example, I was told that men are naturally predisposed to be assertive and women to be shy, tender, and submissive; that men are more guided by reason and rational calculation and women more by their feelings and intuitions; that men are openly confrontational and women likely to resort to subterfuge, flattery, and subtle manipulation from behind the scenes; that men are innovative and willing to experiment and women tend to stick to traditional and time-honoured ways of doing things; that men are firm in their opinions and intolerant of those of others and women less sure of their opinions and more prepared to see another's point of view; that men are egoistic and authoritarian and women unselfish, loving, and caring. At the same time, it is seen as natural for women to arouse men sexually and for men show sexual interest in them. As in other spheres of life, it is considered natural for men to initiate sexual encounters and for women to show restraint before submitting to their sexual advances.

Because men and women are considered to think differently, they are viewed as being naturally predisposed to different tasks. The association of women with the domestic domain and of men with leadership positions in the public domain is culturally constructed as naturally given. It is significant that most self-proclaimed Czech feminists emphasise that they became feminists after they married. As one expressed it, 'The experienced ones say that a woman becomes a feminist when she marries. That, indeed, was my case. Only feminism helped me to find out that I am not abnormal when I do not enjoy housework and that it does not have to be "natural" for me' (Eva Hauserová in *Lidové noviny*, 14 May 1993). Since the feminists emphasise not only the emancipation of women in the public sphere but also the importance of increased participation by men in the domestic sphere, many men and women who openly reject feminism describe it as a movement of hysterical women who hate housework or who demand to be paid for it.

The cultural constructions of gender differences are reflected in attitudes as well as in behaviour. Forty per cent of Czech women prefer a man as their superior in employment and only 6 per cent would prefer a woman in this position. Only 5 per cent of women would prefer a female to a male doctor under all circumstances while 14 per cent would prefer a male doctor. When the question was modified to 'sometimes or depending on the circumstances', 80 per cent of women expressed a preference for a female doctor. In the sociological survey mentioned above, 57 per cent of respondents denied any awareness of sexual harassment, 33 per cent said that they had heard of it, and only 10 per cent admitted personal experience of it in their workplace (*Data a fakta*, no. 13, September 1992). Conduct which in the West would be interpreted as sexual harassment is, however, almost standard practice in virtually every workplace. Although for most Czech women sexual harassment would require more explicit and overt sexual advances than those which they habitually encounter in the average workplace, they do not see it as degrading or offensive. Most of them see it as appreciation of their attractiveness and sex appeal. Even a self-proclaimed feminist admitted that if a man told her that she had beautiful legs she would start wearing miniskirts (*Lidové noviny*, 14 May 1993).

Jokes about women which play on the stereotypes of male and female nature are found objectionable by only by 4 per cent of women; 54 per cent object only to vulgar ones. A greater degree of differentiation appears in attitudes toward the public display of female nudity (table 7). Even women who find the ubiquitous pictures of nude or partly dressed women demeaning are reluctant to protest them: 'I would feel ridiculous, prudish', one said (*Respekt*, 1992, no. 29: 8).

Czech advertisements rely heavily on woman's capacity for sexual

Table 7. *Objection of women (percentages) to displays of female nudity by context*

In general magazines	73
In 'erotic' magazines	28
On posters in the streets	83
On posters in workplaces	75
On posters in homes	80
On packaging of consumer goods	71
In television advertisements	62
In films	34
In doctors' surgeries	49

Source: Data a fakta, no. 13, September 1992.

attraction as the selling point and mostly depict women as subservient or inferior. For example, washing powder advertisements routinely depict a woman as a caring housewife who is persuaded about the advantages of this or that washing powder by the male scientist who has developed the miraculous product. In this rather blatant as well as in other, more subtle ways, advertising fosters ideas about the way a woman should look or behave. This practice has not yet inspired any debate among Czech women, and no campaign has yet been mounted against what would be seen in the West as the commercial exploitation of women. On the contrary, Western-style advertisements in which women were pictured as strong, independent, and successful, which deliberately reversed the traditional roles of men and women, or which ironically commented on the traditional gender roles were seen as unrealistic or downright silly by the people with whom I discussed them.

The degree to which Czech women accept their role as men's helpers and supporters and their association with the domestic domain and the upbringing of children is perhaps best indicated by their attitude to the various stereotypical images of women perpetuated in Czech literature, film, theatre, and television (table 8).

One out of four women considers women abnormal who devote themselves totally to their careers and who do not resign on marrying and having children (*Data a fakta*, no. 13, September 1992).

The association of women with the household, family, and children and the association of men with the public domain is perpetually re-created not only by women's magazines but also by the organisations which represent women's interests. Under the communist regime, typical women's

Table 8. *Objections of women (percentages) to various female stereotypical images*

Guardian of family hearth	7
Man's partner for all seasons	11
Mother	16
Committed office-holder who manages to cope with everything	43
Absent-minded scientist or scholar incapable of finding 'her' man	49
Sex symbol	60
Unintelligent and submissive woman (*slepice*, 'hen')	78
Exhausted worker/wife/mother	83

Source: Data a fakta, no. 13, September 1992.

issues were not only motherhood, the upbringing of children, and the problems of the family but the cumbersome and poorly functioning retail sector and the occasional shortages of food, household necessities, children's clothing, and other items. For the Czechoslovak Union of Women, an improvement in the supply of goods was one of the most important ways to better the position of women in society, and many women's organisations which emerged after the fall of the communist system still called for greater attention to women's roles as mothers and homemakers (Wolchik 1991: 205).

With a full range of food and consumer goods now readily available in privatised Czech shops, however, most women's organisations no longer see women as suffering unduly in the performance of their traditional role of homemaker. The main women's issue is the insufficient representation of women in politics. Only 10 per cent of the members of the Czech parliament which emerged from the 1990 elections were women, and their number dropped to 8 per cent in the parliament elected in 1992. Of the sixteen members of the cabinet formed after the 1990 elections, only one was a woman, and there was no woman in the Czech cabinet formed after the 1992 elections. Politics is the main domain which women see as clearly advantaging men, and 95 per cent of women participate in no political activity. Immediately after the fall of the communist regime, women rejected any suggestion of quotas which would guarantee them greater participation in politics, arguing that 'it would be like under the Communists' or that 'women do not belong in politics'. By December 1991, however, 70 per cent of women favoured quotas which would guarantee a certain number of parliamentary seats to women, as is customary in many European countries (*Data a fakta*, no. 13, September 1992). This change of opinion was due to the campaign of various women's organisations for more active participation of women in public life in general and in politics in particular. These organisations do not necessarily see themselves as feminist, and many of them explicitly distance themselves from feminism. As a female politician has expressed it, 'the question of the representation of women in politics does not need to be a feminist matter. It is the matter of a normal development of democratic society' (Petra Buzková, deputy chairman of the Social Democratic Party, in *Lidové noviny*, 7 August 1993).

Two main arguments are put forward for the desirability of greater representation of women in the main political institutions of the country. The first is that women are seen as better qualified than men to propose legislation on education, child benefits, child care, maternity benefits, and other issues which fall under the rubric of family policy and family law. The second is that greater participation of women would 'soften' and 'clean up' the political game and thus improve the overall political culture of the country. Politics is understood as an arena of competitive confrontation between opposing views and principles, and more participation of women, with their proclivity for care, tolerance for the opinions of others, and reluctance to be drawn into direct confrontation, is expected to yield a more consensual politics to the benefit of both men and women.

Both arguments are predicated on assumptions about the inherent and naturally determined differences between men and women in characteristic traits, inclinations, and ways of thinking. The cultural premises on which the Czech pattern of gender relations is built are constantly invoked in the gender discourse. When the minister of health, in response to a question in a television interview, said that he appreciated and admired the work of women but considered their number in business circles, in top administrative posts, and in the parliament sufficient, there was adverse comment from many women. Asked for his reaction to this, he replied:

Politicians are good and bad, successful and unsuccessful; the division into men and women in various professions is secondary. According to my information, there are many women in business and I appreciate this. My statement was only an expression of the fact that I understand their choice. Luckily, the roles of men and women are different and to a great extent predetermined biologically and historically. A different angle from which to see the world is an indispensable corrective for both groups. Politics requires both views to different degree at different times. There are two ways of dealing with difference, either to accept it or to change it. Because as a surgeon I know the second possibility very well, I recommend the first.   (Lidové noviny, *10 August 1993*)

What makes radical feminism unappealing not only to Czech men but also to the overwhelming majority of Czech women is ultimately the unquestioned assumption that differences in men's and women's roles are naturally determined. Czechs reject feminism not so much because they perceive its ideology as leftist and militant (*Respekt*, 1992, no. 29: 8) as because of its conviction that gender differences and the traditional roles of men and women are not biologically determined but learned and can thus be consciously altered. The conscious redefinition of gender roles which is the goal of the feminist movement in the West is seen as ridiculous or at least excessive not only by Czech men but by almost all Czech women, including the well-educated. It is seen as an inappropriate interference of conscious human design with the givens of nature which, if carried through, would destroy naturally constituted gender relations just as various human projects have destroyed the naturally constituted ecological balance. In consequence, Czech gender politics is aimed not at altering existing gender relations but at better employing existing gender differences for the benefit of society.

The cultural construction of the natural and the artificial

In the Czech conceptualisation, things are perceived as either having emerged naturally (like, for example, gender relations or a market economy) or as the result of deliberate human design (like, for example, gender relations in the West which are the result of feminist agitation, or a planned economy). The dichotomy between the naturally constituted and the consciously created does not simply parallel the nature–culture dichotomy. That the market economy, for example, is seen as natural in opposition to the consciously created planned economy indicates that what is seen as naturally constituted is not limited to cultural constructs that are seen as innate in nature, but also includes constructs that are seen as the result of the evolution of human society and of its historical development. The evolution of human society and of its specific institutions (e.g., the family) is itself seen as 'natural' in the sense that these institutions cannot be attributed to particular human agents as their conscious or deliberate creations. The market economy is seen as natural because 'nobody created it'. Similarly, the course of history is 'natural'; although specific historical events are the result of purposeful human action, those who at any given moment 'created' history did not act alone. Historical events are the result of the interaction of a multiplicity of actors whose goals and purposes were mutually opposed and who were at the time unaware that they were making history. Rather than as a dichotomy between culture and nature, the dichotomy between the consciously created and the naturally constituted can be formulated as a dichotomy between will and nature – between processes designed and controlled by human agents and those outside such control and design. The dichotomy is an anthropocentric one: the naturally given or constituted does not define what can be created, designed, or controlled by the human will; rather what is or can be so created and controlled determines what will be classified as 'natural'.

The cultural constructs which I have mentioned as examples of the dichotomy between the naturally constituted and the humanly created are clearly differently evaluated. The market economy is seen as superior to the planned socialist economy, ecological balance has to be preserved from the human creations that threaten and destroy it, and gender relations based on the natural proclivities of men and women ought not to be altered in the name of deliberately created ideals. This might suggest that a higher cultural value is ascribed to what is seen as natural than to what is seen as the result of conscious human effort, design, or will. The construction of gender relations suggests, however, that this is not the case. In comparison with men, women are seen as more emotional and less governed by reason. This difference is routinely invoked as a justification for the virtually total absence of women from high political offices in particular and from politics, seen as the domain of rational calculation *par excellence*, in general. A politically active woman is seen as lacking natural feminine attributes, a view expressed in the sexist joke that either she is a spinster or there is something wrong with her ovaries. She is a peculiar creature who suppresses her naturally given disposition to nurturance in the name of a deliberately created ideal. Emotions can be provoked or perhaps controlled, but they cannot be created or designed by human will in exactly the same way as certain natural phenomena, although existing independently of human will, can be provoked or controlled by human action (acid rain is a pertinent example). In terms of the dichotomy between the naturally given and the deliberately created, emotions stand at the natural pole.

The Czech language makes a semantic distinction between *city* (such as love, hate, joy, sorrow, grief, etc.), which I gloss as 'feelings', and *emoce*, which I gloss as 'emotions'. Certain feelings may of course be inappropriate to certain situations, but in ordinary speech *city* is value-free, whereas *emoce* always has negative connotations. In ordinary speech, 'emotions' connotes not any particular feeling but rather, as one of my informants formulated it, 'an unsuitable or inappropriate expression of feelings;

unsuitable in the sense of their expression through inappropriate means'. The word 'emotion' acquires its meaning in opposition to 'reason': 'Emotion is an inappropriate expression of feeling or opinion, that is, an expression which is not sufficiently guided by reason', as another informant expressed it. Particularly in political rhetoric, politicians, political commentators, and ordinary people commenting on political events and decisions condemn as irresponsible the appeal to emotions by extremists, both ultra-left-wing and ultra-right-wing populists, and they negatively evaluate 'emotional solutions to problems' and 'emotional answers to complex questions'.

The guiding idea of Czech culture is not the positive or negative evaluation of either the naturally constituted or the consciously created, but the negative evaluation of the excess of one pole of the dichotomy over the other. This notion is expressed in a number of common sayings: *všeho moc škodí* ('too much of anything is harmful'), *čeho je moc, toho je příliš* ('too much of anything is excessive'), and *všeho s mírou* ('everything in moderation'). Shifting from one extreme to the other is bad: it lacks direction or forward movement (*ode zdi ke zdi*, 'from wall to wall'). The root metaphor of Czech culture is the 'centre'.

The Czech lands are seen as part of neither Western nor Eastern Europe but Central Europe. Although Czech pro-government political commentators argue that the Czech Republic is unique among the post-communist states in having elected a right-wing coalition government in 1992 and thus signalling to the world 'We belong to the West' (Jan Patočka in *Český deník*, 27 October 1992), the Czechs I listened to do not share this view. They talk about a trip to Austria, Germany, France, or Britain as visiting the West; they talk about 'Western cars', 'Western goods', 'Western films', 'Western technology', 'Western influences on Czech culture', and 'the penetration of Western capital into Czech industry'. They talk similarly about the 'East' – Russia, Romania, and other countries of the former socialist bloc. They see themselves as belonging to neither the East nor the West – as standing in between. Their country lies on the boundary between East and West, and it has often seen the solution to its political predicament by thinking of itself as a 'bridge' between them. The image of a bridge expresses again the positive value ascribed to centrality: a structure that links the two sides. Czech national identity has been built on this metaphor since nineteenth-century national revival. In the introduction to his *History of the Czech Nation*, Palacký identifies the historical task of the Czech nation as to 'serve as a bridge between German and Slav, between East and West in Europe'. This idea was actively invoked by Czech intellectuals and politicians after World War II in their efforts to prevent the total incorporation of Czechoslovakia into the East. The metaphor of the bridge lends to Czech identity the role of mediator between two distinct European cultures and value systems, and creator of their eventual synthesis (Macura 1992; see also Pynsent 1994: 179–80).

Another core symbol of the desirable mediation between the naturally given and the consciously designed is reason. Nationalism has negative connotations because it is a manifestation of emotions (the naturally given) insufficiently controlled by reason. The Czech–Slovak conflict is occasionally seen as a conflict of reason and emotions (Petr Nováček in *Mladá fronta dnes*, 27 October 1992; Havel 1992: 64; Macura 1993: 40–1). Nationalism is an emphasis on nation as the highest cultural value. As the nation is a naturally constituted entity, nationalism is a manifestation of an undesirable excess: it disturbs the culturally valued balance between the naturally constituted and the consciously created in human existence.

Reason curbs not only emotions but also ideological dogmatism as an extreme expression of unmitigated human intention. One commentator characterised the controversial dam on the Danube at Gabčíkovo as 'a perfect monument to the grand victory of idea over reason' (Jaroslav Veis in *Literární noviny*, 30 October 1992). When the Czechs speak of reason, they mention either common sense (*prostý rozum*) or, more specifically, 'a healthy farmer's reason' (*zdravý selský rozum*). By explicitly invoking the image of a farmer, this particular type of reason aptly expresses the creation of value through cultivation – the transformation of the naturally constituted through conscious human effort. Although this is not its only connotation,[1] 'a healthy farmer's reason' suggests cultivation as another metaphor for the culturally valued harmonious balance between the naturally constituted and the consciously created.

The idea of balance embodied in the metaphors of centre, bridge, and cultivation (the last itself a metaphor for the right kind of reason that mediates between the naturally constituted and the wilfully created) is the guiding idea of Czech culture. The achievement of balance is recognised as the ideal. In various contexts different oppositions, such as those between freedom and responsibility or private and public interest (Jaroslav Veis in *Literární noviny*, 30 October 1992), may be invoked, but the desirable state of affairs is always the balance between them:

Freedom has its inevitable counterpart in personal responsibility, without which it is impossible to achieve a much needed *balance* and *harmony* in society.

(Václav Klaus in Český deník, *15 September 1992)*

An excess of deliberate constructions is as undesirable as an excess of emotions:

In the history of states, it does not often happen that people want to die for the republic as they did in 1938. We should think about that as well, to remember and realise that that should be our highest goal. Such a goal is not a matter of a *rational engineering plan*.

(M. Uhde, chairman of the Czech National Council, in an interview about the new Czech state,
Český deník, *30 October 1992)*

The Communist Party had a slightly different opinion about the building of the prosperity of the state in the framework of the 'world socialist system'. However, this opinion did not agree with what is logical and *natural*.

*(*Metropolitní telegraf, *30 October 1992)*

One of the questions debated in connection with the drafting of the constitution of the Czech Republic was the question of the role of the president in the political system and the way in which he should be elected. In one particular contribution to this debate, the change from his election by the parliament to his election by direct popular vote was criticised in terms of the danger of tinkering with established social practices which might destroy the desirable balance that had naturally developed:

Society is not a laboratory for experiments, and the return to proven forms of parliamentary democracy is more than desirable. The president is non-partisan in his function, and he guarantees first of all a *balance* between the legislative and executive powers. The problem of the direct election of the president and of his non-partisanship is *artificially created*; it is a pseudo-problem.

(Vladimír Hepner in Český deník, *7 December 1992)*

By disturbing the desirable balance between the naturally constituted and the consciously created, the excess of wilful engineering is against nature (*proti přírodě*) or against reason (*proti rozumu*) and can eventually become something that is existentially alien (*bytostně cizí*). Ultimately, the rejection of socialism as a system alien to Czech culture derives alternatively from its excess of deliberate social engineering and planning or from its lack of cultivation, which leads to the excess of the animal-like side of human nature.

The excess of deliberate social engineering and planning is emphasised by contemporary Czech critics of socialism as its most characteristic feature not only in the context of a socialist planned economy but in a number of other contexts:

[The government of one party] overturned the *natural* course of affairs. Specifically, in Prague it started to build hideous concrete boxes and allowed that which at one time breathed with life to die . . . Prague thus turned into some kind of open-air museum, and life moved into lifeless boxes . . . [Another] Czech interest thus must be to defend at all costs the *natural* course of affairs and not to consent to a government by one party.   (*Vladimír Hepner in* Český deník, *26 September 1992*)

The numerous criticisms of socialism which point out the moral devastation which it brought about stem from the recognition of the opposite excess of the socialist system, manifested in its lack of cultivation of human nature:

Just notice the conduct of many old-new bureaucrats in many old-new offices. Just notice the attitude to customers of certain suddenly emerging entrepreneurs. Even those are examples of the omnipresent heritage of the *jungle* in which not only words but also values and relations become degraded . . . Anyone who wants to be successful and to influence the course of events has to perceive and to heed the *natural* trends, norms, and constraints . . . Let us avoid taking *extreme* positions. *On the one hand*, it is a negative identification in relation to a real or illusory enemy; *on the other hand*, it is a worshipping of new idols.

(Petr Havlík in Český deník, *16 October 1992)*

The perpetual striving for balance between the naturally constituted and the consciously created does not mean that the excess of either is always negatively valued. Just as the basic premises of Czech culture make possible and shape ongoing discourses, they also give meaning to the observable changes in Czech culture and to its long-term development. This development is a process of counterbalancing periods of unrestrained dominance of the deliberately created (such as the socialist system) with periods of unrestrained dominance of the naturally constituted (such as the period of aroused emotions, euphoria, and re-emergence of national sentiment following the 'velvet revolution' of 1989). Similarly, the indisputable incorporation of Czechoslovakia into the Eastern bloc has now been replaced by emphasising its Western orientation (see Jan Patočka in *Český deník*, 27 October 1992).

The cultural construction of nation, state, and homeland
In the Czech conceptualisation, the nation is a naturally constituted community. Membership of the nation is, as we have seen, not the result of an individual's conscious decision but determined by the very fact of one's birth – a natural process *par excellence*. To belong to the Czech nation is as naturally given as gender or physical characteristics – something that cannot be changed by a conscious decision. The cultural construction of the nation as a naturally constituted entity is attested to by the fact that many informants mentioned that one was a Czech because one felt that one was a Czech. This is a kind of belonging that also determines mem-

bership of other naturally given categories, such as those of gender. Ultimately, as some of my informants said, one is a man or a woman because one feels that one is one or the other.

Whereas the nation is not something people can build, the state is a deliberate human construction. 'States come into being and disappear, nations remain' (the historian Jaroslav Opat in *Lidové noviny*, 27 October 1992). We are 'building the state', as Czechs have recently been incessantly reminded by the politicians and mass media in connection with the disintegration of Czechoslovakia. 'What kind of state we are going to build' has been one of the issues most heatedly debated in connection with the drafting of the constitution of the Czech Republic and considerations of its future economic and social policy, international orientation, military doctrine, etc.

When talking about their homeland most of my informants described it as the country in which they were born and grew up and in which they had their family and friends – as one informant expressed it, 'where one has one's roots through the relation to one's parents, family, and other people'. Many people found it difficult to define a homeland in general terms, and in trying to do so they often mentioned various tangible symbols which evoked for them the image of the homeland – from family, friends, language, customs, way of life, mentality, culture, history, and traditions to specific familiar places, characteristic landscape, and natural environment. Most people stressed that a homeland was epitomised not by its landscape and natural environment but by the people who lived in it and their culture. The statement of one of my informants that 'a homeland is not a particular place but people' succinctly expressed this generally shared sentiment.

By seeing a homeland as epitomised by the commonality of the way of life, customs, mentality, and traditions of the people among whom one lives, the Czechs construe it as that socio-cultural space in which they understand what others do and others understand what they do. As one informant expressed it, 'A homeland is an environment in which everything is familiar to me and I do not have to learn new ways of doing things, in which I can live without fear of the unknown, in which I know what is proper or improper to say and do.' A homeland is thus the space in which the conduct, expectations, attitudes, feelings, and reactions of others are predictable and in which one knows the rules of appropriate behaviour. An important part of this familiarity is the language. The same informant mentioned specifically that a homeland was a country in which every word of the language had a clearly understood meaning, and another one expressed the same thing by saying, 'If I had to live in a country where people spoke a language which was not mine, it would not be my homeland even if I spoke and understood that language well.'

Semantically, *vlast* ('homeland') is related to *vlastní* ('own') and opposed to *cizina* ('abroad'), derived from *cizí* ('foreign, alien, strange'). People often expressed the meaning of 'homeland' by saying that it was 'their country', 'their home', or a country in which they had 'the right to live'. It is a country which stands apart from all other countries which are *cizina* and in which, as one informant put it 'everything is more familiar to me than it is abroad' (*v cizině*).

Territorially, the Czechs delineated their homeland alternatively as Bohemia, the Czech lands (i.e., Bohemia and Moravia), or Czechoslovakia. The variations in this delineation reflected to some extent the differences in the conceptualisation of the nation of which particular informants considered themselves to be members (i.e., whether they thought of themselves as Czechs or Czechoslovaks), but more than this was involved. The fact that most people considered only Bohemia and Moravia their homeland was of course to a great extent determined by the fact that I did my fieldwork in 1992, when the partition of Czechoslovakia into two separate states was already a foregone conclusion and was constantly being discussed. A few people said that before the partition was mooted they had considered the whole of Czechoslovakia their homeland, but most of them stressed that even before this their homeland was only Bohemia and Moravia; Slovakia was part of the state in which they lived, but it was not their homeland. They said that they had never been to Slovakia and did not know any Slovaks or that, although they knew some Slovaks intimately, their family and most of their friends lived in the Czech lands. Language is also often invoked as the reason Slovakia is not part of a Czech's homeland: although the Slovak language is very close to Czech and Czechs can understand it perfectly, most of them cannot speak it.

Language, customs, traditions, and culture are attributes which make a homeland of a country. At the same time, they are attributes which make a nation of a collectivity. In this respect, the present-day Czech construction of a homeland does not eliminate nationality as did the construction of the nineteenth-century Bohemian nobility characterised as regional patriotism (*Landespatriotism*). If one's homeland is a country in which people speak the same language and have the same traditions and customs as one does, one's homeland is the country in which one's nation lives. This is the reason many of my informants mentioned that even if they lived abroad, the Czech lands would always be their homeland. However, although the same attributes may be used to construct a nation and a homeland, these two terms are not synonymous. In the Czech conceptualisation, the nation is defined by common language and culture and remains a nation whether its members inhabit a particular territory or not. Although played down in the Czechs'·definition of 'homeland', the spatial aspect enters into its conceptualisation as it does not enter into the conceptualisation of a nation. This emerges from the frequent equation of 'home' and 'homeland' and from the statements of many informants that their homeland was not only where they felt at home, but was also their home. 'Home' is not an intangible entity but always and foremost a specific place; the proper question is not '*What* is your home?' but '*Where* is your home?' For most people home is the place where they were born and brought up or, alternatively, the place in which they established their own families and had their children. In relation to the 'proper' home understood in this way, homeland is the familiar space stretching beyond its boundaries and is a 'home' in the wider sense of the term. One woman, who stressed that her homeland was formed by her family and friends and was not merely a territorial concept, expressed it in the following way: 'My home is in this country. I see my homeland as that territory in which I have my home; the centre of that territory is my home.'

In saying that a homeland is a country in which one knows the rules of appropriate behaviour, people mean not only the customary rules which have evolved spontaneously but also the rules stipulated by the state. And when they describe their homeland as either the Czech lands or Czechoslovakia, they again resort to the concept of the state or, even more concretely, of the state's boundaries, to delineate the homeland. Yet, again, the homeland is not synonymous with the state. One can love one's homeland deeply and still be extremely critical of or hostile to one's state. This was the attitude of people who explained to me why they had not emigrated from communist Czechoslovakia in spite of suffering persecution. Although they hated the communist state, they loved their homeland too much to leave it. For most Czechs, the Czech lands were their homeland during the pre-war republic, during the war years when their state was a German protectorate, and during the years of the socialist state, and are their homeland now. States come and go, but the homeland remains. A homeland is a construct which mediates between the naturally constituted nation and the artificially created state; it is that space in which the nation and state intermingle or are linked.

The Czechs make a sharp distinction between patriotism and nationalism. Patriotism is a positive attitude to or awareness of belonging to one's homeland. Most people defined it as the love of one's homeland which manifests itself in the willingness to do something positive for it, ranging from contributing to the development of national culture to having a cultured lifestyle respectful of national customs and traditions. Even people who did not claim strong patriotic feelings and said, for example, that they would never fight for their country maintained that patriotism was a desirable attitude. As some of them argued, it had to be, because love itself was a positive feeling and so, of course, was love of one's country. But first of all, patriotism was a positive attitude because it expressed love for one's country without engendering animosity, hatred, and a feeling of superiority toward other nations.

The latter sentiments are characteristic of nationalism, which most people described as immoderate, fanatical, or exaggerated patriotism – patriotism gone too far. Nationalism stresses the exceptional qualities of a particular nation and belittles the qualities of other nations. It is an expression of a negative attitude and often open hostility to other nations, and it manifests itself in intolerance, the pursuit of national interests at others' expense and the denial of others' rights. Whilst patriotism is solely inward-looking and is thus tolerant of other nations, nationalism is always outward-looking. It is a hatred of other nations which typically leads to violence. Everyone I spoke to condemned nationalism, and most of them expressed the view that while Czechs, or at least most Czechs, were patriots, they were certainly not nationalists. These views were reflected in a survey conducted in the Czech Republic in autumn 1990, in which 52 per cent of respondents expressed the opinion that Czechs had no strong awareness of themselves as a nation (*Aktuálne problémy Česko-Slovenska*, November 1990: 26). Opinions like this give rise to the often-expressed view that Czech nationalism does not exist or, if it does, emerges only as a reaction to Slovak nationalism, with its openly expressed anti-Czech sentiments. The perceived lack of Czech national awareness is to a great extent the result of the fact that Czechs have been the dominant nation in the Czechoslovak Republic; in consequence, Czechness is not felt to be under threat and does not need to be openly asserted. Nationalism is something that plagues others – Slovaks, Serbs, Croats, and the various nations of the former Soviet Union – but not the Czechs. Denial of Czech nationalism is part of the construction of a positive image of the Czech nation, for nationalism, whether as a militant movement or as heightened national feeling, has unambiguously negative connotations.

Identification with the state is also denied a positive value. Czech political commentators on both the right and the left continually criticise the prevalence of party-political interests in Czech political culture, as opposed to the common interest of the state, and ordinary citizens' lack of identification with the state. In pre-war Czechoslovakia this attitude was seen as a survival of the Austro-Hungarian Empire, when Czechs had little reason to identify with the state whose citizens they were but which did not serve their interests. Today this attitude is explained as a survival of the communist regime, when Czechs had every reason to see the state as alien and oppressive. Czechs certainly do not seem to take any special pride in the institutions of their state, whether the parliament, the civil service, the army, or the police. In 1992, when the political institutions of the Czechoslovak federation had been paralysed but not yet fully replaced by the institutions of the Czech state, no one seemed to mind. The situation was viewed not with concern or disquiet but, if anything, with amusement. Everything seemed to be in order, for the homeland with which Czechs identified was still there.

The Czech state and Czechoslovakia: the natural and the artificial

The key cultural metaphors of the natural and the artificial and the notion of a desired balance between the two were actively invoked in the discourse about Czech statehood which emerged soon after the fall of the communist regime in 1989 and gained prominence after the elections in Czechoslovakia in June 1992. This debate was triggered by the reconsideration of the coexistence of the Czech and the Slovak nation in a single federal state which was immediately put on the political agenda.

The problematic nature of Czech–Slovak relations came to the fore in the spring of 1990, when the Federal Assembly debated changing the country's name. There was agreement on leaving out the adjective 'socialist', and as most members of the parliament at least verbally subscribed to the legacy of the pre-war republic it was generally expected – at least in the Czech lands – that the country would once more be called the Czechoslovak Republic. However, this was unacceptable to the Slovak deputies, who insisted on 'the Czecho-Slovak Republic'. This provoked strong aversion among the Czechs because it had been the official name of the truncated republic which came into being as the result of the Munich agreement of 1938. Eventually, a compromise, 'the Czech and Slovak Federal Republic', was accepted.

This official name indicated that post-communist Czechoslovakia endorsed the federal structure set up in 1968. But whereas the communist government might have employed the legalistic rhetoric whilst effectively ignoring its own laws in practice, the post-November regime was determined to build a legal state and in practice had to implement, at least initially, the structure of government and the laws inherited from the previous system. Many of these laws and their underlying principles, such as the principle that neither Czech nor Slovak deputies could gain an absolute majority in the Chamber of Nations, which had to approve any legislation passed by the Federal Assembly, resulted in political paralysis which was eventually resolved only by the division of Czechoslovakia into two separate states. Virtually the whole period between November 1989 and the elections in June 1992 was marked by lengthy, tortuous, and turbulent negotiations between Czech and Slovak politicians about the mode of coexistence of the Czech and Slovak republics in a common state.

The negotiations were complicated by the differing interpretations of Czech and Slovak politicians of the various agreements which they had already reached and by the repeated demands of Slovak politicians that federal laws be subordinated to the laws passed by the parliaments of the respective republics, that a treaty between the two republics be a prerequisite for the adoption of any federal constitution, and that special attention be paid to Slovakia, which would be more adversely affected than the Czech lands by the proposed economic transformation. Some Slovak politicians argued that Slovakia should act as an independent subject of international law and have its own army and currency; there was also the threat that Slovakia would adopt a constitution of its own which would not necessarily respect the existing constitution of the Czechoslovak federation. In coming forward with these proposals, Slovak politicians emphasised that they were not seeking full Slovak independence but aiming only at achieving Slovak sovereignty as a precondition for a treaty with the Czechs (Měchýř 1991).

On the Czech side, the roots of the prolonged political crisis had been widely perceived as lying in the Slovaks' pursuit of national sovereignty. The content of the negotiations changed after the elections of 1992. The growing fear during 1991 that agreement would eventually be impossible was confirmed by their result. The strongest party to emerge from the elections in the Czech lands was the Civic Democratic Party of the former finance minister Václav Klaus, which campaigned for the maintenance of a common federal state with a unified international policy and a unitary economic system based on strict market principles and a minimum of state interference. In Slovakia the elections were won by the Movement for Democratic Slovakia under the leadership of Vladimír Mečiar, which campaigned for recognition of Slovakia as an international subject in its own right (either as part of a loose Czecho-Slovak union or as an independent state linked to the Czech lands by an international treaty) and with an economic system in which market principles would be combined with a strong state role.

In the Czech lands, the negotiations which took place before the 1992 elections were perceived as an effort by Czech politicians to find an acceptable model of a common state in the face of increasing separatist tendencies in Slovakia. After the elections the negotiations took a new turn. The Czechs rejected the Slovak proposal of a loose Czecho-Slovak military, economic, and monetary union in which Slovakia would exist as an independent subject of international politics, insisting on the creation of two independent states whose relations would be determined by treaties. The inevitability of the separation of the Czech and Slovak republics was accepted by both sides, and the negotiations concentrated on guaranteeing the peaceful dismantling of the common state within the agreed constitutional and legal framework. Part of this process was the declaration of an independent constitution for each republic and the termination by the parliament of the Czechoslovak federation. As a result of this legislation, the Czech Republic and the Slovak Republic came into being as two fully independent states on 1 January 1993.

It is not my purpose here to write the political history of Czech–Slovak relations in post-communist Czechoslovakia or to speculate about whether the demise of Czechoslovakia was the result of the unwillingness of the Czechs to abandon their dominant role in the Czechoslovak Republic and their paternalistic attitude to the Slovaks, as most Slovaks and some Czechs argue, or of Slovak separatism and ingratitude, as most Czechs and some Slovaks prefer to see it. According to a survey conducted in September 1992, opinion in the Czech lands was equally divided on the creation of two independent states but 80 per cent of respondents considered it inevitable. Most of those who approved of the division saw it as the result of Slovak nationalism and separatism;[2] most of those who disapproved saw it as the result of the inability of the Czech and Slovak politicians to reach an agreement. For most Czechs, then, the creation of two independent states in place of the Czechoslovak federation was something which they had never wanted.[3] In this situation, the main problem for Czech politicians, helped by Czech journalists, historians, sociologists, and other intellectuals, was to convert the unwanted necessity of creating a new identity into the positive programme of building an independent Czech state. The tacit assumptions of Czech culture gave shape to the discourse both in formulating the problems which had to be addressed and in providing solutions to them.

The first problem was the fact that most Czechs had always treated Czechoslovakia as their state even though most of them considered only the Czech lands to be their homeland. In an interview for a Polish newspaper, in answer to the question 'What does it mean – a Czech state? What is the Czech national interest? It seems that Czech politicians are avoiding this question, and arguing that there will be time enough to think about it in the future', Václav Havel summed up the situation:

This relates to the fact that the Czech state emerges as a result of a certain compulsion. For the past seventy-five years, the Czechs have identified with Czechoslovak statehood; they have felt themselves to be Czechoslovak patriots. The idea of Czech statehood has had no special meaning during the past few decades because it has been merged with the idea of Czechoslovak statehood, and therefore today, as the Czech state approaches the task of establishing itself, we observe a certain embarrassment and hesitation.   *(Lidové noviny, 11 September 1992)*

Communist propaganda had concentrated on building a negative image of the pre-war Czechoslovak Republic as a capitalist state based on the exploitation of the working masses. What was emphasised after November 1989 was its democratic character. Czech newspapers and magazines were full of articles on various aspects of the history, political system, and economy of the first Czechoslovak state; post-1989 Czechoslovakia was construed as the heir to the pre-war republic, symbolically expressed in the fact that 28 October, the day of the establishment of the Czechoslovak Republic in 1918, was once again celebrated as the main state holiday. A significant part of the building of the new Czech state was the emergence of a critical attitude to the pre-war republic. The main theme of this criticism was its artificial character. Although the Czechoslovak Republic was seen by the Czechs as the revival of their historical statehood, that is, the continuation of the Bohemian kingdom, it was in fact created on the basis of temporary pragmatic considerations.

In contrast with the newly created Slovak state, the Czech state was not the result of a nation's aspirations to express its identity vis-à-vis other nations. The Czechs already had such a state in the Czechoslovak Republic. An independent Czech state might thus again be seen as a deliberate construction founded on momentary pragmatic considerations. To preclude this possible construction, political rhetoric seized on the notion of the natural not as innate but as the result of spontaneous historical development, consistently construing the Czech state as natural in opposition to the artificially created Czechoslovak Republic.

In accordance with this meaning imposed on the naturally constituted, what was emphasised was not so much the building of a new state as the re-emergence of the historical Czech state that had evolved naturally and existed within the boundaries of the newly emerging state for a millennium:

Our task is not to search for statehood; that has simply *existed for several centuries.* Our task is only to give this statehood the appropriate form of a democratic state which guarantees civic liberties.   *(Pavel Šafr in* Český deník, *29 September 1992)*

It is necessary to understand the independent Czech state, which is *renewing* itself . . . as a self-evident *continuation* of a millennium-long historical development . . . It is not an easy task because our thinking is still influenced not only by the idea of Czechoslovakism but also by the detrimental continuous suppression of national awareness in the name of a proletarian internationalism.
(Milan Šimek in Český deník, *23 September 1992)*

The fact that Slovakia is separating itself from Bohemia does not mean that the *continuity* of Czech statehood is ending and that it is once more necessary to define our state in some dramatic way . . . It is not at all necessary to redefine the idea of Czech statehood . . . The *continuity* of Czech statehood was preserved in Czechoslovakia, and it will go on even after 1 January 1993.
(Martin Schmarcz in Český deník, *27 October 1992)*

Today it is not the matter of the division of the state, much less of the emergence of some new Czech state, which is the explanation our government coalition has accepted from the current Slovak political representation. *No new Czech state is emerging* after 1 January 1993. The Czech state *has been*, is, and will be here; only the organisation of the state administration is changing, as, of course, has happened many times in the past. And also, of course, a part of the territory will be lost which we never considered to be our own in the true sense of the word; we only loved it as our own.
(Petr Vopěnka, minister of education in the 1990–2 government, at the conference on the idea of Czech statehood held in Prague in October 1992, quoted in Lidové noviny, *20 November 1992)*

A commentator in the daily *Český deník* (7 December 1992) summarised the political rhetoric by pointing out that

during the search for the roots and meaning of Czech statehood a long-known fact has been 'discovered': that Czech statehood has *lasted without interruption* since the Middle Ages and *did not cease to exist* even in the time of the 'Habsburg oppression'.   *(Josef Mlejnek Jr)*

A tangible symbolic expression of the construction of the Czech state as natural was the 'celebration of the renewal of the Czech state' organised in October 1992 by the ruling Czech Civic Democratic Party at Vyšehrad in Prague, the first seat of Czech kings. The demonstration, attended by some ten thousand citizens of Prague, was addressed by the Czech prime minister, the chairman of the Czech National Council (the Czech parliament), and Václav Havel. After the singing of the St Wenceslas hymn and the Czech part of the Czechoslovak anthem, the demonstration ended with the laying of a wreath by the prime minister and the chairman of the council on the grave of Vratislav II, the first Czech king.

The metaphor of the centre

The political discourse which preceded the founding of the Czech state aimed to persuade Czechs of the necessity of having a state of their own. In so doing it played on the higher cultural value ascribed to the naturally constituted over the artificially created by emphasising the fact that the Czech state was not being artificially created for reasons of pragmatic expediency but simply assuming a new shape in its millennium-long natural continuity. It also seized actively upon the Czech cultural notion ascribing a positive value neither to the naturally constituted nor to the deliberately created, but to the harmony and balance between the two. We have already seen an example of such evaluation in the ascription of high value neither to the nation (the naturally constituted) nor to the state (the artificially created) but to the homeland – a construct which mediates between these two terms. The same notion informed the emerging criticism of the pre-war Czechoslovak Republic, which pointed to its artificial character. In linking Slovakia with the historical lands of the Czech crown, Czechoslovakia became a deliberate construction manifesting an excess of the consciously created over the naturally constituted, which was also ultimately the reason for its eventual and inevitable demise. The emphasis on the natural character of the Czech state is aimed at precluding the interpretation that its founding is a similar victory of the consciously created over the naturally constituted. If the state is, on the one hand, something people create and, on the other hand, something that is in itself natural, a desirable balance between the naturally constituted and the deliberately created is achieved.

The discourse about the Czech state contains disagreements about specific issues and about solutions to particular problems under discussion. These disagreements stem from the fact that one text of the discourse may focus on the opposition between the various positively or negatively valued terms, such as the opposition between the positively valued natural and the negatively valued artificial or the opposition between the West and the East, whereas another may focus on the opposition between any pair of these two negatively valued extremes and their positively valued reconciliation. For example, the disagreement about whether the Czech lands are or should be part of the West stems from the invocation of these two different oppositions. However, the disagreements reflect the tacitly accepted agreement on the basic premises of Czech culture. It is this agreement that makes possible the production of particular texts within the discourse and defines the issues which are the subject of either agreement or disagreement among their authors.

The national principle of the Czech state

The main disagreement in the discourse about the Czech state is over the principles on which this state should be built. One of these principles is the civil principle which strives toward the balance between the naturally constituted and the deliberately created in curbing the undue emphasis on the naturally constituted nation and the excess of emotions characteristic of nationalism:

[The new Czech state] can in no way be the state of the Czech nation as some people wrongly imagine. The state has to be built on strictly civil principles so as not to repeat the mistakes which Czechoslovakia committed in relation to minorities after 1918.   *(historian Jan Rychlík in* Lidové noviny, *29 October 1992)*

Although much of the political rhetoric similarly emphasised that the new state had to be built on civil principles and the principle of the market economy, equally strong was the view that it could not be built on these principles alone. In the interview from which I have already quoted, Václav Havel expressed it in the following way:

I am of the opinion that a market economy is an essential condition, an unavoidable component, and a necessary part of the building of this state. But at the same time I think that this alone would not be enough. A market economy is the programme of many countries from Bohemia to Hong Kong, and it is hardly possible to found a state on this idea alone, for the question could then emerge why we could not become the seventeenth land of the Federal Republic of Germany – why is it necessary to have an independent state because of the existence of something which is a universal programme? I think that it is necessary to seek other dimensions of Czech political traditions and Czech statehood.

(Lidové noviny, 11 September 1992)

One of these 'other dimensions' has been the growing emphasis on the national principle of the new Czech state, consistent with the positive value ascribed to the nation as a naturally constituted entity and the negative value ascribed to the state as a deliberate creation. The emphasis on the pursuit of specifically Czech interests in the process of building the new state has been expressed in the context of numerous aspects connected with the dismantling of the Czechoslovak federation, ranging from the division of federal property, through the problem of the structure of the local government of the new state, to its international relations.

The discourse about the Czech state emphasised that the pre-war Czechoslovak Republic, to which the post-1989 Czechoslovak federation declared itself an heir, was an unnatural creation because it was not a nation-state – a form which balances and harmoniously combines the naturally constituted (the nation) with the deliberately created (the state).

The positive identification with the naturally constituted Czech nation was invoked as a principle which would enable the identification of citizens with the state which was being consciously constructed. In his speech at the demonstration at Vyšehrad in October 1992, the liberal and market-oriented Czech prime minister emphasised the necessity of solidarity among those who would together build the new Czech state and clearly defined that solidarity as 'the solidarity among us Czechs' (*Metropolitní telegraf*, 26 October 1992). Stressing the necessity of the feeling of togetherness which makes it possible to find new possibilities in political disagreements and a 'common road', he said:

[To achieve the desirable togetherness] one has to know that there is a community which subsumes every democratic differentiation and lends it a certain meaning. That community is the *Czech nation*. (*Český deník, 26 October 1992*)

An editorial comment in the right-wing *Český deník* stated the position bluntly:

There is no point in philosophising about the creation of the Czech state. Its meaning is given by the existence of the *Czech nation*. (*6 October 1992*)

The invocation of the national principle is not only the prerogative of right-wing politicians. The left-wing opposition also invokes national interests, albeit for reasons of an effective defence against the power of the state. The chairman of the reformed Communist Party of Bohemia and Moravia explained the programme of his party as follows:

I consider the consistent defence of *national interests* and an offer of social self-defence against profiteering, speculation, and the asocial behaviour of the state bureaucracy to be the main pillars [of this programme].

(*Rudé právo, 11 November 1992*)

The different reasons for emphasising national solidarity and the pursuit of national interests stem, however, from the shared cultural premises whereby the nation is construed as naturally constituted and the state as consciously created, each of them thus standing at one pole of the dichotomy which needs to be brought into balance and harmony.

Referendum on the Czech state: reason and emotions

Czech cultural premises were also invoked by the ruling coalition in the Czech lands to justify the specific political means by which it pursued the disintegration of the federation and the creation of the new Czech state.

The main argument of the opposition against the ruling coalition's policy was that the creation of an independent Czech state was not part of the election programme of the Civic Democratic Party which emerged victorious from the 1992 elections and therefore the government coalition had no mandate for the dismantling of Czechoslovakia. Whether the Czechoslovak federation should be preserved or split into two independent states should, it was argued, be decided in a popular referendum. According to an opinion poll conducted in September 1992, this view was shared by more than 80 per cent of the population.

The government coalition opposed such a referendum arguing that as an element of direct democracy it would negate the principle of representative democracy and that it was unnecessary in a well-functioning democratic system in which the political will of the people was expressed by their duly elected representatives in the parliament. In the government's view, the opposition was insisting on the referendum not out of any concern to preserve the federal state but in an effort to change the result of the elections. As the opinion polls conducted in September 1992 showed that only 36 per cent in the Czech Republic and 37 per cent in the Slovak Republic would vote for the end of the federation in a referendum, the opposition hoped that the referendum would reveal disappointment with the government coalition for its inability to preserve the Czechoslovak federation.

The government coalition also used another argument against the referendum which again stemmed directly from the premises of Czech culture. In line with the negative evaluation of emotions in opposition to reason, the government argued that voters who lacked full knowledge of the complexities of the problem of either preserving or dividing the federation would base their decision on their emotions and accused the opposition, which was aware that most Czechs identified emotionally with Czechoslovakia, of arousing those emotions. The referendum would be nothing other than an attempt at an emotional solution of a complex problem which could not be solved emotionally:

The overwhelming majority of citizens are simply not sufficiently informed. The MPs are no wiser than ordinary citizens; they only have a larger amount of information at their disposal. On the basis of this information, they see a little bit farther than citizens. They are more acutely aware of the inevitable consequences of the prolonged agony of the state. They are better informed about the economic and political consequences. They have facts and figures at their disposal. They can evaluate better whether we will pay more for the division of the state or for stubbornly keeping it alive in an atmosphere of permanent instability.

. . . An *emotional* opinion of the uninformed majority should not win over the opinion of informed minority in the decision about the future of the state.

(Pavel Černocký in Metropolitní telegraf, *24 October 1992)*

Should there be a referendum about maintaining or abolishing the federation, many people in Bohemia would vote for the federation because their *sentimental* attachment to the idea of Czechoslovakia prevents them taking into consideration what are or are not the wishes of the Slovaks. A similar problem in orientation to all the twists of the constitutional question exists also in Slovakia, and many people are demanding a common state and the independence of Slovakia at the same time.   *(Václav Klaus, Czech prime minister in* Český deník, *18 September 1992)*

The above texts suggest that a decision taken on the basis of emotions would be an expression of nature uncontrolled by reason. The sense in which nature has been invoked in these particular texts is just one of many senses in which it has been employed in the discourse about the Czech state. Different texts of the discourse use the metaphor of nature in different contexts, drawing variously on the opposition between the naturally constituted nation and the artificially created state, the opposition between the natural character of the Czech state and the artificial character of the Czechoslovak Republic, or the opposition between naturally given emotions and deliberate social engineering. Nature was invoked in yet a different sense in the discussion surrounding the referendum. One commentator argued that to ask people in a referendum whether they wished the Czechoslovak federation to be preserved was like asking them whether they wished never to have a toothache again. This rhetorical device construes the disintegration of Czechoslovakia itself as a natural process which it would of course be folly to oppose. And it would of course be equally foolish to oppose the creation of a Czech state once the Czech state has been construed as a naturally given entity rather than something created by human design.

Conclusions

A specific understanding of politics is of course in the interest of politicians, and they shape the discourse to achieve that kind of understanding. That the Czech government largely succeeded in putting across its policies concerning the creation of an independent Czech state without holding a referendum is attested to by the results of opinion polls. Whereas in

September 1992 more than 80 per cent of respondents favoured a referendum on the question of whether the Czechoslovak federation should be preserved, in October only 42 per cent of the population of the Czech lands (and 51 per cent of the population of Slovakia) considered a referendum to be the best way of terminating the common state. In the end, when the independent Czech Republic was officially declared on 1 January 1993, although the event was greeted without any particular joy, it did not trigger any opposition.

This considerable shift in public opinion clearly suggests that Czechs found the discourse about the disintegration of the federation and the creation of an independent Czech state persuasive. By construing the Czech state not as an artificial creation but as a natural entity, the discourse made sense of and therefore made manageable ideas and actions which most Czechs found not only disturbing but undesirable. The discourse gained its persuasive power by effectively invoking the symbols and key metaphors through which Czechs make sense of the world in which they live. The meanings of these symbols and metaphors, through which the basic premises of the culture are expressed, are not restricted to any particular discourse but emerge in a multiplicity of them. The metaphors of the natural and the artificial are employed in economic, political, ecological, and gender discourses and probably many more besides. In this respect, they are key metaphors of Czech culture.

This culture, however, does not exist in people's heads simply because they have learned it and because what they have once learned simply persists by virtue of some kind of mysterious resilience. It is the various discourses which keep it alive and also change it (Halliday 1978: 124–5; Scherzer 1987: 296, 306). They keep it alive by seizing on the metaphors through which its basic premises are expressed, and by so doing, they achieve their persuasiveness. They change it because each necessarily alters, at least to some extent, the meaning of these metaphors by applying them to contexts to which they have not been applied before. The discourse on the Czech state not only re-created Czech culture by metaphorically employing its key notions of the natural and the artificial but also, at least to some extent, changed it by newly contextualising these notions and thus giving them new meanings. These altered meanings are then themselves used to express the basic premises of culture in other discourses. In this sense, culture is not itself a discourse (in the same way as language is not discourse) but is reproduced, kept alive, and perpetually changed in ongoing discourses.

The basic premises of Czech culture and the way in which Czechs construct their national identity have affected not only the discourses which I have discussed in this chapter but also the way in which communist rule ended in Czechoslovakia and the whole process of transformation on which Czech society embarked thereafter. This process was accompanied by the emergence of a multiplicity of new discourses which, on the one hand, seized on the basic premises of Czech culture and, by positively invoking them, reaffirmed and re-created them and, on the other hand, altered them in many subtle ways. Seen in this way, Czech culture and ideas about what constitutes Czech identity must be conceptualised not as timeless and unchangeable attributes of the Czech nation, as Czechs themselves conceptualise them, but as constructions perpetually re-created and modified in political practice. Moreover, rather than as a harmonious, singular, and coherent ideational system, they must be seen as a system of competing values and concepts which are internally inconsistent and ultimately irreconcilable.

One set of such values and concepts is generated in an overtly nationalist discourse which emphasises the values of egalitarianism and construes individuals as parts of a nation and as emanations of collective Czech nationhood. During the events which led to the fall of communist rule in Czechoslovakia, in the process of subsequent post-communist transformation of Czech society, and during the political crisis which was eventually resolved by the creation of an independent Czech state, the notions, beliefs, and values espoused in what may be called Czech nationalism gained prominence in a number of everyday discourses. However, the nationalist discourse is not the only one that creates and re-creates Czech cultural assumptions, premises, values, and beliefs. It is in constant competition with a discourse which espouses the values of Western individualism and construes individuals not as parts of a nation but as autonomous persons in their own right.

Czech identity is negotiated in these two simultaneous discourses, which, on the one hand, are in competition with each other and, on the other hand, draw upon each other and are occasionally collapsed into each other. In situations perceived as national crises, the values espoused in the nationalist discourse come to prominence and those espoused in the competing discourse on individualism may be temporarily submerged. But in fact both sets of values feed into the premises of Czech culture, and a middle way is ideally sought between them so that neither discourse is ultimately seen to be dependent upon the other. In consequence, Czech culture is a system of values and concepts which are in constant tension with each other and which surface and are argued about in a multiplicity of discourses through which they are perpetually created and re-created.

In chapter 4, I discussed two images of the past, one of which construes the Czech nation as a subject and the other as an object of history. These two images compete and are often collapsed into one everyday discourse. Just as these two images represent two ways of looking at Czech history, the notions of collectivism and individualism, with their associated values, represent two ways of looking at Czech culture. They too are in competition and occasionally are collapsed into each other. For example, in everyday discourse they are represented in the image of the individuality of the leader and the collectivity of the masses or in the celebration of the intellectuality and individualism of leading historical and political personalities and the simultaneous emphasis on the conformity and mediocrity of the little Czech.

This collapsing of competing notions into one everyday discourse is probably most clearly manifested in the fusion of universal European values and particularistic national sentiments in the discourse about the future political and economic orientation of the Czech Republic. The proclaimed goal of the Czech post-communist government is admission to the European Union, and it is doing everything in its power to achieve this. For example, it makes sure that all new legislation passed by the Czech parliament is in line with the European Commission's rules and regulations. This effort is the most tangible expression of the 'return to Europe' upon which Czechs embarked after the overthrow of the communist regime in 1989.

Yet, the notion of the return to Europe emerged in the context of heightened nationalist feelings which accompanied the demise of communism not only in Czechoslovakia but in most of the countries of Central and Eastern Europe. Nationalism is generally perceived as being at odds with the idea of greater European integration, the proclaimed goal of the European Commission. The self-proclaimed European federalist and former president of the European Movement in Britain has pointed to the growth of nationalism and the establishment of independent nation-states as the underlying cause of rivalry and enmity within Europe (Wistricht 1989: 77). A similar view has been echoed by Hobsbawm (1990) and by Smith (1992: 76), who argues that confronting established national identities is the supreme challenge that faces Europe today. The attempts of the European Commission to achieve a higher form of European integration than a common market are based on the recognition of the need 'to change people's consciousness of themselves, including their identity as nationals rather than European citizens' (Shore 1993: 784). In the view of the ideologues of greater European integration, the precondition of European unification is 'the dismantling of the nation-state and its associated ideology of nationalism' (Shore 1993: 787).

The Czechs see their 'return to Europe' as appropriate for a nation which is highly cultured and well educated and possessed of a long tradition of democracy and other characteristics which link it to other liberal-democratic countries of Western Europe. As I have shown in chapter 3, these assumed traditions and characteristics, which embody and emphasise universal European values, are currently re-created through comparisons with the Slovaks, whom Czechs see as lacking any of these values. The ostensibly European values which the Czechs attribute to themselves are thus constructed in the context of an overt nationalism.

It has been suggested that 'if the EU succeeds in shifting the loyalties of large numbers of European nationals toward Brussels or Strasburg and avoids provoking a nationalist backlash, the re-drawing of borders and boundaries that would result from the withering away of the established nation-state is certain to precipitate increased ethnic and regional conflict as those peripheral identities that have been submerged for decades under the political roof of the big nation-state begin to assert their independence' (Shore 1993: 794). According to this scenario, greater European integration would simply mean the replacement of one form of nationalism by another. Before the nation-state withers away, the policy of particular nation-states eager to join the European Union   such as the Czech Republic – might well encourage another form of nationalism, one based on a 'more-European-than-thou' attitude, in which particular nationalistic ambitions are couched in terms of what are ostensibly European values. The Czech self-images which emphasise the tradition of democracy and portray the Czech nation as highly cultured and well educated are precisely such values.

Paying attention to the self-images people have of themselves as nations, to the specific discourses through which these images are created, and to the ways in which they affect political and economic practices is particularly important in studying the process of post-socialist transformation. It prevents us from treating Eastern Europe as a politically, economically, and, to some extent, even culturally undifferentiated whole and as undergoing a single transformation from a totalitarian political system to democratic pluralism and from a centrally planned to a market economy. Although, undoubtedly, this process has many common features (Verdery 1991) which it is useful to bear in mind, it also shows the remarkable differences from one country to another. The Czech case is a special one in that it combines the problem of legitimating a post-socialist state with that of legitimating a new one to its subjects. However, legitimation of a new post-socialist order and of the gradually emerging post-socialist states is a process which, in one way or another, all former socialist countries have to face. The attention paid in this process to the invocation of shared cultural meanings and the key metaphors and symbols through which they are expressed may link specifically anthropological concerns with those of political science, economics, and sociology, the disciplines which have so far dominated the study of the post-socialist countries' current transformation.

Notes

1 Nation against state

1. In October 1945 more than 3,000 enterprises were nationalised, and in March 1947 they employed 61.2 per cent of industrial workers and accounted for almost two-thirds of total industrial output (for further discussion of social and economic changes in Czechoslovakia between 1945 and 1948 see Luza 1973: 387–415; Korbel 1977: 38–41; Teichova 1988: 87–100; Wolchik 1991: 17–20).

2. In 1987 the proportion of total agricultural land left in private hands in the Czech lands was only 3.9 per cent (4.0 per cent in Slovakia) and the proportion of arable land only 1.4 per cent (2.4 per cent in Slovakia) (*Statistická ročenka Československé socialistické republiky 1988*: 284–5). As the average private holding was only 0.5 hectares (1.2 hectares in Slovakia), the income of those who worked it derived not from agriculture but from work in industry or elsewhere. According to official statistics, of the 848,000 people employed in agriculture in the Czech lands at the end of 1960, only 78,000 were considered private farmers, and by 1983 their number had dropped to a mere 4,000 out of 546,000. The number of private farmers remained slightly higher in Slovakia, where there were 178,000 private farmers of 509,000 employed in agriculture in 1960; by 1983 their number had dropped to 5,000 out of 345,000 (ibid.: 282; see also Taborsky 1961: 332–43; Korbel 1977: 261; Wadekin 1982: 85–6; Wolchik 1991: 23).

   The proportion of the population employed in the private sector as a whole was only 27.3 per cent in 1950, and it dropped to 4 per cent in 1961 and 2.5 per cent in 1970. The decline of the population employed in the private sector proceeded more slowly in Slovakia than in the more industrialised Czech lands. In 1950 only 21.6 per cent of the population in the Czech lands was employed in the private sector (39 per cent in Slovakia), and the proportion in private employment gradually dropped to 1.7 per cent (4.8 per cent in Slovakia) by 1969. The share of the private sector in the creation of national income was only 1.5 per cent of the total in 1950 and had decreased to 0.8 per cent by 1965 and 1970.

   The impact of nationalisation was also reflected in the composition of the labour force. For example, in 1960 individual farmers accounted for only 4.2 per cent and private artisans, craftsmen, and those with free professions constituted only 0.1 per cent of the total labour force (Wolchik 1991: 168–70). The only substantial items of national wealth which remained largely in private ownership were dwellings; in 1955, 56.3 per cent of them were in private and 43.7 per cent in state or cooperative ownership (Krejci 1972: 17, 20–1).

3. Collective, nominally voluntary work groups on Saturdays and Sundays ('brigades') were organised to tidy up and improve the appearance of public spaces, build new parks and children's playgrounds, etc. These 'brigades' were recruited either from among the residents of a neighbourhood or, more often, from among the employees of an office or factory. Offices and factories were also centres of collective entertainment and recreation, the organisation of which became the main function of trade unions (Krejci 1972: 95–6). Promoting collective forms of life was the main function of the 'socialist work brigades' consisting of workers and employees of a working unit who pledged themselves not only to work but also to live in a socialist way. A campaign to create these brigades was launched in 1959; by 1961 there were 71,000 collectives competing for the title of brigade and 8,538 such titles had been awarded. By 1963 the number of competing collectives had increased to almost 89,000, and more than 31,000 had been awarded the title. Collectives competing for the title encouraged their members to participate in organisations such as trade unions, the Union of Socialist Youth (the Czechoslovak equivalent of the Soviet Komsomol), the Czechoslovak Union of Women, and the Society of Czechoslovak–Soviet Friendship. Their members collectively attended cultural performances and took an interest in one another's family life; they helped one another to overcome survivals of 'bourgeois morality' such as individualism and preference for the private to the public good, to overcome individual vices such as alcoholism, and to acquire socialist moral attitudes (Krejci 1972: 96).

4. All translations from Czech are mine.

5. The Soviet hero Pavlik Morozov, who denounced his father as a traitor, was set up as a role model and occasionally emulated. During the trials of Rudolf Slánský, the general secretary of the Communist Party, and other leading Czechoslovak Communists in the 1950s, *Rudé právo* published letters in which the relatives of the accused condemned their actions and demanded harsh punishment for them; such letters were intended not only to indicate the heinousness of the crimes and to inculcate the belief that they must be enormous if they were condemned even by the culprits' families, but also to stress where an individual's loyalty should lie. For example, the son of Ludvík Frejka, one of the alleged collaborators of Slánský, wrote to the presiding judge:

Dear comrade, I demand the heaviest penalty, the penalty of death, for my father. Only now do I see that this creature, whom one cannot call a man because he did not have the slightest feeling and human dignity, was my greatest and vilest enemy . . . Hatred toward my father will always strengthen me in my struggle for the communist future of our people. I request that this letter be placed before my father and that, if occasion permits, I may tell him all this myself.

(Rudé právo, *25 November 1952; quoted in Taborsky 1961: 95*)

6. 'Interest organisations' constitute an area which spans the divide between the public and the private spheres but in which particular organisations – depending on the size of their membership, the degree of openness of their recruitment, and the extent to which they were subject to or managed to avoid official control – tended to cluster closer to either the public or the private pole of the dichotomy.

7. Basing his calculation on published Czechoslovak censuses and statistics, Krejci estimates that some 650,000–700,000 individuals, representing about 10 per cent of the working population (Krejci 1972: 140) and called *řídící kádry* ('directing cadres') in official parlance, were entrusted with this kind of management in 1967. Of this managerial class, only slightly over 200,000 were in control of the means of production – many fewer than the 500,000 persons who owned enterprises employing hired labour or farms over 10 hectares before the war (Krejci 1972: 110–11).

   A survey of attitudes conducted in 1974 by a correspondent of the émigré journal *Svědectví* found that only 10 per cent of respondents and only 25 per cent of party members polled felt that they had some influence on political decisions (Paul 1979: 45). Of the respondents with post-secondary education, only 5 per cent felt that they had any political influence (ibid.: 307, n. 93).

8. Statistics on the theft of socialist property are not unambiguous, but its overall trend appears to be one of remarkable stability in the annual figures. The available statistics concerning the value of the stolen goods suggest the following figures for the early 1970s: 1970, 120 million Kčs; 1971, 140 million Kčs; and 1972, 211.4 million Kčs (Paul 1979: 36). The theft of socialist property constituted one-fifth of all criminal activity in the 1960s (Ulc 1974: 92) and one-third in 1971 (Paul 1979: 37). The available statistics reflect only reported crime; many workers and managers certainly failed to report such thefts, and it is estimated that the value of the property stolen and not reported may have exceeded by several times the value given in official statistics (Paul 1979: 37). For example, in 1969 it was reported that, on average, one out of three violators of the law went undetected; for pilfering of socialist property the percentage was 44.7 per cent (Ulc 1974: 92–3). An official of the presidium of the Czechoslovak government estimated in 1988 that at least one-quarter of the materials for the building of family homes came from 'unidentifiable sources' (*Práce*, 18 June 1988). These figures indicate the tacit support which this particular type of crime enjoyed (Paul 1979: 37).

9. A spokesman for the Ministry of Labour and Social Welfare of the Czech Socialist Republic estimated in 1975 that these activities amounted to the loss of 100 million working hours a year and represented the work time of 55,000 workers (Paul 1979: 28). A survey conducted among the workers in the East Slovakia Ironworks in 1972 found that one-third of respondents were of the opinion that work time was used to only 70 or 80 per cent of its capacity; half of the respondents refused to express an opinion; and only 14.6 per cent thought that work time in the factory was fully utilised.

10. Schweik is the hero of the novel *The Good Soldier Schweik* (published in English translation by Penguin Books, 1951) by the Czech writer Jaroslav Hašek (1883–1923). This novel has become the secular 'bible' of most edu-

cated Czechs, some of whom know it almost by heart and quote freely from it in their everyday discourse.

11. As a consequence, according to a UNESCO report, work morale in Czechoslovakia was among the lowest in Europe, and, for example, the utilisation of working hours in West Germany or Japan was three to four times greater (Ulc 1974: 54). In May 1969 the prime minister noted that 'in offices, institutes, and some factories work ends at noon on Friday, and thus the working week is not five days, but often only four and a half, four and a quarter, and so on' (ibid.: 55).

In November 1974 Radio Prague reported that 'hundreds of thousands of workers regularly celebrate their birthdays, name-days, and other anniversaries' with their co-workers during working hours (Paul 1979: 28). This general observation has been confirmed by surveys of the utilisation of work time. 'In one machine-works factory, it was found that fully one-fourth of the 1,200 workers were allowed exemption from the normal working time. In another factory 150 workers were allowed to leave work two hours before the end of their shifts', and on the basis of another survey 'it was estimated that overextended work breaks in one factory caused a loss of production in one year's time equivalent of 7,000 shifts' (ibid.).

Unexcused absence from work and malingering were the targets of perpetual complaints by party and government. The statistics on absenteeism which I have come across are rather old, but they do indicate the scope of the problem: in 1952 almost 3 million shifts were lost through unexcused absences (Evanson 1985: 250). On the average workday in 1970, 51 of every 1,000 workers were absent. Referring to statistics indicating that daily absence from work due to illness alone was 47 per 1,000 during the first half of 1970, the then-prime minister mentioned that study of the problem had revealed that at least 25 per cent of the absentees were faking their illness.

12. It is difficult to determine the extent of this tendency toward withdrawal from the public into the private sphere, but there are some indications. A much greater concern with individual well-being than with the organisation of political life in the country emerged from a public poll conducted by the Czechoslovak Academy of Sciences in February 1968: economic improvement and housing were the top priority of most respondents, and the democratisation of the political system came out seventh (Ulc 1974: 56). In a survey on gender equality and the economic emancipation of women, only 7 per cent of respondents stated that they sought employment for their 'self-realisation' (ibid.: 9); for the overwhelming majority employment was simply an economic necessity. The results of a 1988 survey made public in 1990 showed little interest in participating in local government and a low regard for local government on the part of most citizens. Only 2 per cent of respondents felt that they had any significant influence on local affairs, and only 14 per cent felt that they had some influence; most respondents said that they had rather little (42 per cent) or virtually no influence at all (42 per cent) (Wolchik 1991: 77). In addition, a study of young people conducted in May 1988 indicated their very low levels of political involvement (ibid.: 112–13).

13. Czech dissidents used the term 'post-totalitarian' to describe a society in which

communist ideology had assumed a purely ritual function. Czechoslovak society in the 1970s and 1980s was 'post-totalitarian' in the sense that the ruling Communist Party no longer expected citizens to express their ideological beliefs in participating in its rituals (see Pynsent 1994: 213, n. 35).

14. In the seven elections held between 1948 and 1981, the lowest percentage of votes for the 'candidates of the National Front' was in the elections in May 1948: 87.12 per cent in the Czech lands and 84.91 per cent in Slovakia. In all the subsequent elections the percentage of votes for the 'National Front candidates' oscillated between 97.89 and 99.98 per cent (*Československé dějiny v datech* 1987: 633–4). The voting pattern of the Federal Assembly is probably best demonstrated by the fact that in December 1989 the 323 deputies elected to the Assembly before November 1989 voted unanimously for Václav Havel as president of the republic; in a secret ballot in the subsequent election in July 1990 he was elected president by only 234 votes against 50.

15. For a discussion of the importance of symbols and symbolic opposition for the success of public demonstrations and of the ways in which 'the status and potency of the state is reduced by symbolic means', see Paine (1985).

2 Freedom, nation, and personhood

1. The gender-specific language which I employ here reflects the usage common in Czech. *Člověk* (plural *lidé*, 'people') is grammatically masculine. It is the equivalent of the German *Mensch* (plural *Leute*). English has no adequate equivalent, and I resort to translating *člověk* as 'man' – denoting both 'human being' (which Czechs would render by the grammatically feminine expression *lidská bytost*) and 'human being of male sex' (which Czechs would render as *muž*).

2. A married woman's personal identity may be doubly hidden. She not only sheds her own identity by taking her husband's name but may merge with him by being addressed by his occupation. This usage, fading now, was quite common before World War II, though it was limited to higher-status occupations: an accountant's wife was 'Mrs Accountant' but a shop assistant's wife was addressed by her name.

3 Self-stereotypes and national traditions

1. This is a common Czech parable which I have heard in different variants: when a neighbour's field has a better crop, the farmer does not wish his field to yield as well as his neighbour's but prays for his neighbour's crop to be seized by blight. When a neighbour's wife buys a new fur coat, my wife does not wish to have one as well but wishes her neighbour's to be eaten by moths.

2. When workers in an industrial plant in a small town in eastern Bohemia were asked for their understanding of the expression 'cultural standard', 39.8 per cent mentioned participation in and appreciation of 'high culture' and 22.9 per cent mentioned 'culture of everyday life', including conduct and manners (13.7 per cent), equipment of the household (3.3 per cent), and ways of spending one's leisure time (7.2 per cent) (Maříková, Klus, and Malina 1987: 157).

3. Aš is the western-most town in Bohemia; Znojmo is a town in southern Moravia close to the Slovak border.

4. Levý Hradec, on the northern outskirts of Prague, was the site of the oldest his-

torically documented Christian church in Bohemia, built by Wenceslas's grandfather Bořivoj in the second half of the ninth century.
5. Cyril and Method came as missionaries from Salonica to the Great Moravian empire to spread Christianity in 863. They originally conducted mass in a Slavonic language, but Latin became the liturgical language in 873.

4 National traditions and the imagining of the nation

1. Karel Havlíček Borovský (1821–56), journalist, writer, and politician, was one of the leading protagonists of the national revival.
2. Petr Chelčický (ca. 1390–ca. 1460) was a theologian and a leading ideologist of the Hussite movement.
3. Jiří z Poděbrad (1420–71) was a Czech Protestant king (ruled 1458–71) who, after the disruption of royal rule in Bohemia during the Hussite period, restored power to the Czech kingdom against the opposition of the pope and the European Catholic monarchs.
4. The land office, which carried out the reform and which was abolished only in 1935, was in the hands of the Agrarian Party, which used the reform effectively to create a solid base in the Czech countryside. It was mainly due to the reform that this party remained the strongest party throughout the lifetime of the pre-war Czechoslovak Republic and, paradoxically, played the most important role in every coalition government of a country whose economic strength was based on its relatively developed industry rather than agriculture.
5. The third obvious purpose of the land reforms, which the official political rhetoric of course never mentioned explicitly, need not detain us here: to strengthen the political base of the parties which effectively controlled them – the Agrarian Party in the case of the first reform and the Communist Party in the case of the second.
6. The Czech Brethren (Jednota bratrská) was a religious sect founded in 1457 by the supporters of the teaching of Petr Chelčický.
7. The Czech philosopher and historian Jan Patočka (1907–77) was one of the leading activists of Charter 77.

5 National traditions and the political process

1. In January 1992, a year after the start of the reform, the number of people in the Czech lands who expected prosperity as the end result of economic transformation increased to 71 per cent; 66 per cent thought that the speed of the reform either was adequate or should increase; only 6 per cent believed that reform should be stopped altogether (*Aktuálne problémy Česko-Slovenska*, January 1992: 58–9).
2. I emphasise with italics the key words and expressions in these and subsequent quotations in chapters 5 and 6.
3. In December 1990, before the start of the economic reform, 70 per cent of Czechs and 80 per cent of Slovaks were afraid that it would result in considerable weakening of the social security which they had so far enjoyed. People were also afraid that it would be accompanied by an increase in social injustice (53 per cent in the Czech lands and 71 per cent in Slovakia) and that it would lead to the deterioration of general morality and inter-personal relations (*Lidové noviny*, 28 December 1990).

4. Country cottages and farmhouses became increasingly available during the 1960s and 1970s when cooperative farmers began to build themselves new homes with modern facilities and were willing to sell their old cottages to town inhabitants as holiday homes. Cabins vary from simple one-room frame structures to structures which are, in fact, family houses and which, by circumventing planning and building regulations, have been built with a view to providing a permanent home in retirement and are equipped with modern amenities such as bathrooms and central heating. Those who can afford it spend as much time as possible in their cottages. This offers an opportunity to acquiring all the paraphernalia of luxury, such as fireplaces or bars, which cannot be accommodated in the confined space of a flat – particularly a flat in a prefabricated tower block, which, before the market with flats and houses gradually developed after 1989, was the only kind to which most of those who did not inherit a flat in an old apartment block could have aspired.

In 1934 Prague residents owned a total of 3,000 holiday cabins; in 1974 they owned 65,000 in central Bohemia alone, with many others travelling farther to their cabins in other parts of the country. In 1967 there were 110,000 cabins in the Czech lands; by 1970 their total reached 150,000, and, according to the population census of 1991, there were 206,456 in the Czech lands in that year. The wooded countryside south and west of Prague is virtually littered with these tiny frame structures, the abundance of which has played havoc with the natural environment in recreational areas and caused practical sanitation problems. In 1974 the Czech government felt it necessary to curb the 'dacha mania' by limiting to 25,000 the number of building permits which could be issued in the future. At that time, it was estimated that there was still a possibility of acquiring some 33,000 vacant buildings in the country for conversion into holiday homes; many of them were farmhouses and cottages abandoned after the war by Sudeten Germans forced to leave Czechoslovakia (Paul 1979: 34). Apart from the holiday cabins, 52,622 country cottages and 128,120 flats were being used solely as holiday homes in the Czech lands in 1991. Holiday cabins, cottages, or flats were owned or regularly used by 452,080 households in the Czech lands (12.2 per cent) and 387,198 buildings were used solely as holiday homes. The proportion of households owning holiday homes is unequal throughout the country. In Prague, a full 27.7 per cent of households have a holiday home in the country, and the proportion is even higher in the city of Plzen (28.9 per cent), which lies closer to the border territories inhabited before the war by the Germans.

6 Nation and state in the context of Czech culture

1. The expression connotes primarily a down-to-earth, no-nonsense practicality.
2. The Czech sociologist Josef Alan has captured this view in a collection of essays on Czech–Slovak relations written during the complex political negotiations about the future structure of the state and published at the height of the constitutional crisis in 1992:

> Although the discussion is about the tension in Czech–Slovak relations, the issue has always been Slovakia, and it has, since the creation of the republic, principally been initiated by the Slovak side and almost regularly construed by the Czechs and Czechoslovakists (or 'federalists') as the manifestation of nationalism.
>
> *(Alan 1992: 17)*

It is a view which depicts Slovaks as nationalists while denying the existence of any nationalist sentiments among the Czechs. It is expressed not only by ordinary people but by many Czech intellectuals, including Alan himself:

The Czech lands first experienced a process of the creation of national self-consciousness, building upon the ancient traditions of the Czech state, during the nineteenth century, and national identity has become self-evident, a lived value rather than one sought after. As a result, paradoxically, it has exhausted its culture-creative potential and ceased to be perceived as an ultimate value. It has even 'dried up' or, more exactly, acquired such refined forms that it is no longer defined as specifically national . . . This achieved national identity is accompanied by the emergence of a universalistic and institutionalised value system in which the state is a 'transnational' institution, a set of forms of social coexistence, which can be transferred from one setting to another.   *(Alan 1992: 14)*

[The Czech] side accentuates universalistic values which transcend the horizon of the nation (civic society, free market economy, individual liberties, etc.); the [Slovak] side universalises particularistic values (the nation and its sovereignty, language, Catholicism, etc.). Another dimension: one side emphasises a civilisational-geographical identity (belonging to the West), the other side a cultural-historical identity (faithfulness to traditions).   *(Alan 1992: 16)*

3. The perception in Slovakia was different. The Slovaks wanted a different kind of coexistence with the Czechs in a common state which would truly reflect the equality of the two republics in the form either of a confederation or of some other kind of union. In Slovakia the disintegration of Czechoslovakia was mainly perceived as a result of the intransigence of the Czech politicians who emerged from the 1992 elections and who, arguing that the goal of the Slovak politicians was the creation of 'an independent Slovakia with a Czech insurance company', presented the Slovaks with an ultimatum: either a 'workable' federation (which the Slovaks saw as the maintenance of the old unitary state) or complete separation. As a unitary state, in which they felt themselves to be discriminated against and which was widely perceived as having never served Slovak interests, was no longer acceptable to the Slovak people, the separation forced upon the Slovaks by the intransigent Czechs became the only solution. According to a September 1992 opinion poll, 41 per cent of Slovaks agreed with the division of Czechoslovakia (in October it was only 37 per cent) and 46 per cent did not agree. Most of those who agreed with the division (32 per cent) attributed it to 'Pragocentrism' and discrimination against Slovakia within the federal structure. Most of those who did not agree with it (49 per cent) attributed it to the inability of the Czech and Slovak politicians to reach agreement about the form of the common state.

References

Agnew, H. L. 1992. Czechs, Slovaks, and the Slovak linguistic separatism of the mid-nineteenth century. In *The Czech and Slovak experience*, ed. J. Morison. New York: St Martin's Press.

Aktuálne problémy Česko-slovenska: správa zo sociologického prieskumu. Bratislava: Centrum pre sociálnu analýzu.

Alan, J. 1992. Česko-slovenské vztahy po pádu komunistického panství. In *Dnešní krize česko-slovenských vztahů*, F. Gál *et al.* Prague: Sociologické nakladatelství.

Anderson, B. 1983. *Imagined communities.* London: Verso.

Austin, J. L. 1971. A plea for excuses. In *Philosophy and linguistics*, ed. C. Lyas. London: Macmillan.

Barnard, F. M. 1991. Political culture: continuity and discontinuity. In *Czechoslovakia 1918–88: seventy years from independence*, ed. H. G. Skilling. New York: St Martin's Press.

Barth, F. 1969. Introduction to *Ethnic groups and boundaries: the social organization of culture difference*, ed. F. Barth. Boston: Little, Brown and Company.

Bauman, R. 1986. *Story, performance, and event: contextual studies of oral narrative.* Cambridge: Cambridge University Press.

Beneš, E. 1935. *Světová válka a naše revoluce.* Prague: Čin a Orbis.

Beránek, J. 1988. K otázce česko-slovenské vzájemnosti v letech 1918–1938. In *Češi na Slovensku. Zpravodaj koordinované sítě vědeckých informací pro etnografii a folkloristiku* 7: 55–88. Prague: Ústav pro etnografii a folkloristiku ČSAV.

Berger, J. 1968. The nature of mass demonstrations. *New Society*, 295 (23 May): 754–5.

Biedermannová, C. 1992. *Mstivá kantiléna, aneb rigor magoris aneb feministický nářez.* Prague: Ivo Železný.

Boissevain, J. 1975. Towards a social anthropology of Europe. In *Beyond the community: social processes in Europe*, ed. J. Boissevain and J. Friedl. The Hague: University of Amsterdam.

Bradley, J. F. N. 1984. *Czech nationalism in the nineteenth century.* East European Monographs, Boulder, Colo. and New York: Columbia University Press.

Brown, A. and J. Gray (eds.). 1979. *Political culture and political change in communist states*. London: Macmillan.

Campbell, F. G. 1975. *Confrontation in Central Europe: Weimar Germany and Czechoslovakia*. Chicago: University of Chicago Press.

Československé dějiny v datech. 1987. Prague: Svoboda.

Chaloupecký, V. 1930. *Zápas o Slovensko 1918*. Prague: Čin a Orbis.

Chirot, D. (ed.). 1991. *The end of Leninism and the decline of the Left: the revolutions of 1989*. Seattle: University of Washington Press.

Clark, J. and A. Wildavsky. 1991. *The moral collapse of communism: Poland as a cautionary tale*. San Francisco: Institute for Contemporary Studies.

Cohen, A. (ed.). 1974. *Urban ethnicity*. ASA Monographs 12. London: Tavistock.

Cole, J. 1977. Anthropology comes part-way home. *Annual Review of Anthropology* 6: 349–78.

Collard, A. 1989. Investigating 'social memory' in a Greek context. In *History and ethnicity*, ed. E. Tonkin, M. McDonald, and M. Chapman. ASA Monographs 27. London: Tavistock.

Crump, T. 1975. The context of European anthropology: the lesson from Italy. In *Beyond the community: social processes in Europe*, ed. J. Boissevain and J. Friedl. The Hague: University of Amsterdam.

Csepeli, G. 1992. National identity in post-communist Hungary. In *Ethnicity and conflict in a post-communist world*, ed. K. Rupesinghe, P. King, and O. Vorkunova. New York: St Martin's Press.

Data a fakta: informace z výzkumu. Prague: Sociologický ústav ČSAV.

Devereux, G. 1978. *Ethnopsychoanalysis*. Berkeley: University of California Press.

Dumont, L. 1986. *Essays on individualism: modern ideology in anthropological perspective*. Chicago: University of Chicago Press.

Dunn, J. 1984. *The politics of socialism: an essay in political theory*. Cambridge: Cambridge University Press.

Evanson, R. K. 1985. Regime and working class in Czechoslovakia, 1948–1968. *Soviet Studies* 37: 248–68.

Fairclough, N. 1989. *Language and power*. London: Longman.

   1992. *Discourse and social change*. Cambridge, UK: Polity Press.

Faltan, S. 1986. *Slovenská otázka v Československu*. Bratislava: Vydavatelstvo politickej literatury.

Felak, J. 1992. Slovak considerations of the Slovak question: the Ludak, Agrarian, Socialist, and Communist views in interwar Czechoslovakia. In *The Czech and Slovak experience*, ed. J. Morison. New York: St Martin's Press.

Fidelius, P. 1983. *Slovo a moc*. Munich: Arkýř.

Filip, O. 1989. Rozhovor na dálku s Evou. *Listy* 19, no. 2: 70–81.

Foster, R. J. 1991. Making national cultures in the global ecumene. *Annual Review of Anthropology* 20: 235–60.

Foucault, M. 1972. *The archaeology of knowledge*. London: Tavistock.

   1979. *Discipline and punish: the birth of the prison*. Harmondsworth: Penguin.

Fox, R. G. 1985. *Lions of the Punjab: culture in the making*. Berkeley: University of California Press.

Gál, F. 1992. Problém česko-slovenských vztahov po Novembri 1989 cez prizmu politiky. In *Dnešní krize česko-slovenských vztahů*, F. Gál *et al.* Prague: Sociologické nakladatelství.

Gal, S. 1991. Bartok's funeral: representations of Europe in Hungarian political rhetoric. *American Ethnologist* 18: 440–58.

Galasi, P. and G. Sziraczki (eds.). 1985. *Labour market and second economy in Hungary.* Frankfurt: Campus Verlag.

Geertz, C. 1966. Religion as a cultural system. In *Anthropological approaches to the study of religion*, ed. M. Banton. ASA Monographs 3. London: Tavistock Publications.

1973. *The interpretation of cultures.* New York: Basic Books.

Gellner, E. 1983. *Nations and nationalism.* Oxford: Basil Blackwell.

1987. *Culture, identity, and politics.* Cambridge: Cambridge University Press.

Grečo, M. 1947. *Martinská deklarácia.* Martin: Matica slovenská.

Grillo, R. D. (ed.). 1980. *'Nation' and 'state' in Europe: anthropological perspectives.* London: Academic Press.

Grove-White, R. 1993. Environmentalism: a new moral discourse for technological society? In *Environmentalism: the view from anthropology*, ed. K. Milton. ASA Monographs 32. London: Routledge.

Halliday, M. A. K. 1978. *Language as social semiotic.* London: Edward Arnold.

Halliday, M. A. K. and R. Hasan. 1976. *Cohesion in English.* London: Longman.

Hankiss, E. 1990. *East European alternatives.* Oxford: Clarendon Press.

Hann, C. M. 1993. Introduction to *Socialism: ideas, ideologies, and local practice*, ed. C. M. Hann. ASA Monographs 31. London: Routledge.

Hannerz, U. 1987. The world in creolisation. *Africa* 57: 546–59.

Havel, V. 1990a. *Dálkový výslech: rozhovor s Karlem Hvížďalou.* Prague: Melantrich.

1990b. *Projevy: leden–červen 1990.* Prague: Vyšehrad.

1992. *Vážení občané: projevy červenec 1990–červenec 1992.* Prague: Lidové noviny.

Havel, V. *et al.* 1985. *The power of the powerless: citizens against the state in Central-Eastern Europe.* London: Hutchinson.

Heiberg, M. 1980. Basques, anti-Basques, and the moral community. In *'Nation' and 'state' in Europe: anthropological perspectives*, ed. R. D. Grillo. London: Academic Press.

Heller, A. 1984. *Everyday life.* London: Routledge and Kegan Paul.

Henderson, K. 1993. *Czechoslovakia: the failure of consensus politics.* Leicester University Discussion Papers in Politics, no. P93/4. Leicester: Department of Politics, University of Leicester.

Hervey, S. G. J. 1992. The textual layer-cake: reflections on the unruliness of texts. *Semiotica* 91: 171–83.

Herzfeld, M. 1982. The etymology of excuses: aspects of rhetorical performance in Greece. *American Anthropologist* 9: 644–63.

Hobsbawm, E. 1990. *Nations and nationalism since 1780.* Cambridge: Cambridge University Press.

Hobsbawm, E. and T. Ranger (eds.). 1983. *The invention of tradition.* Cambridge: Cambridge University Press.

Holy, L. 1987. Description, generalization, and comparison: two paradigms. In *Comparative anthropology*, ed. L. Holy. Oxford: Basil Blackwell.

Hrabal, B. 1988. Kličky na kapesníku. *Listy* 18, no. 3: 56–60.

Jirák, J. and O. Šoltys, 1992. Zobrazení česko-slovenských vztahů v tisku v období

17. 11. 1989 až 31. 12. 1991 – státoprávní uspořádání. In *Dnešní krize česko-slovenských vztahů*, F. Gál *et al*. Prague: Sociologické nakladatelství.

Kálal, K. 1905. *Slovensko a Slováci*. Prague: F. Šimáček.

Kantůrková, E. 1989. O etice Palachova činu. *Svědectví* 22: 360–5.

Kapferer, B. 1988. *Legends of people, myths of state*. Washington, DC and London: Smithsonian Institution Press.

Kertzer, D. I. 1988. *Ritual, politics, and power*. New Haven: Yale University Press.

Kohn, H. 1955. *Nationalism: its meaning and history*. Princeton: Van Nostrand.

1967. *The idea of nationalism*. 2nd edn. New York: Collier Macmillan.

Kořalka, J. 1988. K pojetí národa v české společnosti 19. století. In *Povědomí tradice v novodobé české kultuře*. Prague: Národní galerie.

Korbel, J. 1977. *Twentieth-century Czechoslovakia: the meaning of its history*. New York: Columbia University Press.

Krejci, J. 1972. *Social change and stratification in postwar Czechoslovakia*. London: Macmillan.

Kusin, V. V. 1971. *The intellectual origins of the Prague Spring: the development of reformist ideas in Czechoslovakia, 1956–67*. Cambridge: Cambridge University Press.

1983. Dissent in Czechoslovakia after 1968. In *Dissent in Eastern Europe*, ed. J. L. Curry. New York: Praeger Publishers.

Leff, C. S. 1988. *National conflict in Czechoslovakia: the making and remaking of a state, 1918–1987*. Princeton: Princeton University Press.

Luza, R. 1973. Czechoslovakia between democracy and communism. In *A history of the Czechoslovak republic, 1918–1948*, ed. V. S. Mamatey and R. Luza. Princeton: Princeton University Press.

Macdonell, D. 1986. *Theories of discourse*. Oxford: Basil Blackwell.

McFarlane, A. 1978. *The origins of English individualism*. Oxford: Basil Blackwell.

Machonin, P. *et al.* 1969. *Československá společnost: sociologická analýza sociální stratifikace*. Bratislava: Epocha.

Macura, V. 1983. *Znamení zrodu: české obrození jako kulturní typ*. Prague: Československy spisovatel.

1992. Most. *Tvar*, no. 43, p. 6.

1993. *Masarykovy boty a jine semi(o)fejetony*. Prague: Pražská imaginace.

Mali, V. 1983. On the situation of the church in CSSR. In *Martyrdom today*, ed. J.-B. Metz and E. Schilebeeckx. Edinburgh: T. & T. Clark Ltd.

Maříková, I., P. Klus, and F. Malina. 1987. *Kulturní zájmy dělnické třídy v průmyslovém závodě*. Prague: Ústav pro výzkum kultury.

Masaryk, T. G. 1925. *Světová revoluce*. Prague: Čin a Orbis.

1928. *Slovanské problémy*. Prague: Státní nakladatelství.

Měchýř, J. 1991. *Slovensko v Československu: Slovensko-české vztahy 1918–1991*. Prague: Práce.

Meinecke, F. 1907. *Weltburgertum und Nationalstaat: Studien zur Genesis des deutschen Nationalstaates*. Munich and Berlin.

Mezník, J. 1989. O české malosti (a také velikosti). *Proměny* 26, no. 1: 11–20.

Milton, K. 1993. Environmentalism and anthropology. In *Environmentalism: the view from anthropology*, ed. K. Milton. ASA Monographs 32. London: Routledge.

Mináč, V. 1970. *Duchanie do pahrieb*. Bratislava: Smena.

Možný, I. 1991. *Proč tak snadno . . . : některé rodinné důvody sametové revoluce*. Prague: Sociologické nakladatelství.

Nosková, H. 1988. K výzkumu Čechů v oblasti severozápadního Slovenska ve dvacátých letech. In *Češi na Slovensku. Zpravodaj koordinovane sítě vědeckých informací pro etnografii a folkloristiku* 8: 1–18. Prague: Ústav pro etnografii a folkloristiku ČSAV.

Obrazová, P. and J. Vlk. 1994. *Svatý kníže Václav*. Prague: Paseka.

Ossowski, S. 1969. *Class structure in the social consciousness*. London: Routledge and Kegan Paul.

Paine, R. 1985. Ethnodrama and the 'Fourth World': the Saami Action Group in Norway, 1979–81. In *Indigenous peoples and the nation state*, ed. N. Dyck. St John's, Newfoundland, Canada: ISER.

Parkin, D. 1984. Political language. *Annual Review of Anthropology* 13: 345–65.

Paul, D. W. 1979. *The cultural limits of revolutionary politics: change and continuity in socialist Czechoslovakia*. New York: Columbia University Press.

Pecheux, M. 1982. *Language, semantics, and ideology: stating the obvious*. Trans. H. Nagpal. London: Macmillan.

Pekař, J. 1990. *O smyslu českých dějin*. Prague: Rozmluvy.

Pešková, J. 1988. Problém tradice a jejího vlivu na národní charakter. In *Povědomí tradice v novodobé české kultuře*. Prague: Národní galerie.

Piťha, P. 1992. *Čechy a jejich svatí*. Prague: AVED.

Pithart, P. 1990a. *Dějiny a politika*. Prague: Prostor.

1990b. *Osmašedesátý*. Prague: Rozmluvy.

Podiven (P. Rithart, P. Příhoda, and M. Otáhal) 1991. *Češi v dějinách nové doby*. Prague: Rozmluvy.

Pražák, A. 1929. *Česi a Slováci: literárně dějepisné poznámky k československému poměru*. Prague: Státní nakladatelství.

Pynsent, R. B. 1994. *Questions of identity: Czech and Slovak ideas of nationality and personality*. Budapest: Central European University Press.

Rothschild, J. 1989. *Return to diversity: a political history of East Central Europe since World War II*. New York: Oxford University Press.

Runciman, W. G. 1985. Contradictions of state socialism: the case of Poland. *Sociological Review* 33: 1–21.

Rupnik, J. 1981. The restoration of the party-state in Czechoslovakia since 1968. In *The withering away of the state?: party and state under communism*, ed. L. Holmes. London: SAGE Publications.

Rychlík, J. 1988. České obyvatelstvo na Slovensku v letech 1938–1945. In *Češi na Slovensku. Zpravodaj koordinovane sítě vědeckých informací pro etnografii a folkloristiku* 8: 19–36. Prague: Ústav pro etnograii a folkloristiku ČSAV.

Sampson, S. L. 1984. Muddling through in Romania: why the mamaliga does not explode. *International Journal of Romanian Studies* 3: 165–85.

Scherzer, J. 1987. A discourse-centered approach to language and culture. *American Anthropologist* 89: 295–309.

Schlesinger, P. 1987. On national identity: some conceptions and misconceptions criticised. *Social Science Information* 26, no. 2: 19–64.

Schneider, D. M. 1976. Notes toward a theory of culture. In *Meaning in anthropol-*

ogy, ed. K. H. Basso and H. A. Selby. Albuquerque: University of New Mexico Press.

1980. *American kinship: a cultural account*. 2nd edn. Chicago: University of Chicago Press.

Seidel, G. 1989. 'We condemn apartheid, BUT . . .': a discursive analysis of European Parliamentary debate on sanctions (July 1986). In *Social anthropology and the political language*, ed. R. Grillo. London: Routledge.

Seton-Watson, R. W. 1931. *Slovakia then and now*. London: Allen and Unwin.

Shore, C. 1993. Inventing the 'People's Europe': critical approaches to European Community 'cultural policy'. *Man* (N.S.) 28: 779–800.

Šimečka, M. 1984. *Obnovení pořádku*. London: Edice Rozmluvy.

1990. *Konec nehybnosti*. Prague: Lidové noviny.

Skilling, H. G. 1976. *Czechoslovakia's interrupted revolution*. Princeton: Princeton University Press.

1981. *Charter 77 and human rights in Czechoslovakia*. London: George Allen and Unwin.

1989. *Samizdat and independent society in Central and Eastern Europe*. London: Macmillan Press.

Škutina, V. 1990. *Český šlechtic František Schwarzenberg*. Prague: Rozmluvy.

Smetana, M. 1991. *Dvě kariéry Jana Třísky*. Prague: Interpress.

Smith, A. D. 1986. *The ethnic origin of nations*. Oxford: Basil Blackwell.

1991. *National identity*. London: Penguin Books.

1992. National identity and the idea of European unity. *International Affairs* 68: 55–76.

Spiro, M. E. 1982. Collective representations and mental representations in religious symbol systems. In *On symbols in cultural anthropology: essays in honor of Harry Hoijer*, ed. J. Maquet. Malibu, Calif.: Udena.

Statistická ročenka Československé socialistické republiky 1988. Prague: Státní nakladatelství technické literatury.

Stern, J. P. 1992. *The heart of Europe: essays on literature and ideology*. Oxford: Basil Blackwell.

Strathern, M. 1992. *After nature: English kinship in the late twentieth century*. Cambridge: Cambridge University Press.

Suttles, G. D. 1970. Friendship as a social institution. In *Social relationships*, ed. G. J. McCall *et al*. Chicago: Aldine.

Svitak, I. 1990. *The unbearable burden of history: the sovietization of Czechoslovakia*. 3 vols. Prague: Academia.

Szporluk, R. 1981. *Political thought of Thomas G. Masaryk*. East European Monograph Series 85. Boulder, Colo.: East European Quarterly.

Taborsky, E. 1961. *Communism in Czechoslovakia, 1948–1960*. Princeton: Princeton University Press.

Tedlock, D. 1983. *The spoken word and the work of interpretation*. Philadelphia: University of Pennsylvania Press.

Teichova, A. 1988. *The Czechoslovak economy, 1918–1980*. London: Routledge.

Thomas, N. 1992. The inversion of tradition. *American Ethnologist* 19: 213–32.

Thompson, E. P. 1978. *The poverty of theory*. London: Merlin Press.

1981. The politics of theory. In *People's history and social theory*, ed. S. Raphael. London: Routledge and Kegan Paul.

Thompson, J. B. 1984. *Studies in the theory of ideology.* Cambridge, UK: Polity Press.

1990. *Ideology and modern culture.* Cambridge, UK: Polity Press.

Timoracký, M. 1992. Verejná mienka o česko-slovenských vzťahoch. In *Dnešní krize česko-slovenských vztahů,* F. Gál *et al.* Prague: Sociologické nakladatelství.

Ulc, O. 1974. *Politics in Czechoslovakia.* San Francisco: W. H. Freeman and Co.

Urban, G. 1991. *A discourse-centered approach to culture: native South American myths and rituals.* Austin: University of Texas Press.

Urban, O. 1982. *Česká společnost: 1848–1918.* Prague: Svoboda.

Urban, Z. 1988. K některým otázkám historie a vzájemného ovlivňování a soužití Čechů a Slováků v 19. a 20. století. In *Češi na Slovensku. Zpravodaj koordinované sítě vědeckých informací pro etnografii a folkloristiku* 7: 1–38. Prague: Ústav pro etnografii a folkloristiku ČSAV.

Verdery, K. 1991. Theorizing socialism: a prologue to the 'transition'. *American Ethnologist* 18: 419–39.

1992. Comment: Hobsbawm in the East. *Anthropology Today* 8, no. 1: 8–10.

1993. Ethnic relations, economies of shortage, and the transition in Eastern Europe. In *Socialism: ideals, ideologies, and local practice,* ed. C. M. Hann. ASA Monographs 31. London: Routledge.

Vlček, T. 1986. *Praha 1900.* Prague: Panorama.

Vlnas, V. 1993. *Jan Nepomucký: česká legenda.* Prague: Mladá fronta.

Wadekin, K.-E. 1982. *Agrarian policies in communist Europe: a critical introduction.* The Hague: Allanheld, Osmun, and Co.

Wedel, J. 1986. *The private Poland.* New York: Facts on File.

Wedel, J. (ed.). 1991. *The unplanned society: Poland during and after communism.* New York: Columbia University Press.

Wheaton, B. and Z. Kavan. 1992. *The velvet revolution: Czechoslovakia, 1988–1991.* Boulder, Colo.: Westview Press.

White, S. 1979. *Political culture and Soviet politics.* London: Macmillan.

Wistricht, E. 1989. *After 1992: the United States of Europe.* London: Routledge.

Wolchik, S. L. 1991. *Czechoslovakia in transition: politics, economics, and society.* London: Pinter Publishers.

Wolf, E. 1982. *Europe and the people without history.* Berkeley: University of California Press.

Wright, P. 1985. *On living in an old country: the national past in contemporary Britain.* London: Verso.

Index

actors, 2, 128, 139, 141–3, 145–6, 148
agency, 154
  of market, 154–5, 159
  of nation, 114–16
  of society, 20
  of state, 115
Agnew, H. L., 94
Agrarian Party, 210 nn. 4–5
Alan, J., 7, 211 n. 2, 212 n. 2
Anderson, B., 114
artificial vs. natural, *see* natural vs. artificial
Austin, J. L., 53
Austria, 6, 37, 38, 182
Austro-Hungarian Empire, 5, 34, 37, 39, 51, 82, 93–4, 96, 98, 115, 129, 190

Baltic states, 43
Barnard, F. M., 165
Baroque, 125, 128
Barth, F., 64
Baťa, T., 67
Bauman, R., 4
Benda, V., 112
Beneš, E., 17, 82, 95, 134–5, 165–6
Beránek, J., 99
Berger, J., 33
Bernolák, A., 94
Bible, 82, 93
Biedermannová, C., 172
Blaník Mountain, 35
Bohemia, 6, 12, 34–9, 74, 81, 83, 91, 93–5, 101, 104–5, 107, 112, 116, 121–2, 125, 130–1, 161, 169–72, 187, 194, 196–7, 199, 209 nn. 2–3, 210 n. 3, 211 n. 4
Boissevain, J., 12
Boleslav I, 35
Böll, H., 143
Bolzano, P. B., 98

Bradley, J. F. N., 38
Bratislava, 60, 99, 101, 109–10
Brezhnev, L. I., 32
Britain, 11, 12, 43, 49, 56, 81, 86, 182, 202
Brown, A., 1
Budapest, 6, 98
Bulgaria, 2, 151

Čalfa, M., 162
Campbell, F. G., 165
Canada, 68–9
Čapek, K., 65–6, 82
Čarnogurský, J., 109–10
Catholic church, 39, 40, 113, 131–2, 136
Catholicism, 39–41, 100, 212 n. 2
Central Europe, 10, 28, 33, 36, 39, 48–9, 70, 77, 79, 81, 92, 95–6, 105, 107, 119, 126, 129, 151, 165, 182, 202
Čerwenák, A., 105
Chaloupecký, V., 97
Charles IV, 36, 82, 119, 134–6
Charter 77, 29, 30, 32, 46, 55, 60, 133, 148, 210 n. 7
Chelčický, P., 119, 126, 210 nn. 2 and 6
Chirot, D., 18
Christian Democratic Movement, 109–10
Christian Democratic Party, 112, 140
Christian values, 16, 169
Civic Democratic Party, 8, 112, 191, 194, 198
Civic Forum, 8, 16–17, 60, 140, 144, 148–9
civil rights, 108
civil society, 4, 8, 196, 212 n. 2
Clark, J., 18
Clementis, V., 101
Cleveland agreement, 96
Cohen, A., 5
Cole, J., 12

Collard, A., 79
collectivisation of land, 19
collectivism, 13, 20, 63, 66, 122, 160, 202, 206 n. 3
Comenius, J. A. *see* Komenský, J. A.
Committee for the Defence of the Unjustly Prosecuted, 29, 32
Communist Party, 16–18, 20, 23, 26–32, 34, 41, 44, 52, 57–60, 63, 66, 70, 77, 101–2, 111–12, 133–4, 139–40, 162, 197, 206 n. 5, 209 n. 13, 210 n. 5
  general secretary of, 34–5, 63, 70, 144, 206 n. 5
comparison, 11, 141–2, 203
constitution
  of 1960, 19, 101, 140
  Slovak, 111
context, 3, 12, 38, 53, 108, 131, 196, 199–200
coup d'état of 1948, 18, 34, 41, 59, 79, 135, 146, 151, 166
courtesy, 24
Crump, T., 12
Csepeli, G., 50
cultural meanings, 2, 11–14, 204
culture
  defined, 2, 4–5, 12
  of everyday life, 86–7, 209 n. 2
  folk, 103–4, 125
  high, 12–13, 37, 85–7, 209 n. 2
  national, 91–2, 105, 115–16, 189
  nature and, 103, 107, 180–1
Cyril and Method, 100, 210 n. 5
Czech Children, 29, 65
Czech–German relations, 5, 6, 57, 81, 91–2, 126
Czech National Assembly, 96
Czech Republic, 40, 80, 105, 113, 134, 170–2, 182, 184, 186, 192, 198, 200, 202–3
Czech–Slovak relations, 6–9, 34, 57, 92–102, 104, 108, 113, 119, 166, 183, 187, 190–2, 211 n. 2
Czech Social Democrats, 95
Czech Socialist Party, 125
Czech state, 4, 6, 13, 36–41, 44, 51, 92, 94–5, 98–100, 107, 113, 118–20, 137, 190, 192–201, 212 n. 2
Czechoslovak Anarchistic Association, 88
Czechoslovak federation, 6, 8, 112–13, 190–2, 196–200, 212 n. 2
Czechoslovak language, 57, 93–4
Czechoslovak nation, 57, 94–5, 97–9, 103, 187
Czechoslovak National Council, 95–6
Czechoslovak Union of Women, 147–8, 172, 178, 206 n. 3
Czechoslovak Union of Youth, 133, 206 n. 3

Czechoslovakia
  disintegration of, 6–7, 13–14, 125, 186–7, 191–2, 196, 198, 212 n. 3
  foundation of, 5, 9, 39–40, 42, 44, 47, 56, 58, 60, 82, 110, 120, 127–8, 130–1, 193
Czechoslovakism, 98–9, 103, 194

Danube, 97, 109, 183
democracy, 29–30, 53, 70, 74, 79, 82, 84, 88, 108, 113, 118–19, 148, 151, 153, 156–8, 165, 167, 198, 203
Democratic Party, 18
demonstrations against communism, 9, 13, 32–5, 41–2, 44, 46–8, 51–3, 55–6, 58–9, 61–2, 70–1, 73, 139–41, 146–8, 156
Devereux, G., 44
discourse, 2, 9–10, 13–14, 39, 51–3, 61–2, 66–7, 80, 82, 108, 115, 128–9, 136, 171, 195, 199–203
  culture and, 185, 192, 200
  on Czech statehood, 192, 195–7, 199–200, 202
  defined, 3–5
  on ecology, 169, 171
  on economic transformation, 168, 200
  on freedom, 52
  on gender, 172, 179, 200
  on history, 117–18, 125–6, 129, 148
  on individualism, 61–2, 91
  on *kulturnost*, 86–7
  nationalistic, 61–2, 65–6, 89–91, 201
dissidents, 4, 16–17, 19, 23, 26, 29–33, 42, 66–7, 128, 139, 142–5, 148, 169, 171, 208 n. 13
Dobrovský, J., 93
Dubček, A., 21, 34, 44, 48, 56–7, 59, 60, 70, 102, 129, 135–6, 140, 150, 166
Dumont, L., 164
Dunn, J., 18
Dvořák, K., 77, 82

Eastern model of the nation, 49–50
Ecological Committee, 29
ecological movement, 168–9, 171–2, 174
ecology, 155, 169, 171–2, 180–1
economic reform, 13, 25, 27, 106, 149–55, 157–60, 162–3, 191, 210 nn. 1 and 3
economy, 144, 150–2, 154–5, 159–60, 193
  centrally planned, 1, 150, 153–4, 156, 158, 162–3, 168, 180–1, 184, 203
  market, 1, 4, 10, 129, 137, 140–1, 149–51, 153–9, 162–3, 168, 180–1, 192, 196, 203, 212 n. 2
  'second', 19
  of shortage, 7
egalitarianism, 13, 62, 72, 74, 88–9, 91, 160–1, 201

elections, 28, 31, 43, 48, 55, 121, 161, 164,
    209 n. 14
  of 1946, 18
  of 1990, 128, 140, 151, 162, 178
  of 1992, 8, 106, 113, 178, 182, 190–2, 198,
    212 n. 3
emigration, 26, 62, 66–8, 143, 188
emotions, 3, 106–7, 181–5, 196, 198–9
entrepreneurs, 129, 152–3, 159–60, 162–3,
    173–4, 185
environment, 4, 155, 164, 169–72, 186, 211
    n. 4
equality, 1, 17, 22, 72, 88, 90, 102, 104,
    162–3
European Union, 202–3
European values, 10, 202–3
Evanson, R. K., 208 n. 11
experience, 53, 73, 78–80, 84–5, 116, 141
  historical, 115–16, 167
  lived, 78–80, 85, 141–2
  perceived, 79–80

Fairclough, N., 4
Faltan, S., 99
family, 21, 25–6, 28–9, 62, 65, 75, 77, 141,
    161, 172, 174, 177–80, 186–8, 206 nn. 3
    and 5
Federal Assembly, 8, 102, 129, 140, 190–1,
    209 n. 14
Felak, J., 97, 98, 100
feminism, 168, 172–6, 179–80
Ferdinand I, 37
Fidelius, P., 20, 27, 29
Fierlinger, Z., 17
Filip, O., 66
Forman, M., 67
For the True Image of Slovakia, 110–11
Foster, R. J., 12, 14
Foucault, M., 3
Fox, R. G., 4, 5
France, 49, 56, 127, 182
Franz Josef I, 37
free market, 53, 140, 149–51, 158–9, 212 n. 2
freedom, 13, 29, 39, 48, 52–3, 55–7, 61–2,
    70–1, 108, 110, 120, 148, 156–8, 183
French Revolution, 49
friends, 21–4, 26, 62, 104, 186–8
Friends of the USA Club, 29
Fučík, J., 133

Gál, F., 112
Gal, S., 10
Galasi, P., 19
Geertz, C., 2, 3, 84
Gellner, E., 12, 37, 41, 83
gender relations, 4, 172, 175–7, 179–81,
    185–6, 208 n. 12

general secretary of the Communist Party,
    see under Communist Party
general strike of 1989, 16, 45, 139–40, 143
German occupation, 41, 129–30, 132
Germanisation, 39, 98, 120
Germans in Czechoslovakia, 6–8, 95–8, 101,
    121–4, 211 n. 4
Germany, 30, 32, 41, 49, 52, 81, 101, 110,
    122–3, 140, 144, 146, 182, 196, 208
    n. 11
Goldstücker, E., 83
Gorbachev, M., 21, 32
Gottwald, K., 17–18, 58
Gray, J., 1
Great Moravian Empire, 92–3, 105, 210 n. 5
Grečo, M., 99
Grillo, R. D., 5, 12
Grove-White, R., 171
gypsies, 64–5, 122

Habsburgs, 6, 37–40, 51, 120, 122, 124, 126,
    130–1, 194
Halliday, M. A. K., 3, 5, 200
Hankiss, E., 18, 19
Hann, C. M., 16, 18, 28
Hannerz, U., 5
Hasan, R., 3
Hašek, J., 207 n. 10
Havel, V., 16, 30, 40, 48, 55, 63, 82, 109–10,
    119, 123–4, 126, 129, 134–5, 139–40,
    144–5, 148, 161, 163–7, 183, 193,
    195–6, 209 n. 14
Havlíček, K., 118, 126, 210 n. 1
Heiberg, M., 5
Heller, A., 164
Henderson, K., 102
Herder, J. G., 49, 98
Hervey, S. G. J., 53
Herzfeld, M., 14
historical memory, 80, 84, 125
historical narrative, 117–18
historiography, 39, 56, 58, 81–2, 105,
    116–17, 120, 124
history, 10–11, 13, 20, 35–6, 38, 40, 50, 74,
    77, 79, 81–4, 91, 93, 105, 107, 114–30,
    136–9, 145, 163, 180, 183, 186, 193, 202
  discontinuous, 84, 119–20, 123–4, 127–9,
    138
*History of the Czech Nation in Bohemia and
    Moravia*, 38, 81, 182
Hlinka, A., 99–101, 110
Hobsbawm, E., 76, 202
holiday cottages, 26, 28–9, 67, 157, 169, 211
    n. 4
Holy, L., 11
homeland, 65, 68, 185–90, 193, 195
Hrabal, B., 21, 22

Hradčany, 34, 41–2, 44, 48, 56, 58, 103, 145
human rights, 28, 30, 46, 48, 66–7, 154, 171
Hungarians in Czechoslovakia, 8, 95, 97–8,
    109, 121
Hungary, 2, 6, 10, 19, 30, 32, 37, 43, 61, 67,
    80, 93, 95, 97, 105, 140
Hus, J., 34–6, 38–41, 45, 47, 82, 100, 119,
    126, 130–2, 134–6
Husák, G., 102, 110
Hussite movement, 36, 38–40, 81–2, 119,
    134–6, 210 nn. 2–3

ideology
    communist, 1, 7, 32, 48, 66, 73, 158, 161,
        173–4, 209 n. 13
    nationalist, 7, 48, 50–1, 61–2, 66, 70,
        115–16, 124, 127, 136–7
images of the past, 117–20, 124–30, 136, 202
income policy, 1, 160, 173–4
independent initiatives, 29–30, 46–8, 52, 148
Independent Peace Association, 29, 47–8
individualism, 13, 51, 61–2, 64, 66, 160–1,
    164, 201–2, 206 n. 3
individuals and nation, 51, 61–3, 65–6, 68,
    70–1, 85, 89–90, 114, 116, 164, 201
intellectuals, 2, 10, 14, 16–17, 22–3, 28,
    30–2, 50, 59, 70, 77, 82–3, 86, 91–2,
    94–5, 99, 102, 111, 125, 127, 136,
    140–1, 143–5, 148, 157, 163, 182–3, 192
interest organisations, 22, 207 n. 6
invasion of Czechoslovakia, 42, 46, 60, 120,
    124, 129, 134, 142
Italy, 56, 127

Jakeš, M., 63, 111
Janáček, L., 82
Jazz Section, 29, 52
Jews, 64–5, 101, 109
Jirák, J., 112
Jirásek, A., 36, 38
Jiří z Poděbrad, 119, 210 n. 3
Joseph II, 39
Juriga, F., 99

Kálal, K., 104
Kantůrková, E., 45
Kapferer, B., 1
Kavan, Z., 26, 48, 140, 147, 169
Kertzer, D. I., 3, 45, 100
Klaus, V., 110, 151, 153, 155, 161, 163, 168,
    191
Klus, P., 209 n. 2
Kohn, H., 49, 64
Kollár, J., 93
Komenský, J. A., 39, 119, 126, 134–6
Kořalka, J., 50
Korbel, J., 205 nn. 1–2

Kosík, K., 119
Krejci, J., 20, 22, 206 nn. 2–3, 207 n. 7
Kubelík, R., 67, 82
kulturnost, 85–7, 91–2, 113, 136, 144, 151–2
Kundera, M., 69, 82, 120
Kusin, V. V., 29, 102
Kyncl, K., 90

land reform, 17, 121–2, 210 nn. 4–5
Leff, C. S., 40, 97, 98, 102, 165
Left Initiative, 88
legionnaires, 39, 59, 127–8, 130
legitimacy of power, 3, 28, 60, 204
Levý Hradec, 93, 209 n. 4
liberal democracy, 1, 43, 52, 70, 173–4, 203
little Czech, 62, 72–3, 75–6, 164, 167, 202
Lustig, A., 67, 75, 115
Luza, R., 205 n. 1

Macdonell, D., 53
McFarlane, A., 161
Machonin, P., 22, 77
Macura, V., 9, 92, 130, 183
Magyarisation, 94, 98
Major, J., 124
Mali, V., 40
Malina, F., 209 n. 2
Malinowski, B., 82
Maříková, I., 209 n. 2
Martin declaration, 99
Martinů, B., 82
martyrs, 35, 45, 74, 130–6
Masaryk, J., 135–6
Masaryk, T. G., 48, 56–60, 81–3, 94, 98,
    118–19, 127–8, 134–5, 161, 164–5, 167
Matuška, W., 67
Maxwell, R., 67
May Day, 28
Měchýř, J., 191
Mečiar, V., 110–11, 191
Meinecke, F., 49
metaphor, 83, 190, 200, 204
    of birth, 68
    of bridge, 182–3
    of centre, 182–3
    of cultivation, 183
    of kinship, 104
    of nature, 199–200
Mezník, J., 29
Milton, K., 4
Mináč, V., 105
money-changers, 159–60
morality, 16–20, 23, 26, 29, 74, 136, 154,
    171, 206 n. 3, 210 n. 3
Moravia, 6, 37, 69, 81, 93, 101, 104–5, 107,
    122, 172, 187, 197
mother, 65–6, 68, 104, 147–8, 170, 178

224   *Index*

Movement for Civic Liberty, 29
Movement for Democratic Slovakia, 109, 111, 191
Možný, I., 32, 157
Munich agreement, 79, 100, 105, 109, 119, 123–4, 166, 190
myth, 3, 59, 62, 82, 84, 117, 132, 145
mythological charter, 42, 82, 145

nation and state, 38, 50–1, 54–7, 59, 61, 70–1, 115, 143, 147–9, 168, 185–8, 195–7, 199
National Assembly, 18
national character, 72–8, 84–5, 87, 89–90, 115, 126, 163–4, 167
national consciousness, 3
National Front, 17–18, 209 n. 14
national liberation, 10, 51, 120
National Museum, 34, 40, 44
national revival, 5, 34, 37–8, 50, 68, 83, 91–3, 95, 105, 116, 118, 182, 210 n. 1
national sentiment, 2, 6–9, 48, 51, 53, 55, 92, 185, 189, 202
National Theatre, 37, 145–6
nationalisation, 17, 58, 205 nn. 1–2
natural vs. artificial, 153–7, 168, 180–5, 188, 190, 193, 195–7, 199–200
Nejedlý, Z., 88
Nepomucký, J., 42, 131–2
'new man', 20, 24, 26, 28, 73
nobility, 83, 120–3, 161, 187
normalisation, 26–7, 102, 106
Nosková, H., 99

Obrazová, P., 35
October Revolution, 58, 127
Old Town Square, 34–5, 40, 47–8
Opletal, J., 42
opposition to communism, 2, 9–10, 27, 29–31, 48–9, 51, 53, 55, 59–60, 66, 102, 112–13, 134, 137, 141–2, 144, 148, 166, 169
Ossowski, S., 22

Paine, R., 209 n. 15
Palach, J., 42, 44–7, 60, 131
Palacký, F., 38, 81, 83, 93, 118, 124, 126, 128, 130, 182
Parkin, D., 14
Patočka, J., 126, 210 n. 7
patriotism, 53, 187–9, 193
Paul, D. W., 20, 26, 207 nn. 7–9, 208 n. 11, 211 n. 4
Pecheux, M., 53
Pekař, J., 39, 120, 121, 123, 124, 131, 132
personhood, 53, 55
Pešková, J., 114

Piťha, P., 35, 42, 131
Pithart, P., 83, 101, 119, 120, 121, 124, 128, 130, 139
Pittsburgh agreement, 96, 99
Podiven, 82
Poland, 2, 19, 30, 32, 44, 67, 80, 139–40, 151
Poles in Czechoslovakia, 97–8
political action, 3, 33, 43, 53–4, 129
political culture, 48, 77, 108–11, 164–5, 167, 179, 190
political elites, 3, 97
politics as a cultural system, 3, 41, 140–1
Prague Spring, 19, 21, 31, 42–4, 46, 57, 60–1, 73, 77, 102, 119, 129, 133–4, 161
Pražák, A., 93, 98
president of the republic, 1, 17, 56, 121, 123, 128, 134, 140, 163–6, 184, 209 n. 14
private ownership, 10, 19, 123, 156–8, 163, 169, 205 n. 2, 206 n. 2
privatisation, 10, 14, 17, 140–1, 150, 156, 158–9, 162, 178
proletarian internationalism, 7, 194
Protectorate of Bohemia and Moravia, 41, 146, 188
Public Against Violence, 8, 109
public and private spheres, 10–26, 29, 73, 169, 176, 207 n. 6, 208 n. 12
Pynsent, R. B., 35, 36, 40, 45, 98, 105, 124, 125, 130, 133, 134, 143, 167, 183, 209 n. 13

Ranger, T., 76
re-Catholicisation, 39, 41, 120, 124, 128, 131
Republican Party, 166
restitution of property, 67, 149, 156, 162
retirement, 26, 211 n. 4
return to Europe, 146, 151–2, 202–3
right to self-determination, 6, 8, 95, 99
Říp Mountain, 116
Romania, 151, 182
Rothschild, J., 1
Rousseau, J. J., 49
Rudé Právo, 20, 24, 29, 30, 60, 141, 206 n. 5
Rudolf II, 42
Runciman, W. G., 18
Rupnik, J., 102
Russia, 39, 127, 134, 151, 182
Rychlík, J., 99, 100

Šafařík, P. J., 93
Sampson, S. L., 16
Scherzer, J., 3, 4, 5, 200
Schlesinger, P., 5
Schneider, D. M., 2
schools, 12, 14, 20, 23, 36, 50, 57, 65, 69, 117, 125, 157, 170

Schweik, J. (Good Soldier Schweik), 25, 62, 72–3, 127, 130, 207 n. 10
secret police, 32, 120, 129, 156
Seidel, G., 3, 4, 53
Seifert, J., 82
Serbia, 56
Seton-Watson, R. W., 98–9
Several Sentences, 30–1
sexual harassment, 172, 176
Shore, C., 203
Šiklová, J., 49
Šimečka, M., 23, 27, 28, 139, 142
Skilling, H. G., 19, 29, 102, 166
Škutina, V., 37, 40
Škvorecký, J., 67, 68, 75, 172
Slánský, R., 206 n. 5
Slovak Labour Party, 18
Slovak League, 96
Slovak National Council, 8, 101, 111–12
Slovak National Party, 109
Slovak nationalism, 6–7, 97, 112, 189, 192, 212 n. 2
Slovak People's Party, 100, 110
Slovak separatism, 6, 96–7, 100–1, 166, 192
Slovak state, 6, 41, 92–3, 101, 105, 107, 109–10, 193
Smetana, B., 77, 82
Smetana, M., 67, 69, 74, 78, 90
Smith, A. D., 50, 51, 202
Social Democratic Party, 18, 179
socialist property, 24–5, 157, 207 n. 8
Sokol, 63
Solidarity, 30, 44
Šoltys, O., 112
Soviet army, 17, 35, 47–8, 57–8, 60, 73, 146
Soviet Union, 2, 6–7, 19, 21, 23, 32, 41, 43, 57, 139, 146, 167, 189
Spiro, M. E., 2
St Vojtěch, 42
St Wenceslas, 34–7, 39–42, 46, 56, 116, 119, 130, 132, 136, 195, 210 n. 4
Stalin, J. V., 57
Štefánik, M. R., 82, 95, 134–5
stereotypes
  of Czechs, 72, 107
  of Germans, 91–2
  of Slovaks, 73, 92, 103–13
Stern, J. P., 81, 83, 98
Strathern, M., 61, 64
students, 2, 32, 42, 55, 58, 86, 128, 133–4, 139–43, 145–8
Štúr, Ľ., 94
Sudetenland, 79, 123–4, 211 n. 4
Suttles, G. D., 24
Švec, J. J., 134, 136
Sviták, I., 57
Svoboda, L., 134–5

symbol
  of commitment to society, 21, 28–9
  democracy as, 108
  Dubček as, 56–7, 59, 129
  of freedom, 62, 158
  historical event as, 42, 126
  of homeland, 186
  honest work as, 29
  Hus as, 36, 38–40, 45, 100, 131
  invoked in demonstrations, 11, 33
  market as, 151, 153
  Masaryk as, 56–7, 59
  material well-being as, 28–30
  nationalist, 3, 34–5, 38–42, 44, 46, 48, 56, 59, 71, 126, 131, 136
  National Theatre as, 145
  Nepomucký as, 131–2
  political, 3, 13, 33, 39–41, 57–9, 81, 100, 108, 131, 133–4, 145
  Prague as, 34, 100
  of public and private spheres, 19, 21
  reason as, 183
  religious, 39–41, 44, 100
  of resistance, 45
  Slovak state as, 109
  St Wenceslas as, 36, 39–40
symbolic action, 3, 33, 43, 61, 209 n. 15
symbolic manipulation, 9, 14, 33, 40–1, 43–5, 54–5, 58–60, 81, 131–3
symbolic map, 34
symbolic system, 45, 55
Sziracki, G., 19
Szporluk, R., 57

Taborsky, E., 1, 205 n. 2
Tatra Mountains, 103–4
Teichová, A., 205 n. 1
text, 3–4, 14, 80–1, 195–6, 199
Thatcher, M., 20
theft, 24–6, 207 n. 8
Thomas, N., 5
Thompson, E. P., 78, 79, 80
Thompson, J. B., 4
time, 19, 25–6, 207 n. 9, 208 n. 11
Timoracký, M., 103, 104, 105, 106, 109
Tiso, J., 101, 110
'tolerance patent', 39
totalitarianism, 84, 108–13, 148, 154, 156–7, 163, 166, 203, 208 n. 13
tradition, 3, 5, 13, 50–1, 65, 69, 72, 76–81, 84–5, 87, 89, 91, 93, 114–16, 119, 126–7, 136, 138, 141, 149, 152, 163–4, 167, 186–7, 189, 212 n. 2
  creation of, 91
  of democracy, 13, 77, 79–83, 85, 87–8, 92, 108, 113–14, 127, 137–8, 146, 163–5, 167, 203

tradition (*cont.*)
  of high culture and education, 13, 77,
    82–3, 85–7, 92, 114, 127, 132–3, 136–8,
    143–6, 151, 163, 167, 203
Trenčanský, M. Č., 105
Tříska, J., 67–9

Ukrainians in Czechoslovakia, 97–8
Ulc, O., 22, 25, 26, 207 n. 8, 208
  nn. 11–12
United States, 49, 56, 63, 67, 69, 80, 94,
  127
University of Prague, 35–6, 82
Urban, G., 5
Urban, O., 131
Urban, Z., 95, 96

'velvet revolution', 1–2, 8–9, 11, 13, 70–1,
  86, 112, 128, 139, 141, 144–6, 151, 166,
  185
Verdery, K., 7, 8, 203
Versailles, 39, 96
Vienna, 37, 39, 63, 86, 151
Vlček, T., 34
Vlk, J., 35
Vlnas, V., 131
Voskovec, V., 90
Vratislav II, 195

Wadekin, K.-E., 205 n. 2
Washington declaration, 95
Wenceslas IV, 36
Wenceslas Square, 34, 41, 44, 46–7
Werich, J., 90
Western Europe, 50, 151, 169, 182, 203
Western model of the nation, 49
Western values, 16
Wheaton, B., 26, 48, 140, 147, 169
White, S., 167
White Mountain, 38–9, 115, 119–24, 126,
  135
Wildavsky, A., 18
Wistricht, E., 202
Wolchik, S. L., 19, 102, 160, 178, 205
  nn. 1–2, 206 n. 2, 208 n. 12
Wolf, E., 12
women, 147–8, 172–81, 208 n. 12, 209 n. 2
World War I, 39, 56, 58–9, 94, 98, 122,
  127–8, 130, 134
World War II, 17, 79, 83, 114, 119, 122, 126,
  130, 155, 183, 209 n. 2
Wright, P., 43, 116
Wycliffe, J., 36

Yugoslavia, 6, 7

Žižka, J., 130, 134–6

Cambridge Studies in Social and Cultural Anthropology

11 Rethinking Symbolism*
    DAN SPERBER. Translated by Alice L. Morton
15 World Conqueror and World Renouncer: A Study of Buddhism and Polity in
    Thailand against a Historical Background*
    S. J. TAMBIAH
16 Outline of a Theory of Practice*
    PIERRE BOURDIEU. Translated by Richard Nice
17 Production and Reproduction: A Comparative Study of the Domestic
    Domain*
    JACK GOODY
28 Hunters, Pastoralists and Ranchers: Reindeer Economies and their
    Transformations*
    TIM INGOLD
32 Muslim Society*
    ERNEST GELLNER
39 The Fish-People: Linguistic Exogamy and Tukanoan Identity in Northwest
    Amazonia*
    JEAN E. JACKSON
51 Individual and Society in Guiana: A Comparative Study of Amerindian
    Social Organizations*
    PETER RIVIERE
53 Inequality among Brothers: Class and Kinship in South China
    RUBIE S. WATSON
54 On Anthropological Knowledge*
    DAN SPERBER
55 Tales of the Yanomami: Daily Life in the Venezuelan Forest*
    JACQUES LIZOT. Translated by Ernest Simon
56 The Making of Great Men: Male Domination and Power among the New
    Guinea Baruya*
    MAURICE GODELIER. Translated by Ruper Swyer
59 Native Lords of Quito in the Age of the Incas: The Political Economy of
    North-Andean Chiefdoms
    FRANK SALOMON

60 Culture and Class in Anthropology and History: A Newfoundland
   Illustration*
   GERALD SIDER
61 From Blessing to Violence: History and Ideology in the Circumcision Ritual
   of the Merina of Madagascar*
   MAURICE BLOCH
62 The Huli Response to Illness
   STEPHEN FRANKEL
63 Social Inequality in a Northern Portuguese Hamlet: Land, Late Marriage,
   and Bastardy, 1870–1978
   BRIAN JUAN O'NEILL
64 Cosmologies in the Making: A Generative Approach to Cultural Variation in
   Inner New Guinea*
   FREDRIK BARTH
65 Kinship and Class in the West Indies: A Genealogical Study of Jamaica and
   Guyana*
   RAYMOND T. SMITH
68 Tradition as Truth and Communication
   PASCAL BOYER
70 The Anthropology of Numbers*
   THOMAS CRUMP
71 Stealing People's Names: History and Politics in a Sepik River Cosmology
   SIMON J. HARRISON
72 The Bedouin of Cyrenaica: Studies in Personal and Corporate Power
   EMRYS L. PETERS. Edited by Jack Goody and Emanuel Marx
73 Bartered Brides: Politics, Gender and Marriage in an Afghan Tribal Society
   NANCY TAPPER
74 Property, Production and Family in Neckerhausen*
   DAVID WARREN SABEAN
75 Fifteen Generations of Bretons: Kinship and Society in Lower Brittany,
   1720–1980
   MARTINE SEGALEN. Translated by J. A. Underwood
76 Honor and Grace in Anthropology
   Edited by J. G. PERISTIANY and JULIAN PITT-RIVERS
77 The Making of the Modern Greek Family: Marriage and Exchange in
   Nineteenth-Century Athens
   PAUL SANT CASSIA with CONSTANTINA BADA
78 Religion and Custom in a Muslim Society: The Berti of Sudan
   LADISLAV HOLY
79 Quiet Days in Burgundy: A Study of Local Politics
   MARC ABÉLÈS. Translated by Annella McDermott
80 Sacred Void: Spatial Images of Work and Ritual among the Giriama of
   Kenya
   DAVID PARKIN
81 A Place of their Own: Family Farming in Eastern Finland
   RAY ABRAHAMS
82 Power, Prayer and Production: The Jola of Casamance, Senegal

OLGA F. LINARES
83 Identity through History: Living Stories in a Solomon Island Society
GEOFFREY M. WHITE
84 Monk, Householder and Tantric Priest: Newar Buddhism and its Hierarchy of Ritual
DAVID GELLNER
85 Hunters and Herders of Southern Africa: A Comparative Ethnography of the Khoisan Peoples*
ALAN BARNARD
86 Belonging in the Two Berlins: Kin, State, Nation*
JOHN BORNEMAN
87 Power and Religiosity in a Post-Colonial Setting: Sinhala Catholics in Contemporary Sri Lanka
R. L. STIRRAT
88 Dialogues with the Dead: The Discussion of Mortality among the Sora of Eastern India
PIERS VITEBSKY
89 South Coast New Guinea Cultures: A Regional Comparison*
BRUCE M. KNAUFT
90 Pathology and Identity: The Work of Mother Earth in Trinidad
ROLAND LITTLEWOOD
91 The Cultural Relations of Classification: An Analysis of Nuaulu Animal Categories from Central Seram
ROY ELLEN
92 Cinema and the Urban Poor in South India
SARA DICKEY
93 In the Society of Nature: A Native Ecology in Amazonia
PHILIPPE DESCOLA
94 Spirit Possession and Personhood among the Kel Ewey Tuareg
SUSAN J. RASMUSSEN
95 Learning to be Vezo: Identity and Descent among the Vezo of Madagascar
RITA ASTUTI
96 Social Reproduction and History in Melanesia: Mortuary Ritual, Gift Exchange, and Custom in the Tanga Islands*
ROBERT J. FOSTER
97 The Roads of Chinese Childhood: Learning and Identity in Angang
CHARLES STAFFORD
98 Education and Identity in Rural France: The Politics of Schooling
DEBORAH REED-DANAHAY
99 The Architecture of Memory: A Jewish–Muslim Household in Colonial Algeria, 1937–1962*
JOELLE BAHLOUL
100 Contesting Culture: Discourses of Identity in Multi-ethnic London*
GERD BAUMANN
101 Tradition and Modernity in Mediterranean Society: The Wedding as Cultural Symbol
VASSOS ARGYROU

102 Mass Culture and Modernism in Egypt*
     WALTER ARMBRUST
103 The Little Czech and the Great Czech Nation: National Identity and the
     Post-Communist Transformation of Society*
     LADISLAV HOLY
104 Managing Existence in Naples: Morality, Action and Structure*
     ITALO PARDO

* *available in paperback*

9 780521 555845